THE SHOW THAT CHANGED FASHION

Introduction by Heidi Klum | Foreword by Harvey Weinstein

With Eila Mell

WEINSTEIN
BOOKS

ISBN 978-1-60286-178-7
Library of Congress Control Number: 2012939797

E-book ISBN 978-1-60286-179-4

9   8   7   6   5   4   3   2   1
Digit on the right indicates the number of this printing

Weinstein Books, 99 Hudson Street, 4th Floor, New York, NY 10013

CONTENTS

INTRODUCTION BY HEIDI KLUM 4

FOREWORD BY HARVEY WEINSTEIN 6

PART 1: Behind the Scenes 7
    Casting 9
    Making It Work 20
    Location, Location, Location 28

PART 2: One day you're in and the next day you're out 34
    Season 1 36
    Season 2 60
    Season 3 88
    Season 4 108
    Season 5 130
    Season 6 146
    Season 7 174
    Season 8 200
    Season 9 236

PART 3: Beyond the Runway: The Spin-offs 266

WINNERS CIRCLE 282

SEWING IT ALL UP 286

INDEX 291

CREDITS 296

INTRODUCTION BY HEIDI KLUM

Project Runway Season 10. Wow, I can't believe it! Time has really flown! I'm so incredibly proud to be part of this show. Fans worldwide come up to me and are so passionate about it. I love that *Project Runway* is a platform for talented, aspiring designers. Fashion is so hard to break into and a show like ours that helps them get a little positive exposure is great—especially when they have big personalities like our fan favorites.

We have seen our designers create some amazing looks, and together we have had many, many memorable moments. It's about time that we get some of these wonderful memories down in a book. To start things off, here are some of *my* favorite moments, on and off-camera:

HEIDI'S TOP 10 *PROJECT RUNWAY* MEMORIES

- Once the show was sold, knowing it would soon be on TV was amazing! We knew that designing is a really creative, interesting, inspiring process, and that it wouldn't be a boring hour of watching people sew. I think ten seasons in, we've proven our point!

- Getting the show on air leads to another favorite memory—the very first challenge, set at the grocery store. I mean, people still talk about Austin Scarlett's cornhusk dress. That's when we knew this could really work for real and be fun for our audience . . . and for us! It was a revelation and a big sigh of relief.

- The other judges and I have a lot of fun together. Sometimes we're like little kids; if something sets us off we're like the naughty children in church who can't stop laughing. During the WWE wrestling costume challenge, when the wrestlers came out we couldn't help it. We started hysterically laughing! And it wasn't because we were making fun of anyone or anything; it was just so completely different from what we were used to. With the exaggerated poses and the theatrical costumes, it was just too much. We tried for a good

ten minutes to get ourselves under control. But first Michael giggled, then me, then Nina—we were goners. We had to stop shooting for a good half hour to wipe our tears and get ourselves under control!

- The past couple of seasons, I've done a challenge for my New Balance line. I'm pretty specific with the

parameters, like fabrics, thinking about sales and manufacturing, and things like that. During Season 8, when I went into the workroom mid-point to check in on the designers, it was funny because Gretchen had picked all these strange fabrics that did not match the line at all and Mondo had started some garments that were technically all wrong. I tried to fit my head through one of his shirts and couldn't do it! He got kind of huffy and upset. He must have thought I was mad at him but what he didn't know was that I was actually rooting for him and was one of his biggest fans—as we all saw during the finale!

- Some of my favorite memories take place off camera. During breaks, Michael, Nina, and I have what we call "Cheetos chats" because there's always junk food around. Michael tells us funny stories and we gossip about everything from who got too much plastic surgery to making comments while flipping through magazines. We have fun.

- Speaking of, once we had to shoot some promos and we were being goofy. I started literally chasing Michael around and around the judges' chairs! I chased him so hard he fell down and I practically climbed on top of him and we started wrestling! He says I made him pass out but no way! All in good fun.

- One of my favorite challenges was when the designers had to create looks inspired by the beautiful, special hats of Philip Treacy. I had run into him in London and we'd spoken about him being on the show so it was great that it came through. The designers really had fun with such high-fashion, couture inspirations, and though some designers made things that were a little too literal, some of the final designs were absolutely gorgeous.

- One of my favorite finales was when Christian Siriano won and Victoria Beckham was the guest judge. She was great—so sharp and she's a fan of the show, so she was really knowledgeable about the designers' strengths and weaknesses. Christian was so nervous when it was down to two and it was nice to see that moment of vulnerability and how much winning it all really meant to him! Plus Victoria told Christian she was a fan, which made him so thrilled!

- Stilts! I'd been wanting to do a "larger than life" challenge forever, so I was glad we were able to do a big outdoor runway with the stilt-walkers. I think some of the designs were stronger than others, but to see them all displayed fifteen-feet tall was amazing! I think it's good to mix things up like that every once in a while.

- Tim and I set up my challenge at the New Balance track and I expected it to be fairly routine but it ended up being a morning of drama. First, Olivier had some sort of attack after running around the track and he collapsed on the ground. I told him to get up, the show must go on! Then Cecilia decided she couldn't handle it anymore so we said goodbye to her right then and there. And finally, I got Mr. Tim Gunn to run a little bit. That's kind of the equivalent of watching a fish walk for the first time!

You'll discover and be reminded of your own favorite *Project Runway* memories throughout the pages of this book. Enjoy!

Auf weidersehen!

Heidi Klum ♡

P.S. About that "auf weidersehen": Originally I was supposed to say something like, "You are out . . . You are cut . . ." I said, "Well, I have an accent, I'm German, and that doesn't sound nice after the designers worked so hard. I came up with "Auf Wiedersehen," as an alternative. It means "Goodbye, see you again." It stuck!

HARVEY WEINSTEIN, EXECUTIVE PRODUCER:

I have always been intrigued and inspired by the creative process. And I have learned along the way that talent can come from anywhere. I am passionate about cultivating new talent and have often taken a chance on up-and-coming artists with great results. Through *Project Runway* I can take this a step further by giving new designers a platform and the tools they need to further their careers. However, if you know me, you would understand what a fashion novice I was when we first started to develop *Project Runway*. My wife calls me "fashionably challenged" so actually, one of my proudest accomplishments with the show is avoiding Heidi saying "Auf weidersehen, you're out" to me!

If I see passion I am always willing to take a chance. For example, Padma Lakshmi was a model who had a passion for food. Although she was not an experienced chef I could see she had something valuable to offer and published her cookbooks. This was way before the world knew her as the host of *Top Chef*. I similarly supported other talented people in their early endeavors over the years. With that in mind, I did not feel at a disadvantage being an outsider in the fashion world. Model Daniela Unruh and I first conceived of the idea behind *Project Runway*, but it was then shaped by a great team: my TV department, including Eli Holzman at the time, Barbara Schneeweiss, and later Meryl Poster as President of Television for The Weinstein Company; Heidi Klum, Desiree Gruber, and Jane Cha at Full Picture; our early producers, Dan Cutforth and Jane Lipsitz of the Magical Elves, and more recently Jonathan Murray of Bunim/Murray; and the networks Bravo and Lifetime. I can't tell you how much everyone involved has added to the show. So many smart people have helped us, joined us, and contributed over the years; people like Nancy Dubuc at Lifetime, who I thank for having the foresight to expand the show to ninety minutes, even though I thought it was a crazy idea at first!

Over the past ten seasons *Project Runway* has grown in so many ways. We have had the opportunity to introduce the world to great aspiring fashion designers. We've also brought in the best guest judges in the business—Diane von Furstenberg, Tommy Hilfiger, Catherine Malandrino, Francisco Costa, Badgley Mischka, Cynthia Rowley, Betsey Johnson, Rachel Roy, and my favorite judge (don't be jealous Michael and Nina!)—Georgina Chapman. These are people whose advice and critiques have nurtured so many designers along the way. I am proud to see how our designers grow and benefit from *Project Runway*. This has given the show its integrity and is the very thing that has sustained us across ten seasons. I am immensely proud of the designers who have participated in *Project Runway* and hope that we can continue to inspire young fashion hopefuls.

And to the hundreds of people who worked hard on *Project Runway* and make it work—I want to say to all of you, You're in!

PART 1:

BEHIND THE SCENES

HEIDI KLUM

MICHAEL KORS

NINA GARCIA

DESIREE GRUBER

JANE CHA

BARBARA SCHNEEWEISS

ELI HOLZMAN

SARA REA

JONATHAN MURRAY

MERYL POSTER

CASTING

ON HEIDI KLUM

HEIDI KLUM:

I hadn't done a TV show before. If I would do a Victoria's Secret show early on in my career I was just as nervous. As a model I always throw myself out there and do things that are not like walking to the supermarket; I've done so many things that most people don't get to do. With the challenge of *Project Runway* all I could do was try my best. Early on, filming pickups sometimes ran into the middle of the night for me. I had to do pickups because I would not say a sentence right and we didn't have prompters. I had to memorize what I had to say and my brain just wasn't in the mode yet. As a model you don't have to memorize much. For a commercial you say two lines and that's it.

In the beginning I didn't have styling. I would get my hair and makeup done in the morning and then they would leave me high and dry. I would be shiny by the end of the day. In the first episode I wore a KISS T-shirt and jeans. We were on a budget so I wore things that I owned. I was a young model and I didn't own $5,000 Balenciaga blouses. As a model when you go on a set somewhere, there's a stylist and you get shot in whatever clothes are in this season and what the story is about, but now I had to be really stylish on my own, which was a struggle. Models go to shoots in jeans and T-shirts and then change into the clothes that are being shot. I didn't have the whole range in my closet.

In the beginning I couldn't imagine what the show looked like, especially not when I was in front of the camera. It was a real learning curve. I was quite scared when we got the first cuts, but when I watched the show I knew we were on to something. I felt really excited, Michael was really excited, and Nina was really excited, so we said, "Okay, this is good, we can sleep at night!"

MERYL POSTER:

Heidi's multifaceted. She's a fan as well as a judge. As a model she's worn the clothes, but she also admires the clothes. She says what people are thinking. Heidi really is the voice of the audience.

BARBARA SCHNEEWEISS:

Heidi has brought so much to the show, including the signature "auf wiedersehn." She is very passionate about the show and a really fun participant in the whole process. She sometimes comes back to the control room to check on us and see what's happening. And most of all I love her great sense of humor.

JONATHAN MURRAY:

From day one Heidi has been a huge factor in the success of the show. She has great instincts about everything. She is not afraid to express what she thinks and is not afraid to show that she believes in someone. When Bunin/ Murray stepped in to the show in Season 6 she was pretty seasoned. As new producers to the show we saw that what she had to say had a lot of value. Just spending time with her you quickly see how good her instincts are.

ON MICHAEL KORS

HEIDI KLUM:

We thought it was a great idea to have Michael Kors because we wanted the show to be authentic. It was good we got real people who are established to be judges, because if the designers get judged by people who no one knows, no one takes it seriously.

DESIREE GRUBER:

Michael has a great personality, he has an amazing eye, and he is an American icon, so we thought he was the right match. We went after him pretty hard and he turned us down a few times. Somebody who worked with Michael at the time, Anne Waterman, helped us convince him. It was really his way or the highway. It was, "I won't be here this day and that's my summer Friday and I'm in the Hamptons on that weekend . . ." We said we'd shoot around him. We were so lucky to get him.

JONATHAN MURRAY:

Michael is amazing. As a producer you can count on him for not only smart commentary, but also for those incredibly great one-liners. He has such a gift for expressing himself.

MICHAEL KORS:

My reaction when I was first offered *Project Runway* was a firm no. This was going to be a reality show. Were designers going to be eating bugs? This was before everything was explained. I was also concerned because both television and movies had never really been that successful in portraying the fashion world. As someone who's been designing since age nineteen, the last thing you want people to think is, "This show is a joke and it's not hard work."

Desiree asked me if I had ever watched *Project Greenlight*, and in fact I loved the show. I'm not in the movie business, but I thought it was really interesting to see how a project got off the ground, how it started with an idea, and how it actually came to fruition. That swayed me, as well as thinking about the fact that I had been a critic for the senior class at Parsons for many years. Desiree said, "You're going to do what you did at Parsons. It'll just be in a panel situation and it'll be televised." I thought, okay, we can show people the process and the hard work that goes

into it. Fashion people are entertaining to say the least; it's not an industry devoid of characters, myself included. I said we'll give it a shot and we'll see what happens.

HAS BEING ON THE SHOW CHANGED YOUR PERSONAL BUSINESS?

Before *Project Runway*, in my entire life I'd probably been to ten fashion shows other than my own. Sitting in an audience watching a fashion show is just not something most designers are used to doing. Tim Gunn tells the designers "Don't bore Nina." The reality is editors have to sit and look at too many clothes and they can get bored really easily. As a designer it's hard to be empathetic and think, "My God, they have to go to ten shows a day for a month!" The show has taught me what it's like to be an editor, to sit in the audience and say okay, let's edit, let's focus.

The other surprising thing that happened with the show is that it has opened up my demographic to people not only in their teens but in their tweens. I always prided myself in having a very broad age range of clients, anywhere from early twenties and up. I never thought we would have costumers that were twelve, thirteen, fourteen. Now when I walk into our stores I see moms with their daughters. I think the show has brought fashion-crazed kids out of the woodwork. (I was fashion crazed at twelve and would actually die and faint to have a certain designer piece!)

THE SHOW HAS DEFINITELY MADE YOU A ROCK STAR DESIGNER.

The interesting thing is you never get to hear designers talk. You can read what they say in an article, you see a still photograph of them, and you see their clothes and you connect the dots, but the missing part is hearing designers talk about fashion on a regular basis. I think that when people

hear me talk, whether I'm saying something funny or something serious, they know where I'm coming from, so when they see something from me they think, "Oh right, that's what he's talking about." I came of age as designers were first becoming public figures, people like Halston, Calvin Klein, Bill Blass. But the simple truth is other than an occasional guest spot on an afternoon talk show they weren't in your living room weekly. If I was thirteen and Halston would have been on TV every week I would've learned that much more about his clothes and his design philosophy.

ON NINA GARCIA

BARBARA SCHNEEWEISS:

We knew it would make sense to have a magazine editor on our judging panel. When we first started talking to our original magazine partner, *Elle*, one of the things we asked them was if they had an editor in house they thought might be good for the show. Normally we would ask for tape of that person to see how they were on camera. On Season 1 they presented us Anne Slowey and Nina Garcia. They alternated episodes.

DESIREE GRUBER:

The first season it was between Nina and Anne Slowey. I think Nina was available more. It was better for the show to have the three judges united—Heidi, Michael, and Nina—on a weekly basis. At first Nina seemed to be perceived as the mean judge, but when you know her, she's so not mean; she's great. She's very straightforward. When you edit a magazine, there's not a lot of time to be friendly and kind about what works on the pages and what doesn't work.

She gets straight to it and that's what you have to do. That's what you need on a TV show, too. All the judges have different personalities. They're really unique voices that come together to make a great panel.

JANE CHA:

With her natural elegance, smarts, and telegenic style, Nina was the editorial voice we wanted and needed. I sometimes marvel at how lucky we are. The chemistry between Heidi, Michael, and Nina is so rare and amazing, and it truly has only gotten better. They make me laugh hysterically during our breaks. We call those "Cheetos chats" because we eat unhealthy snacks and after the business end of the conversation is done, Michael in particular will regale us with amazing, hilarious stories.

NINA GARCIA:

When they asked if I wanted to be on a reality show I said, "No, I don't want to be on TV." They asked me if I thought if it was a good idea for a show and I said, "No, I think it's a terrible idea. Who's going to be interested?" Then I found out Heidi was involved and Michael had said yes, so I gave it more thought. I'd been looking at designers' work for twenty years trying to find new talent, so it made sense and I took the chance. I did not get involved to become a "personality" myself but instead to nurture young talent. My motivations to be a part of the show were no different than the founding principles of the CFDA (Council of Fashion Designers of America)—to help designers get their visions seen.

DO YOU THINK THAT THE ADVICE YOU OFFER AS AN EDITOR IS VERY DIFFERENT FROM WHAT MICHAEL AND HEIDI HAVE TO OFFER?

Yes, and that's why the dynamic works so well. Michael has the eye for the designs because he has been in the designer's position for years; someone trying to get their designs out there. As an editor I am used to working with designers and watching them grow, and I know what people are looking for.

PEOPLE OFTEN QUOTE TIM SAYING, "DON'T BORE NINA." WHAT DO YOU THINK MADE HIM SAY THAT IN THE FIRST PLACE?

I think Tim knows my day job is spent looking over designers' work and trying to do something new and fresh for the magazine. I easily get "bored" if someone continues to bring the same thing to the table.

We all get along so well and have a lot of fun on the set. Michael, Heidi, Tim, and I are like a family and each season new participants are added to our growing family. It is a stressful environment for the designers but we try to make it fun and let loose when cameras aren't rolling.

ON TIM GUNN

BARBARA SCHNEEWEISS:

When scouting our location I did outreach to FIT and to Parsons. When I called Parsons I got a person named Tim Gunn on the phone. He was very generous with his time. He talked to us on the phone and he allowed us to come in and ask questions. We knew that we wanted somebody to act as a den mother on the show, to be in the workroom with the designers. Because Tim came from academia, we felt he had those nurturing qualities and he might be the right guy for the job.

DESIREE GRUBER:

As mentor we were looking for a woman at first. We thought it would be like a den mother; somebody who would come in and be that confidant/advisor, that friendly face. When Tim Gunn came along we were worried at

first because he had never been on TV before. It wasn't something he had thought about before or needed for his brand. But he became a professional hand to guide the designers and put them back on track when they ran into trouble. From the first few episodes we knew Tim was a star. When we sat in meetings with him, you didn't get the feeling that this is the star of our show, but through him we learned how much we did not know.

ELI HOLZMAN:

We needed a location to film the show, somewhere that had sewing equipment and was cheap. Barbara Schneeweiss found a perfect spot: Parsons The New School for Design. They were closed to students for the summer and consequently readily available. When we toured the school we were first shown to the tiny office that housed the chairperson of the design program: a truly lovely gentleman named Tim Gunn.

As Tim toured us around the Parsons campus he explained the use of the various equipment and enumerated

the challenges of working with certain materials. (Swimsuit lycra can only be stitched once—who knew?) The more he talked, the more we became convinced that we would need a design expert on the show. In order for the audience to play along, they would need someone to explain the nuances of design challenges. Otherwise they, like us, would have no idea whether contestants were attempting the impossible or the mundane.

JANE CHA:

I still remember the first meeting with Tim in his office at Parsons. Tim was, then as now, warm, open, and genuine. Honestly, we had absolutely no inkling that he would take on such a big, integral role on air, but here we are ten seasons later and Tim is rightly beloved. He truly cares so much about the designers, and they do him. Tim gave us hope. Certain other potential mentors we met with were kind of sourpusses and pessimists. We needed someone with Tim's enthusiasm. I remember we took over Tim's office during shooting with racks of Heidi's clothes and accessories during the first couple of seasons of *Runway*, before we had a proper wardrobe budget and Heidi was wearing her own clothes. It made poor Tim's office a mess.

SARA REA:

Tim is a dream to work with! He is invested in the designers, the process, and the show. He is very passionate and gives 150 percent to every season. His background as a teacher truly comes across in his nurturing and heartfelt approach to each and every designer.

ON GUEST JUDGES

BARBARA SCHNEEWEISS:

The first season we were an unknown entity. It was definitely much harder to get the guest judges. People were very concerned about their image. They didn't know what they were walking into. Especially when they hear "reality television," there's a certain perception.

JANE CHA:

Some of the designers who signed up for Season 1 had a more adventurous, irreverent spirit, like Pat Field and Betsey Johnson. I don't think it's any secret that the default position of a lot of the "Fashion with a capital F" world is to regard an unknown quantity with some distance and a deathly fear of being "cheesy." But after that first season or so, when people really discovered the show and we developed a passionate fan base, we were fortunate to amass an incredible guest judging roster, including the likes of Donna Karan, Vera Wang, Francisco Costa, Diane von Furstenberg, Zac Posen, Bob Mackie, celebrities like Sarah Jessica Parker, Victoria Beckham, and Natalie Portman. So many of these people come on because they

are fans of the show. They're knowledgeable, on point, and give some great critiques to our designers. On the other hand, some have expressed that they're fans of the show, but don't want to put themselves in the position of judging other people.

We'd love to have some more European designers on. We've had Roberto Cavalli and Alberta Ferretti, among others, who were great. I would love to have Stella McCartney, Vivienne Westwood, Dries Van Noten, Donatella Versace, Dolce & Gabbana, Gaultier. It's challenging because we shoot in the summer and often they can't make the trip to New York because of their own show preparations.

ON THE DESIGNERS

HOW ARE THE DESIGNERS CHOSEN?

JANE CHA:

We used to do full open calls, but it got a little crazy. Too many people were coming in who were clearly less interested in design than they were interested in being on TV. It was becoming a waste of our time. You *do* need a certain level of technical proficiency to survive on the show, so we changed the process. We have retained a day or two of open calls in New York and Los Angeles, but we now have casting directors do outreach all over the country, to fashion academies, alumni associations, local retailers, past auditioners who have grown, etc. They pre-select a group of twenty to thirty people that the casting judging panel—made up of a *Runway* alum, retailer, magazine editor, Tim, and some of the producers—sees each day in five or six cities staggered over several weeks. The designers tell us about themselves, show their portfolios, and a few complete looks. Then for callbacks the designers have a longer, more involved interview with our casting directors. They also go home and shoot "about me" videos, which we view as part of the whole package before we decide on the cast.

The cast chemistry is one of the absolute most important aspects of the show. We do our best in the casting process, and then it's a bit up to serendipity. Sometimes designers we thought would behave a certain way or add to the group dynamic in a certain way end up being completely different, sometimes for better, sometimes for worse.

WHAT WAS IT LIKE CASTING THE FIRST DESIGN CONTESTANTS?

DESIREE GRUBER:

In our fantasy version of *Project Runway* every designer had their own seamstress, their own showroom. Then Magical Elves told us one seamstress for seven days a week would cost $30,000—and we needed twelve! We realized we were going to have to find designers who could sketch, design, and sew. There are not many designers that can do all aspects of it. It's not imperative for a lot of top designers to have each of those skills, but on *Project Runway* designers

have to be able to sew for the show to make sense. That made it very difficult casting the first season.

We needed people who would be interested in being on television not knowing what we were creating, and willing to and capable of doing all those things, and also be good characters—people who are interesting and fun to watch. When we pitched the show we said we're going to have the housewife from Topeka who sews in her basement, the disenfranchised guy out of the East Village, etc. We had these archetypes in mind and we actually got them.

BARBARA SCHNEEWEISS:

We asked all of our partners to reach out and we brought on an organization called GenArt, which cultivates young talent in the creative community. They did some outreach for us. We sent out flyers to art schools, coffee shops, and the like, and really tried to canvas the land as best we could. We honestly had no idea if twenty people were going to show up. Our first casting was at the Standard Hotel in downtown LA. I showed up at the hotel and saw a line around the block. There were people with garment bags, models with crazy outfits, shy people with just portfolios. It seemed there was every kind of person that's ever sewn for themselves or for anyone else out there. I wanted to thank every one of them for showing up. It was a big relief.

If you see enough people the cream rises to the top. It's very clear to see who's talented. We asked them a lot of questions about their skill sets, whether or not they could cut, sew, and pattern-make. We looked at their articles of clothing to see what their hems and seams looked like. Were their garments done professionally or could they use more time developing their technical skills? We looked at their portfolios and noted what range they had; if they were able to tell a story with their clothes; if they had a particular aesthetic; if they understood movement; if they had a defined idea of who their client is. We also asked them about which designers they like or emulate.

If someone comes in and it seems that all they want is to be on TV we don't necessarily feel that's the right person for us. We're really looking for skilled designers first and usually what comes along with that is an interesting personality. Not always, but a lot of the time. They are creative types. We love a good story where maybe this is someone's second chance or someone who never tried before.

The casting process has definitely changed since Season 1. In the first five seasons we did mass open casting calls. Starting at Season 6 we've asked designers to submit an application, photos, and video of themselves. Then it's decided if they're going to meet with the bigger group of casting people. We have casting calls in a number of cities throughout the country.

DO YOU THINK THE DESIGNERS ARE THEIR AUTHENTIC SELVES ON THE SHOW?

DESIREE GRUBER:

I wouldn't believe it if somebody said they were able to hide their true personality throughout the whole season. It's too stressful. I think one of the reasons the show is so popular is that viewers get into the act of creating along with the designers. We're following people who are authentically very creative; it's not manufactured. They're trying to bring out their best, which is hard to do in a timed experience. Being creative under pressure is not easy.

SARA REA:

The pace is extremely grueling and the pressure so great that they don't really have time to think about "playing a part" or being someone that they're not. They just have to get the job done.

HAVE YOU HAD ANY FAVORITE CONTESTANTS OVER THE YEARS?

JANE CHA:

I still am great friends with Christian Siriano, Nick Verreos, and Laura Bennett, all of whom were invited to my wedding. Christian even made my reception dress—an absolutely gorgeous blush-pink confection that I danced in all night. I also keep in touch with, and think are super-talented: Austin Scarlett, Daniel Vosovic, Mondo Guerra, and Anya Ayoung-Chee.

DESIREE GRUBER:

I love many of our past designers. It's very interesting to see people who are completely unknown become known, to see how fame affects people. Austin Scarlett was such incredible TV—still is. He's so authentic to who he is. He is a man with a dream and I really honor and respect him. Christian Siriano, same thing. Santino Rice is an incredible person and an incredible character.

MICHAEL KORS:

Well different ones for different reasons. There are the people who I think are fantastic at the glamour and drama, like Austin Scarlett, to someone who is very pragmatic and practical, like Chloe Dao, and then someone like Christian Siriano, who I think quite honestly is a combination of the two. I think it's also always interesting to see the difference between some of the women on the show versus the men. I think a lot of the guys are very abstract about how they design, and the women think about themselves, whether it's Anya or Gretchen. As designers, we all bring our life to our work—where we grew up, what our family was like, male or female, our age. Seeing people from diverse backgrounds deal with the exact same questions is interesting.

ARE YOU EVER SURPRISED BY THE CONTESTANTS WHEN YOU SEE THE SHOW?

MICHAEL KORS:

I never know what goes on behind the scenes until I watch the show. I'm surprised sometimes in a bad way and sometimes in a good way. There can be a person who I think is so lovely, then I see the show and he's insane. Or the opposite! There'll be someone who you think, God she's so combative and then when you watch the show you realize, "No, she's not. Perhaps she's uncomfortable standing there while we're talking to her?" I think the best thing is that we don't really know what's going on, that we really are just looking at the garment.

DO YOU THINK OF *PROJECT RUNWAY* AS A STAR-MAKING VEHICLE FOR THE DESIGNERS?

DESIREE GRUBER:

People think that if they get on *Project Runway* they'll be on easy street. To be on the show is to really push yourself to the limit, and when you get off the show designers feel like there should be some relief but there's not. You have to continue pushing. Christian Siriano pushes his butt off. He's amazing—in that studio all the time, working, pushing.

HEIDI KLUM:

I always try to support the designers by wearing their clothes after the show, especially when *Project Runway* has been nominated for an award. It's about the designers really, that's why I'm at those events. I wore a beautiful gray and yellow dress by Christian Siriano for an Emmy telecast that I hosted. He's a great designer. People always ask where certain designers are now. It depends on their personality and their drive and if they're still hustling afterwards. I've learned that you can't tell them, "Go go go," if they don't go

out and make the connections and keep working constantly. The show gives them a kick inside the industry but then it's really up to them. I think that Christian was really smart in doing Payless shoes. So he can go mass; people can have some of his stuff, while he also does $10,000 gowns. He also has the whole package of the personality. Jeffrey Sebelia has also done well. His stuff is really cool.

MICHAEL KORS:

I think the show's responsibility is to prepare designers for how hard this is going to be, how much work you're going to have to put into it, how fast you're going to have to think, and then if they do well, the show is going to shine the spotlight on them. It's a little like a track-and-field situation. Are they strong enough to continue the run and hold on to the baton? The show is not a pure business course, that's for sure. If they're going to succeed they have to be able to balance art and commerce.

ON THE MODELS

HOW ARE THE MODELS CHOSEN?

JANE CHA:

We do a casting a few weeks before the start of the new season. We have to give the models a lot of credit. They have to endure some hard situations. You try standing up in a dress made out of God-knows-what plastic, feather, paper, tile, or other inorganic material for a minimum of six hours—without being able to go to the bathroom or even sit for fear of wrinkling, smashing, or somehow destroying the garment. The models see firsthand what the designers go through and often they really bond with them, are a great source of support, and in the best of cases, inspiration.

HOW DO YOU COME UP WITH THE CHALLENGES?

BARBARA SCHNEEWEISS:

One of the most fun things about working on the show is coming up with the challenges. We all have ideas; they can come from our daily lives. In Season 1 there were a lot of people we spoke to along the way. We definitely had to do some research early on to make sure the designers were able to complete a garment within the timeframe we were giving them. We gave Parsons students some sample challenges. We had to make sure that we ended up with something presentable. Since none of us really knew how to sew or what went into cutting or pattern-making we definitely had to test it out.

The challenges are about what we like and what we feel they will be able to accomplish in the time restraints; other times it's about what is unexpected and what will push them. We've had them go to Michael Kors' studio and talk about how he uses his mood board. They've designed for Nina. These are some of the real world challenges. The unconventional materials challenges test their creativity. We love makeover challenges when they work with clients. The wedding dress challenge was a big favorite too.

ELI HOLZMAN:

All of the producers have contributed to create dozens of wonderfully inventive challenges. In the original pitch we gave an example challenge where the designers would be told they would be shopping for their materials at a store frequented by all of the top designers—the Duane Reade on 7th Avenue. This idea ultimately became the Gristedes supermarket challenge

in the first episode.

JANE CHA:

We only have eleven challenges during the season, so when you take out some of the ones that have become perennials, like our unconventional materials, prints, and uniforms, and take into account the sponsor-input challenges, there aren't many slots left. We really think about what's going on in pop culture, the environment, and what would make an interesting episode, visually and creatively. It's a group effort that involves numerous meetings over a master list and many, many follow-up e-mails and conference calls. Often it's a friendly fight for the producers to secure their personal favorites. For so long I wanted to do the Potato Sack challenge, taking off from that old saying "She'd look good in a potato sack." The designers would use the sack burlap as a base material. That challenge took me quite a while to get through but it was fun when we finally did it. I'll never forget the visual of Tim with his pants legs rolled up, standing in a Long Island potato field.

DESIREE GRUBER:

My favorite call as a producer is talking about the challenges, and how we "up it" this season. For instance,

the Suitcase challenge was my idea. When you're at baggage claim in the airport and watch the luggage go by, you see all these beat-up suitcases and think, "Whose stuff is that?" But then your beat-up suitcase comes out and you think, "There's my suitcase with all my favorite things in it!" I've always thought it's so interesting to see what somebody else's favorite things are in their suitcase. If you opened mine you're certain to find my favorite sweatsocks from college! We have a history with the items we own. They bring back memories. So the idea of that challenge was, "How does the person next to you respect something—maybe a pair of pants—that are meaningful to you? How do you respect that? And hand over something meaningful of your own." I love that.

I like when we team them up too. You see when somebody's a lone wolf, then all of the sudden they have to partner with somebody. You see more sides to their personality. I think on a daily basis I am very anthropological, especially working on this show. I love living in New York City, seeing all the people and how they react to each other. One of the great things about *Project Runway* is that it has so many levels. You could like fashion, but you don't have to like fashion to like the show. You could be into it for the challenges alone, watching what they do, how they handle the stress, what will they pull out of their hat? It's a show with a lot of entry points.

The challenges are riveting because you never know when somebody you're rooting for can have an off day, or somebody was in the bottom three and then all of a sudden they skyrocket up. Somebody comes in first at the end, but maybe they're not as strong as somebody else—that's life!

WHICH CHALLENGES HAVE BEEN SOME OF THE BEST?

JANE CHA:

So many to choose from—I love the plants and flowers challenge, the Hershey's candy-wrapper challenge, the Olympic figure skating costume, Barbie. Prom. Remember Christian Sirano having a hissy fit over his difficult client's choice of a brown color palette and design request for more sequins? Fantastic.

I love Til Dress Do Us Part, when the designers remade the wedding dresses of divorcées into something hot and wearable for future dating, the gorgeous hat challenge with Philip Treacy, the pet store with those fabulous competing hamster bedding and birdseed dresses, the Clothes Off Your Back challenge, in which the designers had to make do with what they themselves were wearing, what the designers next to them were wearing, or the materials and bedding in their just-moved-into apartment.

I loved going to Paris and doing the avant-garde challenge on a stunning riverboat at sunset along the Seine. Remember Jeffrey's beautiful plaid gown? I loved the car challenge, when Korto made a ridiculously stunning cocoon coat somehow, entirely out of seatbelts. The print challenge, in which Mondo shared a really personal story about the meaning of the + sign in his custom-made print, truly moved all of us.

I adore our unconventional materials challenges, which have also become favorites of many of our fans. And I love team challenges, in which the designers must collaborate and their true colors emerge. I remember one challenge, the designers were divided into two even teams, but one team seemed technically and personally at a major disadvantage. We jokingly nicknamed them the Bad News Bears, but they persevered and actually presented a fantastic collection to win that challenge.

MICHAEL KORS:

The most interesting thing for me is when they have to design an entire collection. That's really when I get to see the whole thrust of it and ask myself, "Is it too limited? Too one dimensional?"

The unconventional challenges are always very interesting because I like to see if they can create something not ridiculous out of a ridiculous situation. I think it really teaches you what they're capable of.

I think the most difficult challenges are consistently the menswear challenges. A lot of these people are very used to making dresses and it's very hard tailoring men's clothes. The body is different, the attitude is different.

SARA REA:

I always love the unconventional materials challenges because you just never know what the designers are going to come up with. They surprise us time and time again—

sometimes in a good way and sometimes in a not-so-good way! I loved the newspaper challenge from Season 6. I also love the HP create your own fabric challenge because the designers are literally starting with a blank slate and their imagination.

HOW DOES THE JUDGES' SCORING WORK?

MICHAEL KORS:

When judging, design comes first in importance, then the fit. When you're dressing a model who quite frankly could wear almost anything, if the fit is terrible or does bad things for her body, time is not the issue. Fit shows an understanding of a woman's body and how to cut clothes properly. Then last but still important is construction. When it comes to construction the designer has to be honest about their skill level and manage time well. If you've never made men's clothes before, why on earth would you try to make a beautifully tailored jacket in a day and a half? Construction teaches me how knowledgeable they are about fabric, how experienced they are, how clever, and how honest they are about themselves and what they're good at. It's design first; cut, proportion, and what it does for the body second; and construction third.

I think some of the designers over the years think they can strategize like athletes, which is not stupid because I would tell everyone it's fine to get the attention but you want to be a long distance runner. I think some of them think, "Maybe if I'm just kind of in the middle I'll never get thrown off, and then all of a sudden at the end I'll come out with guns blazing." You can have a few things that are okay, but overall every designer has to make mistakes to go to the next step. If someone said everything you do is "okay" you're never going to progress. I certainly don't want to see a full car crash, but if there's something where they turned the wheel a little too much to the left or too much to the right, that's a good thing because they're going to learn from it and grow by experimenting.

HOW MUCH OF WHAT THE DESIGNER SAYS ABOUT THEIR LOOK DURING THE CRITIQUE INFLUENCES YOU IN THE JUDGING?

NINA GARCIA:

If they show passion and have a strong stance on their work, no matter how "off" the challenge project may be I take what they say into consideration. Their one mishap could be due to just a rough, exhausting day. That is not an excuse but their belief in their work says a lot. What I don't like is stubbornness. If we are telling you something take it in and use it to your advantage for the next challenge.

WHAT ARE SOME OF THE CHALLENGES OF JUDGING?

MICHAEL KORS:

I try hard to make my decision a week-to-week evaluation. If there's a draw in my mind; two people look equally bad or equally good, who will either stay or go, then I start thinking about the body of work. You have to be honest with a designer because when they start having four collections a year, the press is certainly going to be very honest with them. You're not doing them any favors by candy coating anything, but at the same time you don't feel the need to be vitriolic. We have fun. After all these years it's still fun, we're still curious, and still intrigued.

HEIDI KLUM:

In the beginning I was afraid to step on people's toes. Can you say what you really think? Sometimes I thought a dress looked really horrible, but didn't want to hurt the designer's feelings. You have to articulate what is not good about a look so that the audience at home understands why you're saying a certain thing is good or not good; why this is modern; why this is new; and why this is something that we've already seen before.

I eventually got over my fear. Off screen I enjoy time with the contestants when we're not judging and we're goofing around at the snack bar. I always have something positive and negative to say about each and every one of them. When we judge it takes around five hours and it gets cut down to fifteen minutes of airtime. The audience that sees the final version maybe only sees me being harsh, but the designer knows who I am and what I really said on that day.

PEOPLE HAVE SAID TO ME THAT THEY WONDER IF THE PRODUCERS HAVE ANY INFLUENCE ON THE JUDGING. HOW WOULD YOU ANSWER THAT?

DESIREE GRUBER:

The judges are the judges. Those four people wouldn't put their names on the show and say they're judges if they didn't have authority.

JONATHAN MURRAY:

Evidence of the fact that the producers don't have a say was the season where Gretchen beat Mondo, because any producer or writer would have scripted that differently. It was a better story for Mondo to win. But we showed what happened on the air. Nina and Michael really believed that what Gretchen was creating was more commercial, and that she deserved to win. Heidi disagreed. The guest judge (Jessica Simpson) disagreed, but I think the guest judges find it hard to really make their opinions felt when they're going up against Heidi, Michael, or Nina. Heidi lost that battle. As a producer I can root for the contestants and I don't have to make the decision to eliminate them. I was rooting for Mondo. I'm just like everyone else out there watching. It's important that there be people that the audience wants to root for.

WHAT HAPPENS TO THE CLOTHING THE DESIGNERS MAKE ON THE SHOW?

JANE CHA:

The looks get auctioned off on the projectrunway.com

website and proceeds are donated to a few different charities over the years, including Dress for Success and the Robin Hood Foundation. I've heard funny stories about who ends up with these auction items. A friend of Chloë Sevigny's told me that because they both are fans of the show he made a point to get one of the winning looks at auction for Chloë. And Laura Bennett, one of our alums, told me after her season her husband so wanted her to have some of her winning looks that he bid and got them for her.

WHAT IS THE FINALE LIKE?

BARBARA SCHNEEWEISS:

I always get choked up at the finale. When you're in production you're worrying about budget and schedule and it's stressful. When you get to the finale you see the culmination of all of the designers' hard work. What they make is really spectacular and the mood is amazing. You're giving young, talented people an opportunity to live out their dream. It's gratifying and a really special moment.

MERYL POSTER:

It's very exciting. When you're there you see people who you had no idea were fans of the show. There are so many celebrities that follow *Project Runway*. You can feel the energy and excitement in the room. Everyone is rooting for their favorites.

IN THE BEGINNING, WAS THERE A PERCEPTION THAT FASHION WOULD NEVER PLAY ON TELEVISION?

DESIREE GRUBER:

Of course, but we knew how exciting it was. If you're in fashion you know the drama that takes place to get things made. When you see a runway show it seems like the designer decided these things months ago. Behind the scenes people in the industry know they might have changed their minds the night before and stuff didn't arrive in time. They didn't have enough leather to make a long skirt so they sent the models out in minis. There is a lot of last-minute preparation that has the power to change the entire tone of a show.

HEIDI KLUM:

We always thought of *Project Runway* more as a documentary show and not so much what people think of as a reality show. *Project Runway* is really about talent. It was important that we were taken seriously, because when you work very hard for people to think that you are okay in the fashion industry and then you do a show that is terrible or cheesy, you can't show your face anymore anywhere in this industry—might as well do a different job if it goes wrong.

BARBARA SCHNEEWEISS:

My dad, kept saying to me, "You're making a show about sewing." I don't think that's going to be very exciting. He wasn't my test market group so I let him say his piece and kept going. I understood antithetical to what my father said; we had *Project Greenlight*, which gave talented young people a chance to do what they wanted to do, so I knew that some of that drama and emotion would play into what we were doing. Fashion is a really big landscape. We didn't know how well it would take off. But once we saw Austin's cornhusk dress in Season 1, Episode 1, we knew this works. We really felt like we had something. We also had no idea Tim Gunn would take off the way he did.

A big part of the show's success is that we have always had a lot of great people working on it. Jane and Desiree at Full Picture have been wonderful partners and they've brought so much to the table. At the start, the Magical Elves really helped to shape the show and turn it into the format it is today. When Bunim/Murray came on board as production company after we moved to Lifetime, they respected our process and really only thought to add to improve the show instead of to take away. Everyone working on the show is passionate. Everyone from assistants to cameramen to production people have all expressed their passion for the show and their appreciation for what the designers do. We've really been lucky.

WHY DO YOU THINK THE SHOW WORKED?

NINA GARCIA:

Project Runway came at a time when the industry was going through a kind of democratization. H&M and Zara

were just arriving in the U.S. as *Project Runway* started and suddenly the world of fashion became fashionable. People wanted to know how the designers worked.

AT WHAT POINT DID YOU KNOW THAT SHOW WAS A HIT?

MICHAEL KORS:

Slowly, after the show was on for a few weeks, I started hearing about people who have been in the industry for a long time who were glued to the show. Fashion people are very judgmental and very protective of our

world, yet they were having fun with this. Then the next thing I knew I started having people tell me, "Oh my husband, he's an investment banker, he loves the show." Or, "My husband is an attorney, he loves the show, we watch it with the family." I realized for them it was the same thing that had happened for me, not being in the film industry but being intrigued by *Project Greenlight*. To see someone, really as alchemy, take nothing and make it into something so quickly is intriguing regardless of whether you're into fashion or not. I knew early into the first season that we had something that was very special, different—an original.

THE RUNWAY

PARSONS' WORKROOM

HOW DID PARSONS BECOME THE SETTING FOR THE SHOW?

DESIREE GRUBER:

We originally envisioned the setting as some cool loft. Parsons was a last minute decision, and it shaped so much of the show. That's why we shoot in the summer, when school is out and the space is available.

BARBARA SCHNEEWEISS:

They had a lot of the resources that we needed. They had classrooms, which could be good for production, and there was enough space for a sewing room and a workroom, so it fell into place.

THE ACCESSORIES WALL

30

MOOD

BRYANT PARK

LINCOLN CENTER

PART 2:

ONE DAY YOU'RE IN AND THE NEXT DAY YOU'RE OUT...

THE DESIGNERS

DANIEL FRANCO
FROM: LOS ANGELES, CA
STUDIED: OTIS COLLEGE OF ART
AND DESIGN

MARIO CADENAS
FROM: PEMBROKE PINES, FL
STUDIED: THE ART INSTITUTE OF
FORT LAUDERDALE

STARR ILZHOEFER
FROM: CHARLOTTE, NC
CORPORATE LAWYER

VANESSA RILEY
FROM: LONDON, ENGLAND
STUDIED: KENT COLLEGE OF
ART AND DESIGN

NORA CALIGURI
FROM: CHESHIRE, CT
STUDIED: PRATT INSTITUTE

ALEXANDRA VIDAL
FROM: CORAL GABLES, FL
STUDIED: MIAMI INSTITUTE
OF ART AND DESIGN, PARIS
FASHION INSTITUTE

KEVIN JOHNN
FROM: NEW YORK, NY
STUDIED: ART INSTITUTE OF
CHICAGO

ROBERT PLOTKIN
FROM: NEW YORK, NY
STUDIED: FASHION INSTITUTE
OF TECHNOLOGY, POLIMODA
INSTITUTE OF FASHION
DESIGN AND MARKETING

AUSTIN SCARLETT
FROM: COTTAGE GROVE, OR
STUDIED: FASHION INSTITUTE
OF TECHNOLOGY

WENDY PEPPER
FROM: DAYTON, OH
SELF-TAUGHT

KARA SAUN
FROM: LOS ANGELES, CA
SELF-TAUGHT

JAY MCCARROLL
FROM: DALLAS, PA
STUDIED: PHILADELPHIA
COLLEGE OF TEXTILES
AND SCIENCE, LONDON
COLLEGE OF FASHION

SEASON 1

HIGHLIGHTS

UNCONVENTIONAL MATERIALS CHALLENGE

Project Runway's very first challenge was all about innovation. The designers were told to design something glamorous and sexy for a night out on the town. They were shocked when Tim Gunn took them to get their fabric at Gristedes—a supermarket. While other designers scooped up items such as butcher paper, garbage bags, and wrapping paper, Austin grabbed twenty-eight ears of corn. He used the husks to make a dress. At midnight the designers had to leave the workroom. Austin didn't refrigerate the husks, and when he returned in the morning he found that they had shrunk. He doubted his decision, but the judges thought what he created was fabulous. He won the challenge, and showed viewers what *Project Runway* would be all about.

BARBARA SCHNEEWEISS:

"He used something that you would never think you could use. The color was magnificent and the design of the dress was wonderful. That was the first challenge of the first season. We didn't know what we were going to get since admittedly we were holding our breath until we saw the cornhusk dress. When we saw that we felt okay, we're good."

HEIDI KLUM:

"Having the show's very first challenge be the supermarket challenge was a big back and forth between the producers. I thought this can go really, really wrong. If we do an unconventional challenge and they go to the supermarket and pick some weird stuff, it might look like a terrible Mardi Gras float. If they do some baloney stuff right off the bat we're going to look really bad and no one is going to take us seriously. For me, it was always about being taken seriously. We wanted to have a place in the fashion world. We didn't want all the people with their noses up in the sky say that we're doing some crazy arts

and crafts. Then we decided to go for it and take the risk with an unconventional challenge. It worked out because the designers were actually really talented and they came up with amazing things. Austin putting that cornhusk dress together. It was magical and it was real at the same time. There was also Nora, who made a futuristic dress out of plastic from a lawn chair. That was amazing. In retrospect I think we hit a home run leading off with this challenge."

NORA'S ROSES

The models were the clients for the Wedding Dress challenge. The designers were given the task to work with their model to create the wedding dress of her dreams. Nora was paired with Melissa. Melissa came in with a clear idea of what she wanted; since her middle name was Rose, she had to have roses on the dress. She told Nora that this was the dress she had been dreaming about since she was a little girl. Nora thought Melissa's concept was cheesy, but did what Melissa wanted. While Melissa was thrilled with the results, the judges didn't agree. The consensus was that Nora deferred to the client so much that her vision was lost, and she was sent home.

MORGAN DRAMA

All the models showed up for their fittings for the first challenge—except Kara Saun's model, Morgan. She couldn't be reached by phone, so Kara went out on the street to ask passersby if they would model for her. Morgan finally arrived and explained that she overslept. Her mother was out of town, and she usually woke her. Wendy took Morgan aside to console her. Morgan was crying, and told Wendy her agency had just dropped her. Kara came back from the street without finding a model, and got Morgan ready for the runway.

Later, Kevin chose Morgan to be his model for a challenge where the designers had to make a swimsuit sleek and elegant enough to navigate the waters of a fashion industry party at the Hiro cocktail lounge at the Maritime Hotel. After the party Morgan told Kevin that she was going out to a club. He told her he didn't want her to wear his outfit out, and she said she would change. The next day Morgan showed up for the runway show with the swimsuit. She had worn it all night and ripped it. Kevin was upset and Morgan was upset.

HIGHLIGHTS

POSTAL UNIFORM CHALLENGE

The designers donned postal uniforms for this challenge. Their job was to redesign the postal uniform. They were split into two groups and set out with an actual letter carrier to spend the day delivering mail.

KARA SAUN:

"The postal uniform challenge was definitely the funniest. Jay, Rob, and I had the best team and the best time. We had so much fun walking the streets, singing, greeting passersby. It was hilarious and I have a new appreciation for the job postal workers do. It's a lot more complex than one would think."

EVIL WENDY

In Episode 2 Wendy admitted that everything she did was strategic. She said that she knew it was kind of evil to exploit her role as a mother, but she was willing to do it to get to the end. Her strategy worked; she did indeed make it to the final three. However, she didn't make many friends along the way, as most of the other designers objected to her tactics.

AUSTIN THE MODEL

Four hours before the runway show for the Postal Uniform challenge, Jay was informed that his model Julia would be arriving at the very last minute. He was uneasy with the situation. As it got later and later, and Jay was unable to reach Julia by phone he started to think about other options. Robert called a friend to see if his girlfriend would come and do it, but she was unavailable. With no time left, and no Julia, Jay asked Austin to model for him. He figured that Julia and Austin's bodies were very similar. Austin stepped up and saved the day for Jay.

VISITING MICHAEL KORS

The designers had the privilege of being invited to visit Michael Kors at his studio. He gave them a tour, and showed them what was possible for them in the future. Kara Saun called the experience inspirational.

WHO DREW ON WENDY'S DAUGHTER'S PICTURE?

Upon her return from delivering mail for the postal Uniform challenge, Wendy discovered that someone had taken the picture of her daughter she kept on her table and drawn a line on the face. Wendy was extremely upset by this, as she had no other copies of the photo. She never found out who the culprit was.

VANESSA AT THE REUNION

All the designers were present for the reunion special. Everyone ganged up on Wendy, and said they didn't think she deserved to make it to the finale. Vanessa called her a terrible designer. She also accused Wendy of being the one who drew on her daughter's picture. It was revealed during the reunion that Vanessa had given a scathing interview about the show. Finally Vanessa said she didn't want to be there and walked off—after spilling her wine on the floor.

CONTROVERSY OVER KARA SAUN'S FINALE SHOES

Kara Saun's shoes for the finale were given to her by the Dollhouse shoe line as a favor. When Tim Gunn found out he said it was problematic since she hadn't paid for them. It turned out she was in breach of the *Runway* contract, which said that you can't have anything done as a favor that would enhance the collection. Kara got a receipt, showing she was charged $15 for each pair. Tim said the producers would not accept that those shoes would cost only $15. She was given three options: go without shoes; use new shoes which all the designers had access to; or use the shoes, but the judges couldn't factor them in the judging. She chose the third option.

INNOVATION (AUSTIN)   VISION (KARA)

COMMERICIAL APPEAL (WENDY)　　　　　　　　　　　COLLABORATION (KEVIN)

MAKING A SPLASH (AUSTIN)   FINALE (JAY)

IN SEASON 1, WHEN THE SHOW WAS JUST STARTING OUT, THERE WAS NOT A PHOTOGRAPHER ON SET DURING THE FILMING OF EVERY EPISODE. THEREFORE, THERE IS NO PHOTOGRAPHY OF FOUR OF THIS SEASON'S WINNING LOOKS. KARA SAUN WON THREE OF THOSE CHALLENGES NOT PICTURED: "MODEL" CLIENTS, DESIGN A COLLECTION, AND POSTAL SERVICE. WENDY PEPPER WON THE LAST CHALLENGE BEFORE THE FINALE, DESIGN FOR THE RED CARPET.

MODELS

MARY HENDERSON

ALLISON ZEBELIAN

JOSIANE BARBOZA

AUDREY CHIHOCKY

JOY PURSELL

MORGAN QUINN

ERIN DENARDO

OLGA KONONOVA

MARTINIQUE MITCHELL

MELISSA HARO

JENNY TOTH

JULIA BEYNON

PATRICIA FIELD
COSTUME DESIGNER, *SEX AND THE CITY*

CONSTANCE WHITE
STYLE DIRECTOR, EBAY

PAUL BERMAN
OWNER, 30 VANDAM

DEBORAH LLOYD
EVP, PRODUCT DESIGN AND DEVELOPMENT, BANANA REPUBLIC

SARAH HUDSON
MUSIC RECORDING ARTIST

ANNE SLOWEY
FASHION NEWS DIRECTOR, *ELLE*

AMSALE ABERRA
WEDDING DRESS DESIGNER

RICHARD JOHNSON
PAGE SIX COLUMNIST

BETSEY JOHNSON
FASHION DESIGNER

NANCY O'DELL
ACCESS HOLLYWOOD HOST

PARKER POSEY
ACTRESS

EPISODE 8'S GUEST
JUDGE WAS USPS LETTER
CARRIER BECKY NEGICH

SNAPPED!

JAY MCCARROLL

HOW DID YOU HEAR ABOUT THE AUDITION FOR *PROJECT RUNWAY*?

I was involved with a fabulous organization called GenArt which, at the time, was helping to cast the show from their extensive roster of designers. I got an e-mail from them, threw my portfolio together, and the next thing I was on a bus to New York.

WHAT DID YOU THINK WHEN YOU FOUND OUT THAT THE FIRST CHALLENGE WOULD BE USING MATERIALS FROM THE SUPERMARKET?

I think I was still in shock that I was being filmed for a television show. It was all very surreal. The task at hand was to make something from an unusual source. Oddly enough, it wasn't that much of a stretch from some of the projects we had to do in college. I thought it was a fun challenge, but there was the added pressure of the constraints of the show. Make something for no money in a few hours and have it judged by professionals. On TV!

WHY WERE YOU SURPRISED THE JUDGES LIKED YOUR CHRYSLER BUILDING DRESS SO MUCH?

It was the third challenge, and I couldn't quite gauge how I was doing in the competition yet, so I think I was surprised that they were noticing me. But I really loved that dress and the organic nature in which the idea to do something inspired by that building came to me.

WAS IT FUN DELIVERING MAIL?

Not particularly. Conceptually it seems like a fun job, but it was surprisingly challenging. There are so many things you have to be thinking about all at once, and the possibility of it becoming deathly monotonous. Not to mention the threat of dogs biting you! It was also especially hot that day, and we were just starting to figure Wendy out, so there was drama brewing.

WHY WAS JULIA UNABLE TO SHOW UP FOR THE RUNWAY SHOW FOR THE POSTAL UNIFORM CHALLENGE?

Julia was booked on a job. I don't blame her for not coming. A girl's got to make that coin!

WAS IT FUN HAVING AUSTIN AS YOUR MODEL?

It was a blast having Austin model for me. I think he was waiting for that all season long. He did a fantastic job and looked great; is there any question that he wouldn't have? He also saved my ass that day.

WERE YOU SURPRISED BY VANESSA'S BEHAVIOR AT THE REUNION?

At the time, yes. Having gotten to a place in my career where other people are sewing for me, I can now fully understand her questioning why we had to sew. It just doesn't happen in the real world of fashion, but for the sake of the show, we had to sew. Having reconnected with her since the show, I find her to be a thoroughly interesting and highly entertaining individual and I overlook any past lapses in her judgment.

WAS WENDY AS BAD AS IT APPEARED ON TV?

No. I don't think she was bad. She was just a little delusional about the premise of the show. Actually, I think she is a pretty fascinating character.

DID YOUR FAMILY LIKE BEING ON THE SHOW?

Not really. They actually kind of hated being on television. My mother especially.

WHAT WAS THE MOST FUN PART OF DOING THE SHOW?

Meeting and hanging out with the other designers and the amazing crew. I think the most fun I had wasn't in the workroom, but in the interview room. It was the best free therapy! Where else can you just sit in a room for an hour and spill out all of your terrible thoughts and opinions about the people surrounding you, and no one tells you that you are wrong for thinking the way you do. It was amazing!

WHAT WAS IT LIKE BEING THE FIRST WINNER OF *PROJECT RUNWAY*?

It was a great honor and a heck of a lot of fun. The years since the show have had their ups and downs, but what industry or life situation doesn't?

HOW DID WINNING THE SHOW IMPACT YOUR LIFE?

It was a lot of fun for me and my friends and family to experience together. It got me into a lot of really great events and parties that I wouldn't have had a chance in hell of getting into. It opened a lot of doors for opportunity; some good and some totally terrifying in a myriad of aspects. The best way it impacted me was by giving me exposure and name recognition that has helped me to create a fan base that actually buys my stuff and allows me to do what I love every day.

KARA SAUN

HOW DID YOU GET ON PROJECT RUNWAY?

Before the show I had experienced some successes, already designed for various movies and shows and created looks for Queen Latifah, Eve, and Mary J. Blige. I was on a quest to find the next something big. Months before the ad appeared, I had told my mother, my biggest supporter and cheerleader, "Mom, I don't know what it is, but something big is coming. I feel it!" And only as she would respond, confidently and with exuberance, "You know I think you're right. I feel it too. Something big is coming!" So I prepared for that "something big." No one had heard of *Project Runway* or knew what it was. My manager at the time saw the ad in *Elle* magazine. There was Heidi on the runway with the words "Are you the next Calvin Klein or Donna Karan?" Immediately the page was torn and hung on a wall. I knew then and there that I was meant to be on *Project Runway*. It was like a gift from God; I knew that was the "something big".

By the time my manager brought me the ad, New York and Los Angeles auditions were done. The last audition was South Beach Florida in a week. No worries, I was going to pull together an amazing presentation. I created great new samples, re-designed my portfolio, purchased my tickets, booked the hotel, and hopped a plane to South Beach. When I arrived the venue was packed with anxious designers filling out applications. The audition was a three-tier process. If you made it through the first two tiers you were carted upstairs for the big audition in front of Tim Gunn and two other judges. I stood confident and took in every moment. I watched as a cameraman was slowly walking down the line interviewing people on camera. He introduced himself as Rich Bye, asked a few questions, and then moved to the

next candidate. As he reached me, before he could give his usual greetings I spoke up. "Hi, Rich Bye right?" I proceeded to act like he was an old friend and he laughed as he started asking me a number of questions. I told him my story, how I jumped the flight to South Beach and how I just knew I was meant to be there. He stopped and said, "Come with me." He proceeded to pull me out of line and walk me past the first tier of judges, then the second. We went up the elevator to the final and third tier of judges, "You stay here until they call your name,"

he said as he took his camera and disappeared through the crowd. I would find out later, Rich Bye was one of the executive producers of the show.

As I took my leather camouflage portfolio and garment bag of samples through the audition door, there sat Tim Gunn and the other judges. I put on, what I can only describe as an Academy Award-winning performance. I was beyond excited when I was told I was going on through. As I left the hotel, other designers stopped me and asked questions, congratulating me. One of them said, "I had a feeling when I saw you, you were going to make it." I guess even he knew that was my "something big!"

TIM GUNN KNEW WHO YOU WERE WHEN YOU AUDITIONED. CAN YOU TELL ME ABOUT THAT?

Many years ago, when New York Fashion Week was coming I thought, "What can I do? No one knows who I am and I don't have the funds for a show." In Europe they have these renegade fashion shows where you just crash a fashion show with one of your own. I decided to have my own renegade fashion show. A group of friends helped me—a model friend, hairstylist friends, a makeup artist friend. Everyone thought I was crazy and we'd surely be arrested.

The big day we pull up in front of the Bryant Park Tents and say a prayer before we get out of the rented limousine. There were crowds, clamoring outside the show waiting to get in. There were editors, buyers, and fashionistas. When the girls started modeling it was like the world stood still. Everybody stopped and looked in amazement. I saw a police officer walk towards me and I knew it was over. He leaned down and said, "How much time do you need?" Yes! Next thing I know I was being interviewed by *The New York Times*. Everybody was talking about it.

Exactly ten years to the day, I was doing *Project Runway*. On the second day I met Tim Gunn. He said, "Kara Saun, I know who you are." "You know who I am?" I replied. "Yes, I remember your renegade fashion show ten years ago. Everybody at Parsons was talking about it.

You showed them what it took to have guts in fashion." I replayed what Tim Gunn had said to me again and again in my ahead, with each challenge I designed.

WHAT WAS IT LIKE BEING PART OF THE ORIGINAL CAST?

It's a very special and surreal feeling. Being a part of something that would become a groundbreaking part of pop culture is mind-blowing. The original cast is like being in a secret fraternity. Only we know what it will ever feel like. In 2004, reality television was heating up and taking over. But a few of us were thinking, this could be really, really great for our careers or really, really bad. Luckily, in the fine print of the *Project Runway* ad, I saw the production company's name: Magical Elves. I looked them up and was so relieved to see they produced *Project Greenlight*, a show about aspiring filmmakers that I loved. The production value was great and they really focused on the talent of their contestants, so I knew we wouldn't be sewing and then asked to eat worms or cow eyes or bungee jump off of the Parsons roof, before we went on to the next challenge. Once the show aired we began to see the power of *Project Runway*. It was the sleeper, the new "it" show. People of all ages, genders, and from all walks of life, were so truly inspired.

WHAT WAS YOUR FAVORITE AND LEAST FAVORITE CHALLENGE?

It would be a tie. The Envy challenge was my first win, which is always the sweetest. I loved my military-inspired sheer olive cotton dress with hat. The win had greater meaning, as it was designed in honor of my father, Major Clifford Saunders. He would literally sign me out of school to take me fabric shopping and was a very devoted father to me and husband. My other favorite was the 2055 challenge. I absolutely love sci-fi and creating anything futuristic, so I was in heaven. I loved my long, muted maxi coat, with detachable high cowl collar, and the sexy nude silk and lace dress hidden underneath was killer.

My least favorite challenge was the Red Carpet challenge. This was the one challenge I should have killed, as red carpet is my specialty, but by the ninth episode we were all feeling it and it reared its ugly head in some pretty uninspired work. I still can't believe I didn't do what I had done the entire show, which was to heed the warnings of our fashion guru godfather, Tim Gunn. With his trademark, arms folded, hand on chin, Tim cautioned that the leather pants over the dress I created, simply did not work. I should have immediately burned them. He was so right.

DID YOU FEEL ALLEGIANCE TO A PARTICULAR MODEL?

I absolutely felt an allegiance to my top model, the gorgeous Jenny Toth, who was my model seven out of the ten challenges, three of which were wins, and naturally she closed the finale show. She was a chameleon who could change with whatever design I created. Every outfit hung perfectly on her.

WHICH JUDGE DID YOU FEEL GAVE YOU THE BEST ADVICE?

The best advice I received was from the fashion guru godfather Tim Gunn. All the advice he gave was sincere and spot on. It was clear Tim was on the side of the designers and that he truly was invested and cared about the work and assisting us in being the best we could be.

DID YOU HAVE A FAVORITE GARMENT YOU MADE FOR THE SHOW?

Absolutely. An outfit in my "Fly Girls" Bryant Park finale collection—the olive leather military-inspired maxi coat, sweater, and silk wool capri, with aviator hat and goggles. I feel it represents me, my work, and my run on *Project Runway* in many ways. It represents the fight, the hustle, the heart, and the beauty that is poured into each and every challenge.

YOU AND WENDY HAD PROBLEMS LEADING UP TO THE FINALE. WHAT HAPPENED?

I can't help but to laugh a little when I think back to those days. I literally read my quote about "saving your soul" on a billboard. A well known hotel actually used it in an ad. During the taping of *Project Runway* I was friendly to Wendy. She always seemed to be lonely and depressed, so I'd invite her to sit at our table or talk or walk with her. She was always referring to her age, grey hair, and how everyone was younger and prettier. It wasn't until the 2055 challenge that we realized the entire thing was a strategy, and it wasn't until much later, when the show aired, that we learned how deep that strategy ran. The entire time she had ulterior motives. The rest of us were enjoying ourselves and the experience, even though it was challenging and we had to compete against each other. Sadly, she missed out on that aspect of being on the show.

WERE YOU AWARE THAT JAY AND WENDY FELT IT WAS UNFAIR THAT YOUR FRIEND FROM DOLLHOUSE HELPED YOU?

Just to clarify, my dear friend James Howell did not work for Dollhouse. He's an amazing stylist who had a great relationship with them. We were all given the option to have someone come in to help out a bit, as long as it wasn't with the sewing. James even went to the store for Jay to get him some supplies. I had absolutely no idea Jay felt that way until the airing of the finale, when Jay, who was watching from the east coast, called me before I saw it on the west coast to say he felt bad about that and a few other things he'd said. I understand people being under pressure. It was all good though and forgotten.

HOW HAS *PROJECT RUNWAY* CHANGED YOUR LIFE?

Project Runway has truly been a blessing in every possible way. When people say to me, "Kara Saun, you were robbed," my response is, "Losing *Project Runway* was the best thing that ever happened to me." Offers rolled in. I heard, "Had you won we would have never called, thinking you'd be unavailable." To this day *Project Runway* continues to be a wonderful walking resume and a great conversation piece. It's truly the gift from God that keeps on giving.

WHAT WOULD PEOPLE BE SURPRISED TO KNOW ABOUT *PROJECT RUNWAY*?

Everyone is very surprised when they learn that we do

not keep our amazing finale collections. *Project Runway* auctions them off to the public and the proceeds go to a good cause.

WHAT HAVE YOU BEEN DOING SINCE *PROJECT RUNWAY*?

Currently I'm the owner and creative force behind Kara Saun LLC, a fashion and costume design house that specializes in highly-stylized, fashion-driven projects. We infuse a fresh and unmistakable ultra-luxe signature into each and every detail and manage up to thirty employees, depending on the project.

I've been blessed to be the go-to costume designer behind such shows as NBC's *The Sing-Off* (three seasons) and MTV's hit series *America's Best Dance Crew* (five seasons). Other costume design credits include the ABC reality series *True Beauty*, which featured my Red Carpet Collection; Disney's *The Cheetah Girls*; WB's *What I Like About You*, and numerous TV pilots.

In front of the camera I made appearances as a fashion expert on TV networks such as NBC, E!, The Style Network, and Bravo. I'm fortunate to have had celebrities grace the red carpets and pages of magazines in the Kara Saun brand including Heidi Klum, Zoe Saldana, Vanessa Williams, Joy Bryant, Mario Lopez, Lisa Rinna, Keisha Whitaker, Amanda Bynes, Nick Lachey, Vanessa Minnillo, Eve, Mary J. Blige, Eddie Murphy, Lil' Kim, and Queen Latifah.

I feel blessed, exuberant, and continue to boldly expand my emerging brand into the fashion and entertainment realm, where there are no limits to the amazing adventures to come. This is just the beginning!

AUSTIN SCARLETT

YOU SET THE TONE FOR THE SHOW WITH YOUR INCREDIBLE CORNHUSK DRESS. WHAT INSPIRED YOU TO MAKE SUCH A BRAVE CHOICE OF MATERIALS, WHEN SO MANY OTHERS OPTED FOR FABRIC-LIKE ITEMS?

The beauty of nature and the world of organic things have always been one of the greatest sources of inspiration for me. Visions of the husks as petals or feathers began unfolding and layering themselves in my imagination. There is also something so iconic American about the idea of corn that I think everyone responded to. I saw the potential for something chic yet playful, imaginative yet classic, humble yet luxuriant.

DID YOU HAVE ANY IDEA THAT DRESS WOULD BE THE MOST FAMOUS DRESS IN THE SHOW'S HISTORY?

Of course not! At that time I didn't even knew if the show would survive a full season. The art department hadn't even finished stenciling the runway backdrop yet. Somehow, even with the passing of years, people just kept going back to my cornhusk dress as an example of the type of creativity that is the heart and soul of *Project Runway*. Back during the first season, I did feel the sense of taking part in something truly special. It was a pioneer program on so many levels. Watching how much the show has grown over the years, I think my intuition was right. Was a corn kernel the first seed of the show's success? In its own little way, perhaps it was.

WHAT WAS IT LIKE WINNING THE SWIMSUIT CHALLENGE AND BEING MENTIONED ON *PAGE SIX*?

Oh what a fun frolic that was! However, I must admit I did have an unfair advantage, cocktail parties being my natural element. Also, most people don't know that when I drink champagne, I develop superhuman powers—powers that render any other designer utterly defenseless in my wake. Once I downed my first flute, Jay didn't stand a chance.

What else can I say? I always love making women feel glamorous, sexy, and feminine. I would still love to do a full swimwear line one day. A lot of credit on that challenge goes to my model, Melissa Haro, the sixteen-year-old femme fatale. She became a Guess girl shortly after the show, and I'm convinced the sultry Elizabeth Taylor bathing beauty look I created for her cinched the job.

The *Post Page Six* mention was so exciting! That was really the very first form of public recognition I ever received. Oh, I was such an ingénue then! I remember them mentioning something about "star quality" and being a "native New Yorker." Although I am from Oregon originally, I moved to the city as a teenager to study design, and now do feel I am a proper Manhattanite. Sometimes, whenever some smart-aleck asks where I'm from, I reply, "I am a Native New Yorker . . . according to *Page Six*!"

WAS IT FUN MODELING FOR JAY?

First of all, I love Jay. On the show, we developed a true friendship based on humor and a mutual respect for one another as artists. Jay McCarroll is one in the small handful of friends from the show I have maintained contact with over the years. He will always be a brother to me.

Julia, Jay's model, had been booked by her agency for

classic footlight fables where the young understudy gets her big break. The show must go on!

Naturally, I understood this as a *serious modeling career launch*, and envisioned myself jet setting from Calvin Klein Jeans photo shoots to Gaultier Couture runways to Japanese shampoo endorsement commercials. I still can't believe they didn't even offer me a Guess boy campaign along with Melissa. But seriously folks, my friend was in a bind, and it just seemed the most logical thing to do at the time.

Modeling itself was fun, and I tried to project a simple, sporty attitude to suit Jay's design. Let me tell you, modeling postal uniforms was quite more to my taste than actually having to work as a postal serviceperson. When I saw the looks on the judges' faces when I appeared, it was difficult to hold back the laughter. Afterward, Heidi said I did a good job . . . oh, I bet she says that to all the modeling designers in uniform!

HOW DID *ON THE ROAD WITH AUSTIN AND SANTINO* COME ABOUT?

After the second season, Santino Rice and I became friends, having met and hit it off at some show-affiliated party. Each of us had also formed a lasting friendship with Rich Bye, one of the original producers of *Runway*. We all thought it would be fun to capture our mutual enthusiasm for fashion and our unique friendship in a TV program. A few different concepts were bandied about, all revolving around design. I believe I was the first one to suggest traveling from town to town—maybe because I was a child vaudeville star, before transitioning to silent pictures, then reality TV. Anyway, the three of us—Santino, Rich, and I—came up

some big cosmetics shoot, and we all realized the possibility of her not making it in time for the runway show. Luckily, Jay's design was unisex and it fit me perfectly. Also, I can never resist baby blue. It was almost like one of those

with the idea, and I seriously believe it was one of the best shows on television. I was so proud of the joy, compassion, creativity, and empowerment we managed to share each week. The memory of all the beautiful women we met will be treasured always.

May I take a moment to say just how incredible Mr. Rice is? I always adored his style and amazing humor, but through our experience on the road, I discovered he is one of the kindest, most tender, loving, generous spirits I have ever known. He taught me so much about personal truth, never being afraid to be all you can be.

HOW HAS PROJECT RUNWAY AFFECTED YOUR CAREER?

Less than a year after my appearance on *Runway*, I was hired and became the youngest creative director of a couture wedding dress collection in America. While each *Runway* alumni has their own way of measuring success, I am proud to say my work has maintained a certain standard of elegance, craftsmanship, and luxury. As a result, my creations have always commanded the highest prices out of any other *Runway* designer, winner or not.

With the launch of my new collection for fall 2012, I know that the original season of *Project Runway*, was one of the first big stepping stones to bring me there. In addition to my strictly couture work, Runway has also opened doors to collaborations with amazing artists and major theatrical companies for costume design on the international stage, one of my favorite being the amazing Chinese choreographer, Shen Wei, famous for his work on the Beijing Olympics. I worked with him to create costumes for a performance at The Metropolitan Museum of Art. The performance, actually dancing amongst the sculptures of the American Wing, was a first for the museum, and one of the greatest moments in my career thus far.

As for "Scarlett Starlett"? Never in a million years did I foresee television and media being such a big part of my career. Inside, sometimes I still feel like the very timid little boy who always sat alone in the lunchroom,

and the glamorous Austin Scarlett everyone knows is sort of a superhero/alter ego I created for myself to get over the shyness. I think *Runway* helped me realize my own potential as an artist in general.

WHAT WAS THE BEST PART OF YOUR PROJECT RUNWAY EXPERIENCE?

The greatest thing to come of *Runway* has been the opportunity to inspire others to follow their own dream, whatever that may be to him or her. The stories people have shared with me over the years touch my soul and humble my heart. If something that I have said or done has made one person recognize the unique beauty inside themselves, then my journey has been a success. I think people see in me a story of perseverance in the face of misunderstanding, opposition, even defeat. I will never give up what I know in my heart is my calling. *Project Runway* has given me the platform to share a philosophy of life and the ideals I strive toward as an artist.

THE DESIGNERS

JOHN WADE
FROM: REDLANDS, CA
STUDIED: CALIFORNIA STATE
UNIVERSITY NORTHRIDGE

HEIDI STANDRIDGE
FROM: SARDIS, AL
STUDIED: SAVANNAH COLLEGE
OF ART AND DESIGN

KIRSTEN EHRIG
FROM: NEAR BOSTON, MA
STUDIED: UNIVERSITY OF
SOUTHERN CALIFORNIA

RAYMUNDO BALTAZAR
FROM: MORELOS, MEXICO
STUDIED: FASHION
INSTITUTE OF DESIGN AND
MERCHANDISING

DANIEL FRANCO
FROM: LOS ANGELES, CA
STUDIED: OTIS COLLEGE OF
ART AND DESIGN, FASHION
INSTITUTE OF DESIGN AND
MERCHANDISING

GUADALUPE VIDAL
FROM: LOS ANGELES, CA
STUDIED: FASHION
INSTITUTE OF DESIGN AND
MERCHANDISING

MARLA DURAN
FROM: ALLENTOWN, PA
STUDIED: THE CORCORAN
SCHOOL OF ART

DIANA ENG
FROM: JACKSONVILLE, FL
STUDIED: RHODE ISLAND
SCHOOL OF DESIGN

EMMETT MCCARTHY
FROM: NORTH HAVEN, CT
STUDIED: PARSONS THE NEW
SCHOOL FOR DESIGN

ZULEMA GRIFFIN
FROM: NEW YORK, NY
STUDIED: PARSONS THE NEW
SCHOOL FOR DESIGN

ANDRAE GONZALO
FROM: LOS ANGELES, CA
STUDIED: OTIS COLLEGE OF
ART AND DESIGN

NICK VERREOS
FROM: ST. LOUIS, MO
STUDIED: FASHION INSTITUTE OF
DESIGN AND MERCHANDISING

KARA JANX
FROM: JOHANNESBURG,
SOUTH AFRICA
STUDIED: UNIVERSITY OF CAPE
TOWN, SOUTH AFRICA

SANTINO RICE
FROM: ST. CHARLES, MO
STUDIED: FASHION
INSTITUTE OF DESIGN AND
MERCHANDISING

DANIEL VOSOVIC
FRCM: GRAND RAPIDS, MI
STUDIED: FASHION INSTITUTE
OF TECHNOLOGY

CHLOE DAO
FROM: PAKSE, LAOS
STUDIED: FASHION INSTITUTE
OF TECHNOLOGY

SEASON 2

HIGHLIGHTS

YOU'RE OUT BEFORE YOU'RE IN

Sixteen designers showed up for the start of Season 2. A week before each contestant had been given six yards of muslin to create an outfit that represented them as a designer. Upon their arrival the designers learned that only fourteen of them would actually make it onto the show. John Wade and Heidi Standridge were eliminated.

DANIEL FRANCO RETURNS

Season 1 designer Daniel Franco surprised Tim Gunn when he showed up to audition for Season 2. Franco felt that since he was eliminated in the first challenge he hadn't had a chance to really show what he was capable of. Gunn asked him to step out of the room to discuss the situation with the rest of the judging panel. When Franco came back Tim was pleased to tell him he had advanced.

ANDRAE CRIES ON THE RUNWAY (FOR A REALLY LONG TIME)

The Clothes Off Your Back challenge was emotional for Andrae. He started crying almost immediately as he was discussing his dress with the judges. He cried for over nine minutes. At one point Heidi asked him if they were happy tears or sad tears, to which he replied both.

ANDRAE GONZALO:

"I had chosen to use 'clothes off your back' to create a dress that would celebrate a risk I had taken three years earlier to open my own store (the outfit I was wearing I'd acquired at about the same time). In order to participate on the show, I had to shut down the shop, so I'd literally given up everything to be there. I'd thought it would be cool if the clothes from this time were transformed into something new, just as I'd hoped my life would be, after taking the risk of competing on *Project Runway*. The dress I made was even in a Chinese style, and my old shop was in LA's Chinatown.

There's a misunderstanding that people become fashion designers because they love clothes, and that I was mourning the demise of some of my favorite ones. In fact, designers are Rumpelstiltskins, and the clothes themselves don't matter. I design because I believe that there are clothes that don't exist yet, and I want the opportunity to try to make them real. If you take away the opportunity a designer has to spin 'straw into gold,' any designer worth their salt will shed a tear. And if you don't believe me, just ask Raf Simons.

When I found myself in the bottom two, it occurred to me that this new risk might end in failure, and I might go home to nothing, empty-handed; a loser. Add jetlag to that, and you have the kind of human drama that has made Season 2 worth rerunning on Bravo for years."

MODEL WALK-OFF

As the winner of the On Thin Ice challenge, Zulema had the option of switching models for the next challenge. She chose to do just that, and Heidi brought all the models out for her to choose. She surprised everyone by deciding to have a model walk-off between Danyelle, Tarah, and Shannon. The walk-off was dramatic and created tension. Zulema chose Nick's model, Tarah.

HIGHLIGHTS

GRACIOUS DANIEL FRANCO

Daniel Franco was chosen to be a team leader for the Lingerie challenge. He picked Chloe and Kara to be on his team. When they ended up in the bottom, Daniel protected his team, and said if someone had to go it should be him. The judges eliminated him, but respected the way he handled himself on the runway.

DIRTY DIANA

The Social Scene challenge gave the designers the opportunity to design a dress for Nicky Hilton. They met Hilton at a party at the Marquee club, where she previewed their designs. Diana cut loose and had a good time dancing, which earned her the nickname Dirty Diana.

BARBIE

The designers were thrilled to have the opportunity to design an outfit for the My Scene Barbie doll line, which would be mass-produced. In addition, they were to create a life size version of the outfit for their models to wear on the runway. The designers each received their own Barbies at Toys"R"Us. Kara lost her doll's hat on the escalator and stayed behind to look for it. For the runway show the designers were given the option of using Barbie wigs for the models. Andrae was the only one who didn't use the wig. The judges thought that was a bad decision. The elated winner of the challenge was Nick.

NICK VERREOS:

"Winning the Barbie challenge was heaven! You can see in the episode how happy I was. All I kept thinking about was how proud my mom and dad, my partner, and friends would be when they saw the episode. But, especially my niece; that was a win for her. The fact that I could give her a Barbie (she loves Barbie) that was designed by her uncle—amazing!"

NICK MEETS SASHA COHEN

Season 1's Robert Plotkin showed up at Atlas to deliver the designers' wardrobe for the On Thin Ice challenge—skating outfits. They were taken to a rink where they found Olympic figure skater Sasha Cohen, which thrilled Nick.

NICK VERREOS:

"In the episode you could see that I was jumping up and down like a fourteen-year-old meeting Justin Bieber! I was the only designer/contestant who even knew who she was. All my fellow contestants kept looking at me and asking, 'Who is she?' And I almost slapped them saying, 'Don't you know! It's Sasha Cohen!' Here's a little back-story: At the time I was a closet figure skating fan, with my partner, who really *loves* figure skating. But I made fun of his extra love of the sport. So, you could say I was a figure skating fanatic's wife. Cut to me being on *Project Runway* and ending up in a skating rink, Olympic figure skater Sasha Cohen skates up to us and announces that we are to create a costume for her. Well, I almost had a triple axel heart attack! All I kept thinking about was, 'My partner and his skate-watching buddies are going to give me years of grief now for making fun of them for liking the sport and here I am!'"

CRY & CUT

Zulema and Kara were paired off to work on the Window Shopping Banana Republic challenge. The pairing was problematic from the start. The two designers didn't agree; they had two different styles. When Tim came into the workroom to check on their progress he was surprised to see how off the mark they were. Kara was extremely upset; she felt their look was not coming together. Eventually she just couldn't help but cry. Zulema didn't want them to be eliminated and decided she needed to take over. She told Kara that she didn't care if she cried, but she had to "Cry and cut!"

KARA JANX:

"It was close to midnight and we hadn't gotten things resolved. People don't see that you get called into the confessionals at the most inopportune times, for about an hour at a time. I was called into this confessional when we had nothing, and when I came out and I was crying. Zulema said, 'I don't care if you cry,' and maybe it was good. We were presenting the next day, so Zulema was like, 'Get the shit done.' She wasn't very sensitive. I'm a sensitive people and I don't approach things like that, but sometimes you need a kick in the ass."

HIGHLIGHTS

VISITING FERN MALLIS

The designers were thrilled when Tim Gunn took them on a field trip to meet Fern Mallis at her office at IMG. Mallis, the creator of New York Fashion Week at Bryant Park, gave them valuable advice.

FERN MALLIS:

"The very first time I was on the show I was Executive Director of 7th on Sixth and VP of IMG. Tim brought the four finalists to visit my office and told them they were going on a surprise field trip to meet me. It was fun when I watched the show and saw the way it was edited, and their comments and their excitement when they realized where they were going. I had no idea they even knew who I was. They came into the conference room and I hadn't known or seen any of them on the air yet, so I had no knowledge of who was who, or their eccentric or controversial personalities.

Their first question to me was: 'What advice would you give us to succeed in the business?' and I said the most important advice I can give you is to be nice. They looked at me as if I had four heads. Tim just smiled from ear to ear. I explained that at the end of the day there are a lot of designers out there all doing good work. Ultimately, we all want to do business with people we like. You can get much more accomplished by being nice. You don't have to be a diva or a bitch to succeed in this business. People remember and gravitate to the nice people. Tim was so appreciative that I said that. I'll never forget right after that episode aired I went to a screening and Sarah Jessica Parker grabbed me and said, 'I loved what you said to them. I loved it. That was the best advice I think that was ever given to them.' I got great feedback from that over the years."

THE DANIEL FRANCO SONG

With one hour left to work on Sasha Cohen's skating outfit, Santino composed an impromptu song about Daniel Franco:

"Daniel Franco, where did you go?

Daniel Franco, where did you go?

Maybe next season you'll come back again.

Daniel Franco where'd you go?

Twenty step shuffle from your form,

Pin another swatch on.

Take a look, Daniel Franco.

I think you're insane.

Maybe you should just start sewing that dress.

Daniel Franco, where did you go?

Season 1 you were out on the first challenge and

Season 2 well you didn't do much better but,

there's always the third time. Maybe you should

come back again.

Daniel Franco

Daniel Franco

Daniel Franco

Daniel Franco

We love you Daniel Franco.

TIM AND ANDRAE AT RED LOBSTER

One of the show's most famous and hilarious highlights was Santino's impression of Tim Gunn. He eventually created an entire scenario where Tim and Andrae have a romantic dinner at Red Lobster. Santino was surprised when an amused Tim confronted him about the impression.

ANDRAE GONZALO:

"Tim Gunn will always be a special person to me. His approval on the show always mattered more than that of the judges because he was one of the first people with aesthetic authority in our culture that believed in my ability. As far as Santino's dramatization of our 'relationship' goes, I have no complaints. 'What happened to Andrae?' or 'Where's Andrae?' as is commonly said, is something I've totally embraced. It's to me what 'People' is for Barbra Streisand. With some luck, that meme has the power to rescue my work from creative obscurity long after I'm dead. Thank you, Santino!"

ROAD TO THE RUNWAY (SANTINO)

CLOTHES OFF YOUR BACK (CHLOE)

ALL DOLLED UP (NICK)

TEAM LINGERIE (DANIEL V.)

SOCIAL SCENE (SANTINO)

WINDOW SHOPPING
(ANDRAE AND DANIEL V.)

ON THIN ICE (ZULEMA)

INSPIRATION (DANIEL V.)

FLOWER POWER (DANIEL V.)

MAKEOVER (CHLOE)

WHAT'S YOUR LINE? (DANIEL V.)

FINALE (CHLOE)

MODELS

MARIA LUCIA SANTIAGO

ALYSSA DAUGHERTY

MELISSA BRAISER

ALLISON MCATEE

CLAUDIA

ELIZA JANE

CARA ROBERTS

LESLEY ANN WILLIAMS

SHANNON FLUET

TARAH RODGERS

DANYELLE VILMENAY

RACHAEL HARTZOG

EDEN HENDERSON

HEATHER BROWN

REBECCA HOLLIDAY

GRACE KELSEY

DIANE VON FURSTENBERG
FASHION DESIGNER

LILY MARTINEZ
HEAD DESIGNER, MY SCENE BARBIE

CYNTHIA ROWLEY
FASHION DESIGNER

ALESSANDRA AMBROSIO
VICTORIA'S SECRET MODEL

NICKY HILTON
SOCIALITE/FASHION DESIGNER

DEBORAH LLOYD
HEAD OF DESIGN, BANANA REPUBLIC

ANNE SLOWEY
FASHION NEWS DIRECTOR, *ELLE*

SASHA COHEN
2002 OLYMPIC FIGURE SKATER

JAY MCCARROLL
PROJECT RUNWAY SEASON 1 WINNER

MARK BADGLEY AND JAMES MISCHKA
FASHION DESIGNERS

FREDDIE LEIBA
FASHION STYLIST

IMAN
MODEL/FASHION ICON

DEBRA MESSING
ACTRESS, *WILL & GRACE*

CHLOE DAO

DID YOU PLAN ON AUDITIONING FOR THE SHOW FOR A LONG TIME?

It was very last minute. I woke up that morning and decided I wanted to try out for the show. The reason I waited so long was because I was afraid I wouldn't be able to compete. I watched Season 1 and couldn't imagine how they made garments so quickly. My sister reminded me that I make clothes quickly all the time. I definitely scouted my competition out in line. I felt like I had a strong portfolio. I made it through the first round and got to see Tim Gunn, Wendy Pepper, and two CFDA representatives. I was a bit scared when they asked me what I thought made me the next great American designer. I didn't think that way at all. I said something, and I guess they liked it because they put me through.

WHO DID YOU BOND WITH MOST ON THE SHOW?

Emmett McCarthy. He's 6'6", but somehow it just worked that he and I were best friends. I was the shortest one on the show and he was one of the tallest. Dirty Diana was another close friend. I loved all of the designers, but they were the closest.

WHO DID YOU THINK WAS YOUR TOUGHEST COMPETITION?

I always thought my toughest competition was Andrae, an amazing designer. The piece that really blew me away was the Inspiration challenge. I always thought he should have won that one. He made a beautiful gown out of gutter inspiration; his inspiration was the sewer, the gutter. He was also very well informed about fashion history.

WHO WAS YOUR FAVORITE GUEST JUDGE?

My favorite guest judge was Diane von Furstenberg. She was a judge for the Clothes Off Your Back

challenge. I love her as a person and as a designer. She's very nurturing with young designers; she understands what we go through.

WHAT WAS THE BEST ADVICE YOU GOT ON THE SHOW?

It was from Diane von Furstenberg who said to follow your dream, be who you are, follow your own voice.

WHAT WAS YOUR FAVORITE AND LEAST FAVORITE CHALLENGE?

My favorite challenge was Clothes Off Your Back. I had so little to work with; I'm super tiny—5'. My model was 6' tall. I really didn't have a lot of clothes on that day, so it was difficult to make something that didn't look like I was scavenging fabric and pieces to fit such a tall girl. I was very impressed with myself. You know that's when you're happy—when you impress yourself. My least favorite was the Barbie challenge. I loved it, but we had to spend so many hours making clothes to fit the doll, and the judges didn't even use that as criteria to judge us. Nobody really saw all that work.

YOU HAD A GREAT MODEL TO WORK WITH, GRACE KELSEY.

I was completely loyal to Grace throughout the entire competition. I don't think anybody realized I had the best model. She walked for Gucci, Tom Ford, Bill Blass—definitely a highly successful model before she went on *Project Runway*. She was a chameleon. She was able to embrace and enhance all my different looks.

WHAT WAS IT LIKE BEING THERE WHEN ANDRAE CRIED ON THE RUNWAY?

Clothes have a lot of memories, so I understood where he was coming from. I didn't think he was faking it at all. I think at that moment he was under so much stress to create that garment it just all came out on the runway. It was a little uncomfortable but that's life. You can't predict things, you can't control things. Reality TV is definitely something you can't control.

HOW DID YOU LIKE MODELING DANIEL'S DESIGN?

I hated it! I love Daniel, but I was afraid I'd have a Janet Jackson moment, with not just one breast showing, but two! That was definitely not a piece I'd wear off the runway.

DID YOU THINK ANY ONE JUDGE WAS PARTICULARLY IN YOUR CORNER?

Michael Kors loved my aesthetic, and a lot of times he commented about how well my garments were made. I know Nina Garcia loved my Banana Republic garment. I heard she actually wanted to wear it (I will send it to you, Nina!). From what Tim Gunn said I wouldn't have won the show if Nina was not in my corner. She supposedly rallied the troops to choose me over Daniel Vosovic to win. I want to thank her for that. I love her for being in my corner.

WERE YOU SURPRISED WHEN NONE OF THE OTHER DESIGNERS SAID THEY WOULD CHOOSE YOU TO GO TO FASHION WEEK?

Yes, most definitely! I wasn't surprised about Santino. If you watched the episode before that you saw that Daniel was very upset. Kara Janx was also very upset that Nick was sent home. Everybody was shocked that Santino didn't get sent home. There was a moment where me, Daniel, and Kara had a talk and agreed to help each other out. Santino would do his own thing, and maybe he would be sent home. It was just a conversation, but I definitely felt we were all in agreement that Santino should have gone home, and that Nick was unfairly dismissed.

So what they did on the runway was a bit surprising. I had watched Season 1, so I wasn't surprised that the question was coming. I wasn't going to let them see I was upset. I knew the judges were going to send me to Fashion Week; I knew my pieces were not the worst.

WHAT WAS WINNING LIKE?

I think the best thing about winning is having a platform. The show is aired in countries all over the world. I have a big fan base in Russia now. It's a show that never ends. I win every month because it never stops airing.

DID YOU HAVE A FEELING YOU WERE GOING TO WIN?

Definitely not. At that point I was super exhausted. I had two nights of no sleep. All I kept hearing was Daniel Vosovic you're the best thing that ever happened to fashion, your style is so amazing. I thought, I am screwed. Then they said, Chloe you're such a great businessperson. I thought I'm definitely not going to win. I was preparing myself to not be the winner. I won, thank God. It was nice that they fooled me and made me think I wasn't going to win.

WERE THERE OBLIGATIONS YOU HAD TO MEET AS THE WINNER OF *PROJECT RUNWAY*?

Not technically, but there are expectations. Your fans expect you to be in all the stores, Neiman Marcus, Saks. They think you're a millionaire already and that you dress all the celebrities. Being in the industry for eight years before I went on *Project Runway*, working in New York, I understand getting to that level doesn't happen overnight. It doesn't happen just because you win Project Runway. You have to have your own definition of success, and be okay with it if you're not doing what the fans think you should be doing.

WHO HAVE BEEN SOME OF YOUR FAVORITE PROJECT RUNWAY DESIGNERS OVER THE YEARS?

Rami and Leanne Marshall are amazing, couture designers. I love Jay McCarroll's personality and his collection was amazing. I love Kara Saun, Austin Scarlett. But the one person that people might be shocked to hear that I love, love, love is Vincent Libretti. He was so funny. I loved when he made that hat out of a basket and he thought it was the coolest thing. I was completely entertained by him. Vincent brings a smile to my face. I could watch him all day long.

WHAT WOULD PEOPLE BE SURPRISED TO KNOW ABOUT *PROJECT RUNWAY*?

We shot every day for a month. It is physical, emotional, and mental boot camp. You'd better know who you are as a person and as a designer. It's brutal. There's no time to rest, there's no vacation, there's no day off. But I think people would also be surprised to know that we are so supportive of each other. I never felt it was a competition against the other designers, I felt it was a competition against myself. You can't control who likes your designs, but you have to be proud of them. Another thing is my season was very true to form. There was no weird editing; what you saw is what happened. It was my reality.

WHAT HAVE YOU BEEN DOING SINCE *PROJECT RUNWAY*?

I think the biggest thing is getting married. I married my boyfriend, who you saw on the show. Now he's my husband. The other big thing is working with Nuo with my laptops and luggage. There's nothing cooler than going to the airport with your own luggage, knowing that it's online and in stores. The biggest of all is changing my store name from Lot 8 Boutique to DAO Chloe DAO. I realized that it was time to embrace that Chloe Dao is a brand. *Project Runway* really did change my life. The biggest changes are the vast amount of opportunities and doors that are open to you. I have been invited to the White House twice, shown at the Smithsonian Museum, was a Dove spokesperson for a year. I had a line on QVC, Simply Chloe Dao, for three years. My boutique DAO Chloe Dao has become a tourist location in Houston. My website gets a lot of international hits. I think it is quite wonderful that a designer like me, based in Houston, can sell limited original designs all over the world.

DANIEL VOSOVIC

Yes—very small world. I remember that I had been in the casting panel for *Runway* and I had seen him come through, but the judges are only the first round. He's always had such a strong point of view. He's very bold and it's very editorial, which is great for a young designer.

WHAT'S IT LIKE BEING ON THAT PANEL AFTER
HAVING BEEN ON THE SHOW?

I felt I could be very empathetic towards the designers who are at different phases of their careers, young designers like myself as well as people twenty, thirty years older

who are trying to make it happen. It's a little bittersweet because you realize how many people have dreams and want to follow them. When you see them in minute intervals, in the hundreds if not thousands, it really was a bit of a shock—to see that many people chasing the same dream, and to know in reality only a handful of them will actually even get a chance. And out of that handful, who will actually be successful?

IS WHAT YOU LEARNED AT FASHION SCHOOL
DIFFERENT FROM WHAT YOU LEARNED FROM
BEING A CONTESTANT ON *PROJECT RUNWAY*?

Absolutely. On *Project Runway* I learned it's about the overall perspective. It's not about a garment. It's about your point of view. That's what makes a designer different, not one who makes a good dress. It's who's saying something that's worth listening to. And that's what I think schools have a hard time with. It's a hard thing to teach. It's why you feel great when you put on a certain blazer. Why do you feel sexy when you wear a red dress? It's just fabric sewn together. Understanding the psychology of want as opposed to need, that's sales. That's a whole different thing.

DID THE SHOW PREPARE YOU TO RUN YOUR
BUSINESS?

Yes. You have to wear so many hats on *Project Runway*, from stylist to cutter to patternmaker, to seamstress to salesman. I have a small staff, but I still have to have an understanding of those things before I can direct someone to do them the way I want them done. The show was definitely a template for me.

DO YOU FEEL LIKE YOU WERE PORTRAYED
FAIRLY ON THE SHOW?

What you saw is very much what happened.

YOU GUYS ARE PRETTY HONEST IN THE
CONFESSIONALS.

Those confessionals happen during your eight-hour

challenge. We get eight hours minus a forty-five minute interview. You learn after the fourth or fifth time, the sooner you give an answer, especially a big one, the sooner you go on to the next question. Why would you just sit there and hem and haw about an answer when you're potentially jeopardizing yourself and missing out on finishing the garment that could potentially win you $100,000 and make you America's next great designer?! It was a great skill on the production end; it literally lit a match under your ass.

YOUR SCHEDULE WAS SEVEN DAYS A WEEK?

Yes! You finish a challenge, someone voted off, and you do not see them again. Heidi goes to hair and makeup. We bring a change of clothes and it's literally the next day, or the next week as it appears on TV.

WHEN YOU HAD IMMUNITY DID YOU FEEL FREE TO DO ANYTHING YOU WANTED?

Absolutely, and I remember there was this one time when it did bite me in the butt. It was the Makeover challenge, where we had to make garments for each other. I got Chloe. I remember thinking I could definitely make her pretty, but I'd rather really go balls to the wall and try something different. It totally backfired, but the reality is I had immunity and luckily that was the risk that I earned.

DID YOU HAVE A FAVORITE CHALLENGE?

My favorite challenge was definitely the Inspiration challenge because it was the first time we had a chance to get out of the workroom. This was back when we could film in the streets of New York and people didn't know what it was, so we were running around the city with different camera crews running all around. I won the challenge for this orchid blouse and skirt and that is still one of my favorite pieces years later. It's a hard thing to say as a designer, that I love that piece.

Looking back, the Inspiration challenge is absolutely one of the most gratifying. It was later in the season, and it was a nice invigorating moment. I could go from "What the hell did I sign up for?" to "Okay, at least I'm still being creative." The last challenge many just call in because your brain is just so scraped. You don't have magazines, you don't have television, you don't have a walk in the park. That is a hard environment for a creative person to be in. You're so sleep deprived, so hungry. I lost ten pounds. I am a skinny little motherfucker, I do not need to lose ten pounds. Do you take a half hour lunch break or do you shove as much food in your mouth as you can in ten minutes? It makes for great television.

IS THERE ANY ONE JUDGE THAT YOU DESIGNED FOR?

I think aesthetically I overlapped with Nina more than with Michael or Heidi. I design for chic women, but there's a little bit of a hook—an edge—to it. Nina can do pants and a little jersey top and look as put together as if she was in a Lanvin cocktail dress. That's not clothes, that's style.

TALK ABOUT WINNING THE CHALLENGE IN WHICH THE PRIZE WAS HAVING IMAN WEAR YOUR DRESS?

I was twenty-four years old. I did not know how editorials worked. I did not know how dressing a celebrity worked. The show finished airing around March and I was contacted maybe three months later. I got an email from *Elle* saying Iman was going to an event and it would be a great pairing with the dress. I show up on time, I'm super excited, and the assistant says to me, "So where's the dress?" I said, "Why would I have the dress? It's a TV show, they don't let us keep *any* of it—any of it." So Iman is literally five minutes away and there's no dress and we're calling people. I don't have direct access to the executive producer of *Runway*! I don't have access to this. Iman and then Nina arrive. We tell her the situation and she says, "This is a problem." I'm looking like such an idiot, like this young student. At that point I realized I am the designer. I was no longer a contestant. This was my job. I took responsibility and said I must've messed up somehow and let's figure this out.

The dress turned out to be in someone's closet behind the door. This silk gown born for a supermodel is wadded up behind a closet door in LA—in LA! Nina suggested we reschedule the fitting. The dress arrived maybe three days later. We got the dress on and Iman is in a hurry and it doesn't fit right. It was a silk gown so if it lays wrong, you'd see it. I go back to Mood for fabric and the dye lot is different. Can't find anything to match! I remake the entire dress. Take note I'm still living up in Harlem with four roommates. I didn't win, I have no money, I just graduated, I have $55,000 in student loans, and I'm making a dress based off measurements I took on the fly.

We have a third fitting and it technically fits, but it's big. Iman is almost over it at this point. She was always professional but you can tell that she is business, and I love that. The fitting took place on location. I think she was shooting with Patrick Demarchelier at Chelsea Piers. In between changes she tries on my dress. The entire staff watched me. I looked like this stupid kid with this random rag of a dress. We ended up missing the deadline for the event, which turned out fine. We eventually got another event for her to wear the dress to. I finished the dress the morning of the event. I borrowed a friend's sewing machine.

Iman told me to come to her house. I was so nervous. You had to be called up in the elevator. I had the dress, had looked at the shoes, and everything is ironed, steamed. I went in the elevator and nothing happens. I'm just standing there in an elevator that's not closing, and I'm pushing penthouse and it's not closing. I walked back out to the doorman. He told me to go back in; she's going to call you up. I see the numbers go all the way up to penthouse and then all the way back down. I thought she was going to be livid. So I get back in, wait another ten seconds. The doors close and she's there propped against the door like "mhmm." She was sick as a dog. No makeup, sweatpants, still looked amazing. She only had five minutes. We talked for a minute and then she went into the bathroom to try the dress on and I'm thinking "Please let her come out and be amazing. Please let her come out and be amazing . . ." It fits like a glove! I left the dress and thanked her. She showed up at the event later that evening in full hair, full makeup, and walks the red carpet. I thought "I'm done!" I can't believe she went beyond and above and stayed with me for what, four fittings—for some stupid young designer? She's amazing.

HEIDI'S BEEN SUPPORTIVE OF YOU.

Heidi has been very good to me. She wore two looks from my Spring/Summer 2012 collection, probably within two months. It's been great to build these relationships through the show. The show is a platform for you to do what you want with it. I realized a lot of people thought that the show would make them. To me the show was simply going to speed up the plan I was going to do anyway. After the show, everyone wanted to know if I was going to capitalize on the momentum. I started to really mull things over. This is something Tim and I discussed: ultimately I would look at my career and have *Runway* be a blip—a great blip—in a fifty-year career. I was only twenty-four. I did not know the least about a business plan, about manufacturing, production, or accounting. I would have been completely consumed if I tried jumping in and starting a legitimate business, right after the show.

MIRANDA KERR WALKED IN YOUR FINALE COLLECTION. DO YOU FEEL LIKE YOU DISCOVERED HER?

Absolutely. When she walked in and smiled I turned to [casting director] John Pfeiffer and said, "John, that girl will be a Victoria's Secret supermodel." The caliber of models back then was pretty amazing.

WHAT HAVE YOU DONE SINCE *PROJECT RUNWAY*?

I wrote a book—*Fashion Inside/Out*. Then I started my company. We sell all over the world. Our main focus is original photographic/digital prints that we take ourselves. We tailor for the very confident, edgy woman and the company is continuing to grow. We've explored film and combining a new platform for fashion shows. I don't want to just be a cog in the machine. I want to be a part and become a big player. I mean to compete now; you have to be thinking big. The impression I want to leave on the fashion industry is as a trendsetter.

KARA JANX

HAD YOU ALWAYS WANTED TO BE A DESIGNER?

I always sort of expected to go into fashion, but I had come to New York because I was working in architecture. Then I realized there was a way that I could do this; I could go to night classes. We don't have that luxury in South Africa. I tried it, and it just felt like it was my calling to do fashion. It made sense.

DID THE ARCHITECTURE BACKGROUND HELP YOU AS A DESIGNER?

It helps because you are so disciplined in a craft already.

DO YOU THINK YOU ALSO HAVE A BETTER UNDERSTANDING OF SHAPES?

I think so. I don't sketch, I just imagine it; I can see it. I think that's something from architecture. You're always drawing flat plans, but it has to be realized in a three-dimensional form.

HOW DID YOU FIND OUT WHEN AND WHERE THE AUDITION WAS FOR SEASON 2?

I kept my eyes and ears open. I was very determined that I was going to be on the next season. I just knew that it was going to happen. Months later my brother was getting married in Israel, and the show was actually starting the day after he got married. They phoned me in Israel to let me know that I was going to be on the show.

HOW EXCITING WAS THAT?

It's mind blowing. I'd just come from South Africa to New York. New York was the place I wanted to be a star in—in some capacity, especially in the design world. It was like a dream realized.

DID YOU HAVE ANY FAVORITE CHALLENGES?

I loved the Flower challenge. I really related to it. You grow so much in the process that at that point I was very comfortable with my skill and what I was doing, and sort of past the point of insecurity. I'm a Virgo, I have a lot of self- doubts. I think it's inherent. A lot of the work I produce is a process of panic, panic, panic—beautiful work—panic, panic, panic—beautiful work. At that point I was less panicked so I loved the challenge. It gave me the strength to get through the next few. I loved the design I did for Santino, and I really thought those were two challenges I should've totally taken. Santino designed for me, too. He made me a jumpsuit.

WHAT WAS IT LIKE WORKING WITH HIM?

Santino is hilarious, and he's such a big personality. He can drive you mad but he can make you laugh at the same time. He's very good—and very in your face. There's no holding back; he doesn't care what people think. He was an amazing person to have around. He was comic relief.

DO YOU THINK THE VIEWERS LEFT SEASON 2 WITH A STRONG SENSE OF WHO YOU ARE AS A DESIGNER?

I think my best was the kimono. That became my signature. It's still a very big presence in my business. It was both serendipitous and bizarre, because I literally had nothing, no clothes. It was something I took in to the audition, and brought with me for filming thinking we should bring the clothes we had in the audition. Michael Kors pointed it out. I really think that shows my point of view; very wearable, very real. I sold thousands of them; I still get an email a day about the kimono. Yesterday someone in Brussels ordered it.

DID YOU HAVE A FAVORITE GUEST JUDGE?

Diane von Furstenberg. She is such a dynamic force in this business, in the world. Whenever she judges, she doesn't do it at our expense. She respects us, she respects what we're doing and she's sensitive.

DID YOU FEEL THAT ANY ONE JUDGE WAS PARTICULARLY IN YOUR CORNER?

For me, Nina was my go-to girl. I think she really understood my point of view. She told me things and I learned to really digest it and translate it. She was very instrumental in my growth throughout that season.

ANY FAVORITE CONTESTANTS OVER THE YEARS?

Austin was a favorite. I love Jay. Rami was a favorite. I love Christian Siriano. I also liked these people as people as much as designers. You gravitate toward them as a person and then you really respect them as a designer. I love Daniel, Nick Verreos, and Emmett McCarthy.

WHAT HAVE YOU BEEN DOING SINCE *PROJECT RUNWAY*?

Since Season 2 my business really did take off, so I've been selling to the majors like Neiman Marcus, Bloomingdale's, and Saks. I sell all over the world. I have showrooms and I have very capable people in factories that I work with. I got married and I have two beautiful children, Dylan and Calum. I've been very blessed. I just can't believe that I'm truly living the dream. People say I just want to be a reality TV star. No, I don't want to be a reality TV star, but that is the format that has helped me get to where I need to be. I chose the shows to catapult my brand.

NICK VERREOS

WHAT WAS YOUR *PROJECT RUNWAY* AUDITION LIKE?

The audition process for the second season was still being done "old school" and very *American Idol*-esque. As long as you had some knowledge of sketching, sewing and draping, you could just show up—whether you were a working designer or a mom who liked sewing her daughter's cheerleading costumes. I almost didn't come because I was scared that I would run into some of the students I was then teaching at FIDM (Fashion Institute of Design & Merchandising). I thought they would look down at me and say, "Mr. Verreos, what are you doing here?!"

When I did decide to go to the casting (what did I have to lose?), I called a model friend of mine who was my muse at the time—a 6' tall African American beauty by the name of Amara. I knew that my designs did not have "hanger appeal" and therefore I needed to have them be worn on a real live mannequin. Not many people thought of bringing a live model to the castings back then. In fact, when I showed up to the castings I was the only one among hundreds with a model. I thought to myself, "Are these people for real? You only get one chance and you drag a dress form up in here? Call your tall, skinny cousin for goodness sakes!" Well, of course, what happened was that my model—who was wearing one of my "daywear" cocktail ensembles, was stopped by one of the production assistants working the castings. They asked, "Who are you?" She then told them, "Oh, I'm not the designer, but *he* is!" (pointing to me). We were immediately pulled up the front of the line and then I heard this: "Mr. Verreos! What are you doing here?" My heart just dropped. It was a former student of mine who happened to be working the casting audition. The

next thing I heard was her talking into her walkie-talkie and saying, "We have Nick Verreos, a fabulously talented fashion designer and instructor. We're sending him right up to the holding room to see the judges!" I went up with my model. She decided to change and put on one of my very dramatic silk charmeuse gowns and then we went in.

I introduced myself, showed my design on Amara and the next thing I heard was Tim saying, "Well, we love you! You're In!" Done and done, as they say.

HAD YOU AUDITIONED BEFORE?

No, this was only the second season so this was my first and only time. It was kind of a "Dare" from friends who loved the show and said "Oh Nick, you would be so perfect . . ." I just wanted to be able to tell them "Look, I did it, went to the castings and unfortunately, they didn't pick me!" Well, they actually did pick me, much to my dismay (and delight of my friends).

WHO DID YOU BOND WITH MOST ON THE SHOW?

I instantly bonded with John Wade. It all began at LAX when we were both supposed to be on the same flight to NYC, yet we didn't know that either of us was going to be on *Project Runway*. We both missed the flight! He approached me and said, very quietly, "Are you going to New York to do a very special show?" Now, granted I was warned by many a lawyer from the network, and the casting people, not to breathe a word to anyone. But in that moment, being that we were in the same predicament of missing our very important flight, I broke that pact and said yes. After that, we immediately bonded. I was saddened, however, when he was one of the first two contestants out. With him gone, I subsequently bonded with my roommates, Daniel Vosovic, Santino Rice, and Andrae Gonzalo. I also had great fun with Raymundo Baltazar (my Spanish-speaking partner-in-crime) and Kara Janx—loved her!

WHAT WAS YOUR FAVORITE AND LEAST FAVORITE CHALLENGE?

My favorite challenge was the one I won: the All Dolled Up/Barbie challenge. That was the most fun challenge to do, and the one that I was the most confident about, especially after looking around at what my competitors were creating. In terms of the least favorite, I have to say I had two: the unconventional challenge was very stressful for me. We had to make a garment out of fresh flowers and plants. I think I sat in the workroom for four hours just spraying water on my plants after I got them, not having a clue what to do. The other one was naturally, the challenge in which I was "Auf'ed" from the show. I made a complete suit—jacket, pants, dress shirt, and scarf in one day, for my fellow contestant Daniel Vosovic. And well, it was deemed the worst one by the judges. So, yes, this was definitely not a favorite challenge for me. I didn't think I should have gone home for that.

WHO DID YOU THINK WAS YOUR TOUGHEST COMPETITION?

I would say it was a toss up between Chloe Dao, Daniel Vosovic, and Santino Rice. I knew that the judges would keep Santino to the end because he was the token "meanie," but Chloe and Daniel were competition because they were both quick with their creations and had wonderful design skills.

DID YOU FEEL ALLEGIANCE TO A PARTICULAR MODEL, OR DID YOU LIKE TO CHOOSE YOUR MODEL DEPENDING ON THE CHALLENGE?

Yes, I did feel allegiance to one model—the one I was originally given, the gorgeous Tarah Rodgers. When I was shown her composite card and then I met her I thought I had won the model lottery! She was stunning, tall, perfect sample/runway size, and walked so elegantly. I also loved that she was a model of "color." I've always felt a bond with my "sisters"!

WHICH JUDGE DID YOU FEEL GAVE YOU THE BEST ADVICE?

Nina and Michael were the best. And I listened to them. They are industry professionals and were very on point with their comments with all of us. I never questioned them.

DID YOU HAVE A FAVORITE GARMENT YOU MADE FOR THE SHOW?

Several. But I have to say, I was proud of every garment except the ones that were "collaborative"—the Banana Republic and Lingerie challenges. Those didn't really have

for show and that my fellow contestant, Zulema, wanted to take my model since she didn't like hers. I just didn't feel the need to go through the for show model walk-off aspect. But of course, it made for great TV.

AT ONE POINT YOU FELT THAT YOU MIGHT NOT CONTINUE IN THE COMPETITION. WHAT LED TO THOSE FEELINGS, AND WHAT CHANGED YOUR MIND?

The feelings began soon after Zulema took Tarah from me. It felt like I had lost one of my sails, as it were. The next challenge was a bit tough for me and yes, I almost wanted to quit and voiced this to my fellow designer and roommate, Daniel Vosovic. He quickly snapped me out of my funk and made me realize that I had come this far, so why stop now. Now, of course, I realize I was just being a drama queen.

WHAT WAS IT LIKE DESIGNING FOR DANIEL VOSOVIC?

I was really excited to design for Daniel Vosovic because he was such the ideal model for a menswear challenge. At the time, the look for men—on the Milan and Paris menswear show runways—was all about the uber-skinny boys, a "Twinkie" as my gays like to say. Daniel had that frame. So I wanted to accentuate this by creating a very skinny suit, very 1960s-like, think Mick Jagger with a nod to the disco '70s.

my "Nick Stamp" and therefore I was not comfortable with them.

WHAT WAS THE MODEL WALK-OFF LIKE IN PERSON?

A little stressful, just sitting there trying to hold it all in and remain composed through it all. I knew what the outcome would be and knew ahead of time that it was all

DID YOU LIKE THE OUTFIT CHLOE MADE FOR YOU?

I liked the outfit Chloe created for me. It had a pop of color, which I love. And I was very much into vests at the time so she really took elements of what I would normally wear. I also liked that I looked like a very well-dressed British Airways flight attendant—in the first class cabin of course. At one point, she thought about possibly bedazzling the shirt collar or cuffs but I intervened and reminded her that, yes, I'm gay, but not Elton John gay!

WHAT WAS IT LIKE BEING ON THE PANEL DECIDING WHO MADE THE CUT FOR SEASON 3?

I have been very lucky, honored, and humbled by the fact that for every season since mine, the producers and casting executives, have invited me back to be on the panel of judges who cast the upcoming season. I was looking for talent above all. I wanted to see who could be the next great American fashion designer. What did they have to offer in terms of newness, freshness, and original design that would make the fashion world shake with excitement. I always kept this in my mind: "Can I see his/her designs in a world stage like New York Fashion Week?" And then, I also looked for the passion, drive and yes, a little bit of that TV personality that might make it enjoyable for viewers.

HAVE YOU KEPT IN TOUCH WITH ANYONE FROM THE SHOW?

I am happy to say that yes. John Wade—my LAX buddy—is still one of my best friends. He is very successful working for Marc Jacobs in New York and we keep in touch all the time. I also kept in touch with my Latino "brother," Raymundo Baltazar, Chloe Dao, and Kara Janx.

WHAT WOULD PEOPLE BE SURPRISED TO KNOW ABOUT PROJECT RUNWAY?

One of the most popular questions I get is, "Do you really only get ten hours to make an entire outfit?" Actually we get less time! All those "To Camera Interviews" can take a couple of hours out of our time working, so therefore we really only have six or seven hours. Besides that, the other question I get is that, "Are the confrontations manipulated?" Viewers think that they are and when I tell them that they were not, that surprises them. It's surreal to be in that environment. It heightens people's feelings, emotions, etc. and extra drama just happens naturally.

WHAT HAVE YOU BEEN DOING SINCE PROJECT RUNWAY?

It has been a crazy ride since 2005, when I filmed the show. I did the show to have more women all over the U.S. get to know my designs and hopefully get more exposure for my brand. Things took a different, added twist when TV networks began contacting me for my fashion design expertise as a style guru/commentator for red carpet award shows, etc. I have been to Torino, Italy to comment on the figure-skating costumes for the Olympics, I've been on E!, and covered the Academy Awards red carpet for the *TV Guide* Network.

I have my line, NIKOLAKI, with my partner, David Paul. NIKOLAKI (which means "Little Nick" in Greek) consists of high-end cocktail and evening gowns. I've shown in many Fashion Weeks. I am in the works to produce a diffusion line of Nick Verreos dresses that will be more affordable and available across the country. Several years ago, I released a Nick Verreos prom dress line for Windsor, a mass retailer with stores across the U.S. I also continue being the Spokesperson for the Fashion Institute of Design & Merchandising/FIDM—my alma mater. For the last three years, I have been privileged to be invited by a U.S.-based university to lecture in Florence, Italy on fashion. In terms of TV, I continue being one of the style experts for *TV Guide* network. You can also watch me on a Style Network show *Style Star*.

I have dressed celebrities and singers; Katy Perry and Beyoncé have worn NIKOLAKI designs, as well as Heidi Klum, of course. I filmed a national commercial for Sears, as well as Orbit Gum. Many opportunities came my way after the show but it was definitely up to me to seize the opportunities. My parents taught me that nothing ever comes your way (well, rarely) and that you must work, work, work for it.

THE DESIGNERS

STACEY ESTRELLA
FROM: FOLSOM, CA
STUDIED: STANFORD UNIVERSITY,
HARVARD BUSINESS SCHOOL

MALAN BRETON
FROM: TAIPEI, TAIWAN
SELF-TAUGHT

KATHERINE GERDES
FROM: MINNEAPOLIS, MN
STUDIED: RHODE ISLAND
SCHOOL OF DESIGN

KEITH MICHAEL
FROM: BROOKLYN, NY
STUDIED: PRATT INSTITUTE

BONNIE DOMINGUEZ
FROM: DREXEL HILL, PA
STUDIED: FASHION INSTITUTE
OF TECHNOLOGY

BRADLEY BAUMKIRCHNER
FROM: LAKE HAVASU CITY, AZ
STUDIED: ORANGE COAST
COLLEGE, OTIS COLLEGE OF
ART AND DESIGN

ALISON KELLY
FROM: CAPE COD, MA
STUDIED: INSTITUTO DE ALLENDE,
LORENZO DE MEDICI SCUOLA DE
ARTE, MASSACHUSETTS COLLEGE
OF ART AND DESIGN

ROBERT BEST
FROM: UTAH
STUDIED: PARSONS
THE NEW SCHOOL FOR
DESIGN

ANGELA KESLAR
FROM: PENNSYLVANIA
STUDIED: CARNEGIE MELLON
UNIVERSITY, PENN STATE
UNIVERSITY

VINCENT LIBRETTI
BROOKLYN, NY
STUDIED: FASHION INSTITUTE
OF TECHNOLOGY, PARSONS
THE NEW SCHOOL FOR DESIGN

KAYNE GILLASPIE
FROM: NASHVILLE, TN
STUDIED: FASHION
INSTITUTE OF TECHNOLOGY

MYCHAEL KNIGHT
FROM: NUREMBERG, GERMANY
STUDIED: GEORGIA SOUTHERN
UNIVERSITY

LAURA BENNETT
NEW ORLEANS, LA
STUDIED: UNIVERSITY OF
HOUSTON, COLUMBIA
UNIVERSITY

ULI HERZNER
FROM: EAST GERMANY
FASHION STYLIST

JEFFREY SEBELIA
FROM: LOS ANGELES, CA
STUDIED: LOS ANGELES
TRADE TECHNICAL COLLEGE

SEASON 3

project RUNWAY

HIGHLIGHTS

VINCENT'S HAT

For the unconventional materials challenge Vincent made a hat out of a basket in an effort to keep his simple dress interesting. The judges were thrown by the hat. Michael Kors said, "With the hat you're wondering how many drinks she had." Vincent admitted that he had second thoughts about it himself.

TRASHING THE PLACE

The first challenge of Season 3 was an unconventional materials challenge in which the designers had to use materials found in their apartments. They completely ripped up everything they could find, using things such as drapes, blankets, sheets, chairs, lamps, picture frames, plants, pillows, ironing boards, bed frames, and silverware.

WASTE NOT WANT NOT CHALLENGE

The designers were taken to the Waste Management Recycle America materials facility in Newark, New Jersey for the Waste Not, Want Not challenge. They had to create an outfit from recycled materials. This challenge was about innovation and creativity. Mychael won with an outfit made from a peanut sack, gold Mylar, and a plastic tarp.

KEITH DISQUALIFIED

Kayne saw patternmaking books in Keith's room, which was against the show rules. He was disturbed and went to the other designers with the information. The producers were informed about the situation. Keith also left without permission for a few hours and used the Internet, which was also not allowed. Tim came to tell Keith he would have to ask him to leave the show. Keith claimed he never used the books to get an unfair advantage, but was still disqualified.

JANE CHA:

"Collectively, as a team, we felt that something inappropriate had gone down and that was that. What we did seemed the cleanest, quickest remedy to an unusual situation—and we didn't want the show to become about that."

HIGHLIGHTS

SURPRISE!

The designers' mothers and sisters were the models for the Everyday Woman challenge. Joan Kors, Michael's mother, was on hand to talk with the designers and their family members. Laura surprised everyone, especially her mother Lorraine, by telling Joan Kors she was pregnant with her sixth child.

MICHAEL KORS:

"My mom's fun, she's smart, she has taste, she's opinionated. She's been critiquing my shows since the early '80s, and she *doesn't* love them all. She loves me unconditionally but she doesn't necessarily love the clothes unconditionally. I thought that she brought the experience of someone who has sat through a million fashion shows, also the perspective of a real woman—not a model or fashion editor—who dresses in designer clothes in real life. She had fun with it, she was great.

She also got Laura Bennett to come out about her pregnancy. It was interesting to see my mom with Laura's mom, and I can tell that the mothers and relatives of the designers looked at my mother like, you could be my guide—how does it work being the mother of a successful designer? My mom's lived through all of my reviews for all of my shows. She knows you work hard on something and criticism is hard, but at the same time, without the criticism how are you getting to the next step?"

JEFFREY MAKES ANGELA'S MOTHER CRY

The designers were not allowed to design for their own family member for the Everyday Woman challenge. Jeffrey ended up with Angela's mother Darlene as a model. Darlene was disappointed with the color Jeffrey chose for her and told Tim. Jeffrey told Darlene he didn't appreciate her saying that to Tim, which resulted in her crying.

JEFFREY SEBELIA:

"It was no secret that Angela and her mother were manufacturing friction. Some people saw the show as more of a reality show and less of a design competition. My mom spent a lot more time with Angela's mother than I did. She said that as soon as I left the room she stopped crying."

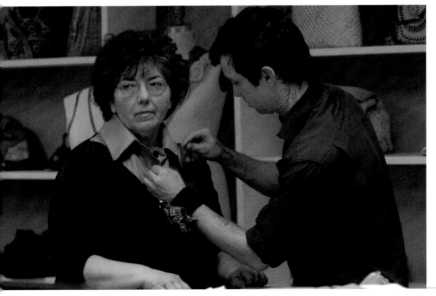

PARIS

For the High Flying Fashion challenge the designers had to make an outfit for themselves. No winner was chosen, but the designers were sent on a trip to Paris from the runway. They had to travel wearing the outfits they made.

DOGS

The designers had to design an outfit inspired by a dog for the challenge called Designer's Best Friend. They went to Central Park, where Tim brought thirteen adorable little dogs for them to choose from. Clearly not a dog person, Laura put her dog in her bag so she, "didn't have to touch it." They also had to design a complimentary outfit for the dog.

LAURA ACCUSES JEFFREY OF CHEATING

The four designers to make it to the finale were Uli, Jeffrey, Laura, and Mychael. Laura had serious doubts that Jeffrey did all his own sewing. She mentioned it to Mychael, who shared her concern. Laura spoke to Tim, who took the issue to the producers to investigate. Laura told Jeffrey what she had done. He was saddened, and defended his work. Tim asked Jeffrey if he had extra help, and believed him when he said no. It was decided that Jeffrey hadn't done anything wrong, and he was allowed to continue, eventually winning the competition.

WALL TO WALL FASHION (KEITH)

FIT FOR A QUEEN (KAYNE)

DESIGNER'S BEST FRIEND (ULI)

REAP WHAT YOU SEW (ANGELA)

ICONIC STATEMENT (MYCHAEL)   WASTE NOT, WANT NOT (MYCHAEL)

EVERYDAY WOMAN (VINCENT)   HIGH FLYING FASHION (JEFFREY)

COUTURE DU JOUR (JEFFREY)

BLACK AND WHITE (LAURA)

WHAT THE *ELLE*? (ULI)

FINALE (JEFFREY)

MODELS

CANDACE PRITCHARD

MOON YUNG

TONI HEATH

KATIA BIASSOU

KATIE CHAMPION

DANIELLE SCHRIFFEN

ALEXANDRA DONHOEFFNER

JIA SANTOS

JAVI HAIRSTON

AMANDA FIELDS

LINDSAY BIEN AIME

CLARISSA ANDERSON

CAMILLA BARUNGI

NAZRI SEGARO

MARILINDA RIVERA

GUEST JUDGES

VERA WANG
FASHION DESIGNER

IVANKA TRUMP
VP OF DEVELOPMENT,
TRUMP ORGANIZATION

KATE SPADE
FASHION DESIGNER

TARA CONNER
MISS USA

MEHMET TANGOREN
MACY'S VP OF SPORTSWEAR

DIANE VON FURSTENBERG
FASHION DESIGNER

RACHEL ZOE
CELEBRITY STYLIST

JOAN KORS
MICHAEL KORS' MOTHER

FRANCISCO COSTA
CREATIVE DIRECTOR,
CALVIN KLEIN

**CATHERINE
MALANDRINO**
FASHION DESIGNER

RICHARD TYLER
FASHION DESIGNER

ZAC POSEN
FASHION DESIGNER

TERI AGINS
LEAD FASHION WRITER, *THE
WALL STREET JOURNAL*

FERN MALLIS
CREATOR OF NEW YORK
FASHION WEEK

FERN MALLIS

WHAT WAS THE BUZZ ON *PROJECT RUNWAY* IN THE FASHION INDUSTRY WHILE THE SHOW WAS BEING DEVELOPED?

Everyone in the industry was intrigued as to what this would and could be. It was the first reality show on TV that featured fashion. I had heard a little bit about what was going on because I was working at IMG at that time, there were many shows about fashion being pitched to us and our broadcast division. Heidi was also a client of IMG models. I think everyone was curious at the beginning and watched it to see if it would work. We can be a very critical audience, so it was a pleasant surprise. Everyone watched it, even if they didn't want to admit it. *Project Runway* became the standard and set the bar for other reality competition shows—whether they're about food, interior design, or art.

WHAT WAS IT LIKE BEING ON THE SHOW?

It was very exciting and very rewarding. I couldn't believe how many people watched it and commented on seeing me. It was a privilege to be invited on the show—three times. I think the show educated a lot of people about the fashion industry, and introduced many designers to the TV audience.

HOW DO YOU THINK HEIDI'S ON-SCREEN PERSONA HAS EVOLVED?

She's become tougher. I don't think she was as critical at the beginning. She seemed to defer a lot to the designers at first. She always had an opinion and great instinct, but now she's equally if not tougher than her co-judges, and is very demanding—and has every right to be.

She's seen a lot of good and bad clothing walk that runway. Heidi Klum has become quite a formidable celebrity, in addition to her supermodel status. She's now a big business all by herself.

I DON'T THINK ANYBODY COULD HAVE PREDICTED WHAT HAPPENED TO TIM GUNN.

Tim Gunn became a breakout star of the show. He does endorsements, commercials, books, red carpet commentary, and whatever he wants to do. I don't think anybody could have predicted this—least of all him. There are probably a lot of people at Parsons kicking themselves in the pants that they didn't step up to the plate. But Tim has also brought some needed credibility, intelligence, exposure, and compassion to the fashion game, and he deserves his success; he's good for fashion.

AS A JUDGE, WHAT IS THE MOST IMPORTANT THING YOU LOOK FOR?

You're always looking for talent, potential, a spark or an idea. I think seasoned designers and professionals can spot that pretty quickly. The audience can also see if something is not made well, is falling apart, or if the finish is bad. When you judge the thing that's interesting, and that the audience doesn't realize, is you have no idea what's been going on up to that point, or who has consistently been delivering good garments or concepts, because none of the episodes have aired yet. So there is no history of what they've done the week or weeks before. Heidi, Michael, and Nina know, but not the guest judge. Then when you watch the episodes on the air, you see what they've been doing; and you also see the shenanigans behind the scenes, and their real personalities—which would probably influence the final decision if I (or another guest judge) had known what was going on. So sometimes the audience is surprised because they've see the progression the guest judge has not seen throughout the competition.

It's difficult trying to pick a winner and a loser when you're comparing people on a single execution of a garment for a very specific challenge (which could be ridiculous). But in the final analysis it's usually pretty clear who is out front, who has real potential, and who needs to "pack their bags."

WHY DO YOU THINK CHRISTIAN SIRIANO IS THE ONE WHO'S HAD SO MUCH SUCCESS AFTER THE SHOW?

Christian has true talent. I think he really has a point of view as well as that central casting "Send me a designer!" personality. On the show he was edgy enough, but not too bitchy, and he knew how to play it. He was a clear winner in his season. Now he has a successful business because he's good, works really hard, is very committed to his business, and has made some very strategic partnerships and licensing deals. He also has many visible celebrity friends who have become clients. He's produced some terrific runway shows and is carried in all the leading stores. He parlayed his TV fame well, and has now evolved beyond that.

HOW DO YOU THINK THE SHOW HAS EVOLVED OVER NINE SEASONS?

What has changed over the seasons is that the designers are not "kids" anymore. One of the biggest changes to me is the amount of "working" designers who are now contestants or competitors. At the beginning I liked that they were younger and really kind of green, didn't know how to make things, yet still very ambitious, and they really wanted to learn how to become a designer. Now you have Bert and Rami Kashou. I think the exposure is great for them, but Rami has shown his collections on the runways at Fashion Week in Los Angeles, and I think he's a great designer. They are seasoned pros and for them to compete with people who've never made clothing before is somewhat unfair. Then again you have people like Laura Bennett, who was fantastic. She'd never made a dress in her life before she was on the show. She has five young sons running around, and she made some really fabulous dresses. I remember because it was the year I was the finale judge. I really thought that Laura deserved to win because consistently she delivered a beautiful product. But the consensus of the judges was it's a one act—"just dresses." I remember speaking to that point, and expressing that if you do one fabulous thing and you're known for that, that's perfectly fine in our industry. There are very few designers who can make everything from bathing suits and evening gowns to sportswear, menswear, and so on in their own firms.

Over ten seasons the show has introduced the public to many very successful, well-known designers who've been judges. They have also been introduced to celebrities they admire, and who dress well, and it's interesting for the audience to learn that some of these stars and designers are very bright, nurturing, and informative—or snarky, and some of them can't put a sentence together. I personally prefer when the guest judges are from the industry as opposed to celebrities. When I was the judge in the finale show, Robin Givhan, who was the fashion reporter from *The Washington Post* wrote a really lovely article about how fantastic it was when they announced I was the judge. She said something along the lines of, "Fern has probably seen more fashion shows than most people in the industry, and she comes from the industry and she cares and she nurtures." I was very proud of that.

WHAT ARE YOUR FAVORITE TYPES OF CHALLENGES?

I prefer the challenges that are for specific types of people and their bodies. Nobody's ever going to wear a collection out of used car parts, garbage bags, party materials, or vegetables. I understand the sense of seeing where their head is, and challenging the designers to think and "create." I do, however, remember Austin and his cornhusk dress. That was pretty fabulous.

DO YOU THINK PEOPLE CAN LEARN ABOUT FASHION FROM WATCHING THE SHOW?

Yes, absolutely. They can observe the process of solving a challenge, making a drawing, shopping for fabric, draping, watching the sewing, and seeing a garment come together. Then they also see the fittings, the hair, makeup, and accessories that complete the look—and maybe learn how to explain it all to boot. I also hope the audiences will learn how to work with others and not throw their colleagues "under the bus."

I think the audience (and designers) can also learn a great deal from the constructive criticism. When we are judges, you have no idea how long we deliberate and discuss each look. We talk about every single person's outfits, and what they've done. We talk about every single designer standing on the runway, and what they've done. But in the final edit the viewer may see the twelve designers on the runway, and six of them are told they are safe and off they go. I think everybody's who's worked their ass off for 24–48 hours deserves to have some sort of input. They don't necessarily know why they were safe. We really take the judging seriously. You don't want to hurt anybody's feelings and you usually want to be encouraging. The deliberation is edited down to sound bytes and ultimately it's all about keeping the audience in suspense. I believe a lot can be learned from the professionals' comments and criticism. I personally find that part the most interesting.

DO YOU THINK THE SHOW PREPARES DESIGNERS FOR A CAREER?

I don't think that's the show's responsibility or real intent, and that's okay. I think they've always set out to create a successful TV show, and they've done that. This is not boot camp for designers.

To be a successful designer takes a great deal of time, talent, schooling, and apprenticeships. There are many terrific fashion design programs in schools all over the country. I hope that *Project Runway* inspires those who are passionate and really want to make this their life work. They should get the proper training and learn fashion history, and develop the discipline they will need to succeed. I hope more of these participants work for established designers and companies. I don't think they need to have their name on a label before it's their time. The show could be more of a clearinghouse for design jobs.

I asked Donna Karan in an interview with her what advice she'd give young designers. She said, "Work in retail. You have to understand what the customers want, how to relate to customers, how to talk to them, and how to sell something." That's great advice.

MYCHAEL KNIGHT

WHAT WAS YOUR *PROJECT RUNWAY* AUDITION LIKE?

My *Project Runway* audition happened twice. I first auditioned in Miami for the second season. Tim Gunn, along with the other judges, said I needed to grow. I was disappointed, but not broken. So the whole second season I prepared. I even went as far as taking on the season's challenges myself with full-on sketches and actual designs. It was good practice. When it was time to audition for the third season I was ready. I had a plan: I gave myself an "edge" in my appearance. I wore a fitted baseball cap, a huge white tee, denim shorts, and sneakers. What made it effective was the garment I chose to present, which was a beautiful wedding gown that had hand-cut floral detail covering the gown. I remember one of the judges, Chloe Dao, pointing and saying, "You made that?!" Brilliant, it worked—well, at least for her. The rest of the judges saw something in me too, and the rest is history!

WHO DID YOU BOND WITH MOST ON THE SHOW?

Laura and I for some reason just hit it off. I think it was her no-nonsense approach—to everything. That's how I am. Angela is one of the sweetest, gentlest people I have ever met. She was completely pure, and not trying to put on. Kayne is just a big ball of fun. I love that dude. We still talk and work together frequently.

WHAT WAS YOUR FAVORITE AND LEAST FAVORITE CHALLENGE?

My favorite challenge was the Recycle challenge. It was just fun to be an artist. No rules, just create! My least favorite was the What the *Elle*? challenge. It was the last and the deciding challenge as to who was going to Fashion Week. So much pressure! I couldn't focus; I kept going back in forth with the design. But, I "made it work."

WHO DID YOU THINK WAS YOUR TOUGHEST COMPETITION?

I think Alison Kelly and later Jeffrey Sebelia were my biggest competition. Although we didn't get to see much from Alison (to this day I think she was sent home way too early). Just thinking back to some of her sketches/drapes, she had some amazing pieces. I told her I thought she was the "freshest" point of view out of us all. I only thought of Jeffrey as a tough competitor when we were narrowed down to the final four.

DID YOU HAVE A FAVORITE GUEST JUDGE?

My favorite guest judge, hands down, was Rachel Zoe. This lady knows fashion! Rachel is on the pulse of what's hot, now and next. She gave such rave reviews on my piece. She even said, "I would put that on one of my clients right now!" How dope is that?

WHICH JUDGE DID YOU FEEL GAVE YOU THE BEST ADVICE?

Nina Garcia was the judge that had the best advice for me. Being a fashion editor, she knows what's hot, the industry, and most importantly, what sells. Her advice was always very multidimensional in all of those areas. In addition, she's a woman. She is the potential customer for whom I'm creating. As designer, your number one rule: listen to your customer. I really appreciated her constructive criticism.

WHAT WAS IT LIKE HAVING TIM GUNN COME TO YOUR HOME?

He is as gracious of a guest as he is as a host at Parsons. That gentleman is such a class act.

WHAT WAS THE MODEL CASTING FOR THE FINALE LIKE?

It was interesting. For everyone else, it was about wanting the same models. It actually turned into an auction, designers trading "this model" for "that model." Too funny. My issue was having enough models of color. Black, Latina, Asian, whatever, there wasn't enough to chose from. As a designer, I want to dress all women. And when I present collections, I want *all women* to see themselves in the clothes.

YOUR PAM GRIER LOOK WAS INCREDIBLE. WAS SHE YOUR FIRST CHOICE FOR THAT CHALLENGE?

Yes! Pam Grier was definitely my first choice. I've always loved her and the characters she played; her strength, confidence, and sex appeal. She personifies the "Mychael Knight Woman."

HOW COOL WAS IT BEING NAMED THE FAN FAVORITE, AND GETTING $10,000?

Winning fan favorite (the first fan favorite winner, I might add) was the raddest thing ever! I truly and honestly did not expect it. I really appreciated (and needed) the $10,000. What was even more amazing to me is that close to 10 million people voted for me. I remember Andy Cohen whispering to me, "You won by a landslide." Amazing.

YOUR STREET SAFARI COLLECTION SEEMED TO BE THE CROWD'S FAVORITE AT FASHION WEEK. WHAT WAS IT LIKE GETTING TO SHOW AT BRYANT PARK?

Showing for the *Project Runway* finale was and is one of the most iconic moments in my career. Finally getting something you fantasize about for so long is mind blowing. I think about that moment every season when I present a collection. I think I'm secretly chasing that same high. I knew it would happen. God (and hard work) made it happen.

WHO HAVE BEEN SOME OF YOUR FAVORITE *PROJECT RUNWAY* DESIGNERS OVER THE YEARS?

Santino, Mondo, Anthony Ryan, and Leanne. All for the same reason: they're just dope.

WHAT HAVE YOU BEEN DOING SINCE *PROJECT RUNWAY*?

I have been busy. I've continued to create collections every season. I've been blessed to do commission work with Starbucks, Nike, and Coca-Cola in addition to designing for celebrities such as Jennifer Hudson, Khloe Kardashian, and Toni Braxton. I also designed a high-end diamond jewelry line and my signature, unisex fragrance, Majk. This year, I'm introducing handbags and will open my first showroom and boutique.

THE DESIGNERS

SIMONE LEBLANC
FROM: SAN FRANCISCO, CA
STUDIED: CALIFORNIA COLLEGE
OF THE ARTS

MARION LEE
FROM: TYLER, TX
STUDIED: PARSONS THE NEW
SCHOOL FOR DESIGN

CARMEN WEBBER
FROM: CHARLOTTE, NC
STUDIED: SAVANNAH COLLEGE
OF ART AND DESIGN

JACK MACKENROTH
FROM: SEATTLE, WA
STUDIED: UNIVERSITY OF
CALIFORNIA AT BERKELEY

STEVEN ROSENGARD
FROM: CHICAGO, IL
STUDIED: COLUMBIA COLLEGE,
CHICAGO

ELISA JIMÉNEZ
FROM: EL PASO, TX
STUDIED: THE UNIVERSITY
OF TEXAS AT AUSTIN, THE
UNIVERSITY OF ARIZONA

KEVIN CHRISTIANA
FROM: FAIRFIELD, NJ
STUDIED: FASHION INSTITUTE
OF TECHNOLOGY

CHRISTINA "KIT PISTOL" SCARBO
FROM: LOS ANGELES, CA
STUDIED: FASHION INSTITUTE OF
TECHNOLOGY, POLIMODA INSTITUTE
OF FASHION DESIGN AND MARKETING

VICTORYA HONG
FROM: SEOUL, KOREA
STUDIED: UNIVERSITY OF
CHICAGO, PARSONS THE NEW
SCHOOL FOR DESIGN

RICKY LIZALDE
FROM: ESCONDIDO, CA
STUDIED: CALIFORNIA STATE
UNIVERSITY, LONG BEACH

**KATHLEEN "SWEET P"
VAUGHN**
FROM: LOS ANGELES, CA
STUDIED: LOS ANGELES
TRADE-TECHNICAL COLLEGE

CHRIS MARCH
FROM: SAN FRANCISCO, CA
SELF-TAUGHT

JILLIAN LEWIS
FROM: SELDEN, NY
STUDIED: PARSONS THE NEW
SCHOOL FOR DESIGN

RAMI KASHOU
FROM: JERUSALEM, ISRAEL
STUDIED: BROOKS COLLEGE

CHRISTIAN SIRIANO
FROM: ANNAPOLIS, MD
STUDIED: THE AMERICAN
INTERCONTINENTAL
UNIVERSITY

SEASON 4

HIGHLIGHTS

RACE FOR FABRIC

Season 4 began with the challenge Sew Us What You Got. The designers were taken to Bryant Park, where they found three tents full of $50,000 worth of fabric across the lawn. They had to make a run for it and grab as much fabric as they could. Chris was the slowest, and was still making his way over while the other designers were already taking their fabric. It made no difference; he still got exactly what he wanted.

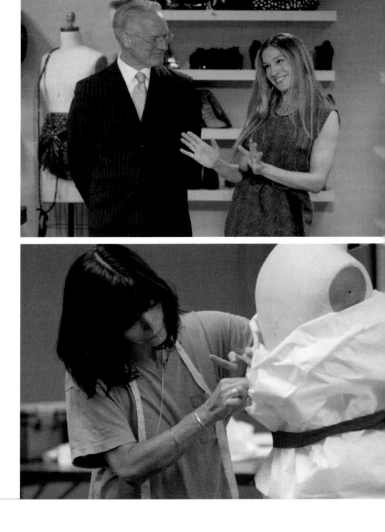

SJP IN THE WORKROOM

Tim revealed that a fashion icon was coming to see them in the workroom. They were both shocked and thrilled when they saw it was Sarah Jessica Parker. Chris started to cry. He explained that he moved to New York because of her series *Sex and the City*.

SPIT MARKS

Elisa and Sweet P were paired as a team to create a look for Sarah Jessica Parker's line Bitten for Steve & Barry's. Sweet P was startled to learn that Elisa made spit marks on her clothes to imbibe them with energy and essence. When Heidi learned of this she advised Elisa to not tell people that.

CANDY CLOTHES

Tim brought the designers to the Hershey store in New York City. Their mission was to create a look using items from the store. Rami won for his dress made from a Twizzlers plastic pillow case and York wrapping paper.

TIKI BARBER

Tim brought the designers to the set of *The Today Show*, where they found anchor Tiki Barber waiting. Their challenge was to design an outfit for him to wear on-air. Barber thought that Jack was smart in his design, and was awarded the win.

JACK LEAVES; CHRIS RETURNS

During Episode 5 Jack was distracted by a staph infection on his lip. He called his doctor, who wanted him to come to see him. Jack had a talk with Tim and eventually made the heartbreaking decision to leave the show. He broke down when he had to tell the other designers he was going. His infection was very serious. He was hospitalized for five days, but made a full recovery. The recently eliminated Chris was brought back in his place.

EMOTIONAL RICKY

The stress and pressure of being on *Project Runway* took a toll on Ricky, who cried in almost all of the episodes he was on.

CHRISTIAN AND THE PROM GIRL

For the What a Girl Wants challenge the designers were assigned to design a prom dress for high school students from St. John Vianney High School in Holmdel, New Jersey. Christian was paired with Maddie. Maddie told Christian that she too was a designer. Christian was surprised that she picked up a pencil and drew on his sketch. They discussed what her dress should be like. Christian didn't completely agree with her vision; he felt what she wanted was somewhat tacky. Maddie wasn't thrilled when she came in for her fitting. On the runway Christian told the judges she was very opinionated. Nina said that Maddie had a right to want what she wanted, and didn't like that Christian blamed her for the problems they had.

WWE DIVAS

For a change of pace the designers were given the task to design an outfit for six WWE Divas to wear in the ring.

CLOTHES MADE FROM HAIR

Tim showed up at Chris's apartment to check in on how his final collection was coming along. He was quite surprised to find out that Chris was using human hair to make his clothing.

RAMI VS. CHRIS FOR THE FINALE

The judges were deadlocked and could not choose between Chris and Rami for elimination for the final challenge to decide who would compete at New York Fashion Week. The decision was made that both of them would create collections, but only one would compete in the finale. It would be Rami.

CHRISTIAN AND CHRIS'S AVANT-GARDE DRESS

Christian and Chris worked as a team for the On Garde! challenge. They had to create an avant-garde look inspired by their model's hairdo. They won the challenge, and were featured in a TRESemmé ad in *Elle* magazine.

VICTORIA ♥ CHRISTIAN

Victoria Beckham was the guest judge for the finale. At judging she told Christian that she would be honored to wear any of his clothing.

CHRISTIAN SIRIANO:

"That was great. She was amazing and really supportive. I went to her house and did a private fitting and it was pretty fabulous. That was probably the most surreal thing ever, which was really cool. It was two weeks after the show ended. I was doing Ellen and Craig Ferguson and all the talk shows, and part of my schedule was to go do a fitting with Heidi and a fitting with Victoria. They don't live far from each other. It was really, really fun playing dress up with her. She was really supportive. She bought a couple of pieces and I just gave her a bunch of things. It was awesome."

SEW US WHAT YOU GOT (RAMI)

I STARTED TO CRY (VICTORYA)

FASHION GIANT (JACK)

TRENDSETTER (JILLIAN)

WHAT'S THE SKINNY? (CHRISTIAN)

EYE CANDY (RAMI)

WHAT A GIRL WANTS (VICTORYA)

EN GARDE! (CHRISTIAN)

EVEN DESIGNERS GET THE BLUES (RICKY)

RAW TALENT (CHRIS)

THE ART OF FASHION (CHRISTIAN)

FINALE PART 2 (CHRISTIAN)

MODELS

WENDI SULLIVAN

CHERON SMITH

ANNA LITA PEREZ

CHRISTINA ANDERSON
MCDONALD

ASHLEY EVANS

KATIE NELSON

AVIVA BROCKS

MARIE SALTER

JACQUELINE MIRANNE

AMANDA ALTER

LEA RANNELLS

MARCIA MITCHELL

LAUREN BROWNE

SAMANTHA RUGGIERO

LISA NARGI

GUEST JUDGES

MONIQUE LHUILLIER
FASHION DESIGNER

TIKI BARBER
TODAY SHOW CORRESPONDENT

DONNA KARAN
FASHION DESIGNER

SARAH JESSICA PARKER
ACTRESS/FASHION ICON

PATRICK ROBINSON
HEAD DESIGNER, GAP

ZAC POSEN
FASHION DESIGNER

GILLES MENDEL
FASHION DESIGNER

CAROLINE CALVIN
SENIOR VP OF DESIGN, LEVI
STRAUSS AND COMPANY

ALBERTA FERRETTI
FASHION DESIGNER

ROBERTO CAVALLI
FASHION DESIGNER

**TRAVER RAINS &
RICHIE RICH**
DESIGNERS, HEATHERETTE

VICTORIA BECKHAM
POP ICON/FASHION DESIGNER

SNAPPED!

CHRISTIAN SIRIANO

DID YOU GO INTO *PROJECT RUNWAY* WITH A PLAN?

No. I went to design school in London so I actually hadn't watched the show because it didn't air there. I didn't know much about it. My friend's mother worked for Bravo and said they're doing this open casting call and I went. I found out the day before so it was totally random and it was just one of those things—something fun to do. It was an open call; you wait in line and it's not so serious at the very beginning. Then as you get through more and more steps you realize this is real. I think that's part of what made it fun for me—that it wasn't such a serious, planned thing.

WHAT WAS THE PROCESS LIKE AFTER YOU FOUND OUT YOU MADE IT ON THE SHOW?

The process was really interesting. I had to do a video diary of what I did on a daily basis. Then they did the references and then I had to take a psych test, which I thought was really funny. It was a process but once you're done with all of that it's quick.

AFTER FINDING OUT YOU MADE IT ON DID YOU RESEARCH THE SHOW SINCE YOU HADN'T WATCHED IT?

There was a season airing at the time and I thought it was great. I had seen some of those contestants around the city. I was starting slowly but surely to get what it was and how it was portrayed.

YOU'RE THE CONTESTANT SO MANY OTHERS SAY THEY WANT TO BE LIKE. DID YOU HAVE ANY IDEA THAT WOULD HAPPEN FOR YOU?

That's so nice! On the show even though I came off as being super confident, there was also plenty of time when we filmed that I was very *not* confident, super-tired, depressed, and not interested in anything, so I don't think I had any idea. Everyone was older than me, so I think they didn't let me know that I was good sometimes. Sometimes they would, but those were the people that left early. As I went forward the people that were left didn't really ever acknowledge that I was good. What I knew all along was that taste is something that can't be taught. I think that's where you differentiate the designers on the show—because taste level is the biggest thing in this business. I knew that I had a different perspective, not even necessarily a different design perspective, but a perspective on how to match a shoe or hair and makeup and all those things, that was never an issue of mine. I grew up with ballet dancers. They have a very sophisticated way of thinking and dressing that's just different.

DO YOU THINK THAT YOUR WORK WAS OR IS INFLUENCED BY DANCE?

Sometimes yes, for sure.

AND YOUR STYLING TOO?

Not as much styling anymore because I like more of an edgy girl. I don't necessarily think a ballet dancer is edgy, but definitely the romance is there. I like movement and I like the theatrics of ballet.

YOU AND CHRIS WORKED TOGETHER ON THE AVANT-GARDE CHALLENGE. WAS IT A REALLY SUCCESSFUL PAIRING CREATIVELY?

The results were amazing. No one would ever be able to recreate that.

LATER IN THE SEASON HE WAS CRITICIZED BY THE JUDGES FOR RECYCLING THAT LOOK IN ANOTHER CHALLENGE.

I didn't actually think that it was that similar. It's probably because the part that the judges knew is that he made the

shoulder piece; that's the only thing he made in that look. I made everything else so that's why I think they brought up that reference. It was very hard because he had to build this under-wire corset jacket. It was made out of ropes and buckles. I think that was why they were a bit annoyed that he created the same shoulder piece again. He had to do that same under-wire corset construction to create it, which is boring to the average person to hear about so they didn't show that part. It was kind of sad because his dress was quite cool; I liked it.

AS SUCH A YOUNG DESIGNER, IT MUST HAVE BEEN SUCH AN HONOR TO BE ABLE TO SHOW YOUR WORK IN FRONT OF MICHAEL KORS AND GET HIS FEEDBACK.

At the time I was just so naïve, I didn't know anything about anything. I've since read tons of interviews with Michael about his business and career. I would actually feel more honored now because I know more about him.

He is such a nice person.

DID YOU HAVE ANY FAVORITE GUEST JUDGE?

I think most of them were interesting in their own way. I obviously think Victoria was amazing and stunning and quite fabulous, very nice, and very supportive. I think Roberto Cavalli was really cool, I think Alberta Ferretti was quite fabulous. Sarah Jessica was really fun. I dress her now but at the time she didn't like what I did! We had some really outstanding judges. It was a really great, great season in general.

WHAT IS THE COLLABORATION LIKE WHEN WORKING WITH A CLIENT?

In terms of a celebrity usually it's very collaborative. I wouldn't even change a neckline unless they knew about it because those things are so personal. A celebrity going to an event is so scrutinized for what they wear. That's what's cool about Heidi. Not everyone loves how she dresses

on the red carpet, but she says, well there will be another Emmys next year, and I'm going to an event tomorrow and the next day. I wish that more actresses would think that way—knowing there's something tomorrow, the next day, the next day. There are other chances to have your great moment so you should experiment.

DID YOU FEEL THAT THE CHALLENGE WITH THE WRESTLING DIVAS WAS ABOUT FASHION OR PURE COSTUME?

That challenge was fun, but totally random, weird, and funny. It was more about costume, which is okay. I've dressed musicians like Lady Gaga, Rihanna—musicians do like clothes that are a little more showy, not necessarily full fashion. The wrestling women were really sweet. It was good that this challenge was toward the end because we were tired. But then on the other hand it was bad because it wasn't really representative of a designer's work, and to be eliminated for that challenge—it's kind of sad.

YOU ALSO HAD TO WORK WITH A GIRL ON THE PROM DRESS CHALLENGE WHO GAVE YOU A LOT OF TROUBLE.

It was fine and she was fine. She really wanted to be on TV. She was having a big flashy moment and was quite intense. We didn't have dress forms that were her size. It's hard when they do any challenge with real women because you're not equipped in the proper way, unless your dress form is the size of that woman. To pad the dress form and to make the garment and alter it to fit that person's measurements is very hard. It's a technical thing that just would never happen in real business. I have clients that we need to do $10,000 gowns for. They can be a size 12 or 14, but it's different because we're basing it on a real size chart and actually grading a pattern. You start with your basic pattern and you mark it and grade to any size you need. That's a technical industry form. I get those challenges and they make sense because it's for real women but it's kind of frustrating because real women's clothing at a mass retailer get made in a real woman way. I had nothing to physically drape on and it's the same for every one of those challenges. I remember in Season 3, they did the mom challenge and all the moms were bigger

women. Without the proper tools I wouldn't want that challenge either. That's a big part of why clothes are made on models and presented that way. It's almost like making a model of a building—you're making a miniature version of what the larger scale could be.

YOU DISCOVERED SESSILEE LOPEZ.

Yes, Sessilee. I also had Iris Strubegger, who is quite a famous model too. She was the face of Valentino. She opened my show in the feathered hat. It's so funny that I had Iris open and Sessilee close. Sessilee was awesome, she was so quiet and sweet and she looked so beautiful. I love girls of different ethnicities. That's always been my thing so it was fun to have her. I still love her.

WHAT WAS IT LIKE WHEN SARAH JESSICA PARKER CAME INTO THE WORKROOM?

It was really exciting. Sarah Jessica will always be the most iconic girl in fashion. She's quite fabulous, and wears clothes really well. She looks beautiful in clothes and is creative with what she wears.

YOU'VE BEEN SO SUCCESSFUL AFTER *PROJECT RUNWAY*. HOW HAVE YOU BEEN ABLE TO MAKE THAT HAPPEN?

That's the golden question that no one really knows. There are a lot of things that go into it. It was a very strong, powerful, exciting season. I think it was a time when *Project Runway* hadn't been on for a while. There had been a long period in between so when it came back there was a lot of promotion. I think the designers were probably some of the most talented there will ever be. Some people like to watch a success story; maybe that's what it was. I was young and the clothes were exciting and exuberant so you remembered them a bit. Because I had a funny personality and I like to be eccentric, I think that helped the media world get behind me. While that was happening I was working on a collection, and I showed my first season five months after *Project Runway* ended. I wanted to show I'm going to make this a real business.

HOW DID YOU GET THE MONEY TOGETHER SO QUICKLY?

I guess because I was fun and a personality and had these big exuberant clothes, I was getting lots of offers. It started slowly but surely, just happening more and more and then I was getting offers to do design collaborations. My first big collaboration I did with a company was for LG phones. I designed accessories for a new phone that they were launching. I did a huge tour with them and they supported me at Fashion Week and that helped fund the business. When we showed my first collection, the salon that I worked at (for my whole life basically) sponsored, gave money, and supported all the stylists and that was really helpful. The production company that put on *Project Runway* did my show because I became friends with them, so everyone helped out a little bit in their own way. I think the main thing is—and it's what every other designer has had a hard time with—it's a lot of money to start a business and to start a fashion label. If you don't do it right after your show, your season's over. It's like you have one chance and in fashion, even for the biggest brand in the world, it's season to season sometimes. I think that the biggest thing is I showed up, clocked in; I was going to really have a brand. I also am a psychotic worker too; I'm so crazy hands-on and pretty business-savvy. I grew up that way. I make quick decisions, I'm pretty decisive. A young designer nowadays in this business has to have all of those qualities. You can't just be creative, it's really not as important as you think—it's like 40 percent, maybe even less. It's still hard for me every day, but you have to move forward every season and really work at it and figure out the kinks and be decisive.

WHO DO YOU GO TO FOR ADVICE?

I've had kind of an advisor, a manager friend who's been amazing. We've done all of my collaborations and deals together. She's awesome. Then friends. My best friend's father was my attorney when I first started. You have to be the best person you can be because you need all of your life supporters. I've had a lawyer do so much work for me and then I made his daughter's eighteenth birthday party dress. You have to give back.

DID THE SHOW PREPARE YOU FOR THIS BUSINESS?

It prepares you a little bit. You leave aware of what you can do and how you work with people. It prepares you in that way but it can hinder the actual business a little because you're put on a very massive platform and then you have to go backwards; you're starting. As a designer everyone knew who I was, everyone knew my name, everyone wanted clothes, but I had nothing to give them and I had no idea how to start that. That's a very scary thing; you're thrown into this business very abruptly and I think that's why some designers have a hard time being successful.

It's not enough to be known, you have to figure out how to make product and sell it. People ask me why aren't you in Barneys? Do they know what the process to get into Barneys is? Just to get to them on the phone is impossible; it's a hard thing to do. It's those types of things that the average person wouldn't think about. As a young designer I didn't know about that either, I thought, maybe I can just call every retailer. You're on this massive platform after the show and you think you're good or you think you're creative but none of those things really matter, actually, until later on. You have to get the business end of it down first because even if you think about a young designer that is in a store one season and the clothes don't sell or they ship late or the quality is not good, then they're done. That's happened to me. I've made mistakes.

AS THE WINNER OF THE SHOW, DID YOU FEEL THIS ENORMOUS PRESSURE TO BE SUCCESSFUL RIGHT AWAY?

I don't know if everyone feels that but I felt it. I didn't know what to give Victoria when she asked for clothes. I didn't even own that finale collection. The pieces were auctioned off. We had to remake the dresses for Victoria, but I didn't even remember how I made them. When you have someone like Victoria Beckham asking for your clothes you have to figure out how to make it work!

WHAT ARE SOME HIGHLIGHTS OF YOUR CAREER POST-*RUNWAY*?

Since *Project Runway* I've gotten to show my collection through ten seasons of New York Fashion Week—and counting! I created a makeup line for Victoria's Secret and have had great design partnerships with Payless, Starbucks, Spiegel, LG, and Puma. My collection has been carried in some of the top retailers around the world, including Saks Fifth Avenue and Neiman Marcus. I've had the honor of dressing stars of film, music, and fashion, such as Sarah Jessica Parker, Emily Blunt, Christina Hendricks, Emmy Rossum, Lady Gaga, Victoria Beckham, Nicki Minaj, Taylor Swift, Miranda Cosgrove, Rihanna, and Heidi, of course. The Christian Siriano brand has been featured in many publications, like *The New York Times*, *The Wall Street Journal*, *Women's Wear Daily*, *Vogue*, *Vogue Italia*, *Harper's Bazaar*, *InStyle*, *Elle*, *People*, and *Marie Claire*. I also wrote a book, *Fierce Style: How to Be Your Most Fabulous Self*, which released in 2008. I'm doing what I've always dreamed of doing and it feels great!

JILLIAN LEWIS

HAD YOU EVER AUDITIONED FOR *PROJECT RUNWAY* BEFORE?

I was in the running for Season 3. When I showed up to audition for Season 4, I was immediately plucked from the back of an extremely long line of hopeful designers and was brought into the room pretty quickly. It really boosted my confidence.

WHO DID YOU BOND WITH MOST ON THE SHOW?

Rami Kashou.

WHAT WAS YOUR FAVORITE AND LEAST FAVORITE CHALLENGE?

My favorite was the Art of Fashion challenge. It was amazing to be able to have a private viewing at The Metropolitan Museum of Art. My least favorite was the second challenge, Money Changes Everything. It is never fun to be limited by such a miniscule budget and such a limited sensibility.

WHO DID YOU THINK WAS YOUR TOUGHEST COMPETITION?

From the very beginning it was both Christian and Rami. They were confident and consistent from the beginning to the end.

WHO ARE SOME OF YOUR FAVORITE DESIGNERS?

Internationally, my favorite designers are Riccardo Tisci for Givenchy and Karl Lagerfeld for Chanel. In America, my favorite designer is Ralph Lauren. I am constantly blown away by the way he is able to keep reinventing while remaining painstakingly true to himself. I have had the pleasure of working for him for several years.

WHAT WAS IT LIKE HAVING SARAH JESSICA PARKER COME INTO THE WORKROOM?

It was incredibly exciting to get to work with Sarah Jessica Parker. I have loved her since *Girls Just Want to Have Fun* in the '80s. On the other hand though, that was my least favorite challenge.

DID YOU HAVE A FAVORITE GARMENT YOU MADE FOR THE SHOW?

My favorite garment was the exaggerated trench coat I designed for the En Garde challenge. I have since made many renditions of this coat, which ended up being my best seller and was worn by Beyoncé four times, including in the video "Halo." Ciara has worn it as well.

I was oddly inspired by human anatomy for that dress. Months after the show finished I happened to go into the Hershey store in Times Square and there it was on display! I was shocked and excited. People still remember me for that dress.

It was so fun! I just remember the self tanner staining all the clothes, but they were fabulous. And it offered a diversion from all the seriousness.

The show may air once a week but in real life the challenges were being filmed consecutively, without even a moment's break. We were up as early as 4:00 in the morning some days and back to the apartments usually around 1:00 a.m. Beyond that, I had essentially stopped eating. By the time the seventh challenge came along, I was exhausted and drained. It was that simple.

After I was declared the "clear winner" of the fourth challenge, which was a group challenge, I knew that I was going to make it. I was in the top for the next few challenges and it became more and more clear to me. Even the one time I was in the bottom, there wasn't a moment of concern. I surprised myself at how much I was able to do with such little time. The look I created for the last challenge before the finale exceeded my expectations of myself and I knew for sure that I nailed it and was going to make the final three.

Not so much. The reality is, we only knew each other for a little over a month. There are certain things that only someone who lived it would understand. That is a true bond but I prefer to just move forward and not look back.

I think people would be surprised to know that the entire eleven episode series, including the commercial and photo shoot, was filmed in about thirty days.

Truck drivers stopping traffic in the middle of midtown Manhattan to tell me they loved me on Project Runway, a young girl excitedly ripping off her shoe for lack of anything else for me to sign, the clicking of numerous cameras and paparazzi calling out, "Jillian, over here." It was if I was living someone else's life. It faded after about three years but it was fun while it lasted.

Immediately after Project Runway ended I launched my own namesake collection with my husband Lewaa. We showed during fashion week each season and sold the line to about twenty top tier boutiques in the US, Canada, and Hong Kong. We had placements in Vogue, W, Harper's Bazaar, Marie Claire, Lucky, Women's Wear Daily, and more. Beyoncé, Ciara, Lucy Liu, Victoria Beckham, and the Kardashians were among my celebrity clients. I also costumed several contemporary dance performances, including A Two Part Affair for Works and Process at the Guggenheim Museum. I rang the NASDAQ bell, was a spokesperson for Brother International, hosted St. Louis Fashion Week, appeared on the news several times, spoke on the radio, and was flown around the country to be a guest at many exciting fashion events and in-store trunk shows. I reached a point where I could not sustain the company that I had built. I ran out of options and could not refuse an amazing offer to return to Ralph Lauren as a Design Director. To date I am still working happily in that role. I know that I will pick up where I left off with my business in the future. That has always been and will always be my dream.

THE DESIGNERS

JERRY TAM
FROM, BUTTE, MT
STUDIED: PARSONS THE NEW
SCHOOL OF DESIGN, FASHION
INSTITUTE OF TECHNOLOGY

WESLEY NAULT
FROM: BLACKSTONE, MA
STUDIED: FASHION INSTITUTE OF
TECHNOLOGY

EMILY BRANDLE
FROM: SACRAMENTO, CA
STUDIED: OTIS COLLEGE OF
ART AND DESIGN

JENNIFER DIEDERICH
FROM: SYRACUSE, NY
STUDIED: FASHION INSTITUTE
OF TECHNOLOGY

KELLI MARTIN
FROM: COLUMBUS, OH
STUDIED: FASHION
INSTITUTE OF DESIGN AND
MERCHANDISING

DANIEL FELD
FROM: EL PASO, TX
FROM: THE BERKSHIRES, MA
STUDIED: PRATT INSTITUTE

KEITH BRYCE
FROM: SALT LAKE CITY, UT
SELF-TAUGHT

STELLA ZOTIS
FROM: ASTORIA, NY
SELF-TAUGHT

BLAYNE WALSH
FROM: YAKIMA, WA
STUDIED: THE ART INSTITUTE
OF SEATTLE

TERRI STEVENS
FROM: CHICAGO, IL
STUDIED: COLUMBIA COLLEGE
CHICAGO

JOE FARIS
FROM: TROY, MI
STUDIED: PARSONS THE
NEW SCHOOL FOR DESIGN

STEPHEN "SUEDE" BAUM
FROM: SEVEN HILLS, OH
INTERNED AT GEOFFREY
BEENE

JERELL SCOTT
FROM: HOUSTON, TX
SELF-TAUGHT

KENLEY COLLINS
FROM: POMPANO BEACH, FL
STUDIED: FLORIDA STATE
UNIVERSITY

KORTO MOMOLU
FROM: MONROVIA, LIBERIA
STUDIED: L'ACADEMIES
DES COUTURIERS DESIGN
INSTITUTE

LEANNE MARSHALL
FROM: YUBA CITY, CA
STUDIED: FASHION
INSTITUTE OF DESIGN AND
MERCHANDISING

SEASON 5

HIGHLIGHTS

DESIGNING FOR BROOKE SHIELDS

Brooke Shields was on hand for the Welcome to the Jungle challenge. The designers had to create a day to night look for her character on the show *Lipstick Jungle*. The winning look would be worn by Shields on an episode of the series' second season.

DRAG QUEEN FASHION

The assignment for the Good Queen Fun challenge was to design an outfit for a drag queen. All of the looks would be auctioned off to benefit the Broadway Cares Equity Fights AIDS charity. Suede was paired with Hedda Lettuce, who criticized the outfit he was making. Hedda asked Suede if he made gloves for the outfit because he was too lazy to make sleeves.

HEDDA LETTUCE:

"I fucking hated the costume. It was like the worst piece of shit I ever saw in my life. What drag queen doesn't have sleeves? You have to, no matter what. So I said, 'You're too lazy to make sleeves.' Suede broke down backstage I heard. Even Tim Gunn, who likes everybody, didn't like me. The funny thing was that later they would mention me as an adjective for a difficult client. They would say, 'I hope she's not the Hedda Lettuce this week.' I loved it."

AUSTIN RETURNS

Let's Start from the Beginning was a nod to the show's very first challenge, in which the designers famously had to shop for materials at Gristedes supermarket. The innovative Austin Scarlett, who won that challenge with his incredible cornhusk dress, came back to announce the task to Season 5's crop of designers. Austin was also the episode's guest judge.

JERELL SCOTT:

"First up was the Gristedes challenge, so Austin was guest judge. He came floating across the street. I swear his feet never touched the ground, like Mary Poppins is here. It was hot outside but he was flawless."

AUSTIN SCARLETT:

"Being a guest judge in Season 5 was, of course, a tremendous honor. I felt I made a good judge because I really do love all fashion and appreciate different points of view, not just my own personal romantic style. I remember Kenley Collins from the scene where I explained to the designers their challenge. She definitely made an impression at the time. I am still captivated by her ever-flawless red lipstick.

After Season 5, I also traveled to Korea to judge their version of *Project Runway*. It was like *Lost in Translation*. They had to hook up to at least three different microphones, so I would speak and my words would be translated in Korean to the other judges and the designers on the runway. Then someone else would interpret their comment into English, via one of the microphones in my ear. I thought the Korean designers were all adorable and extremely talented."

APOLO OHNO

The designers went on a field trip to The Armory Field & Track Center. They arrived to find Olympian Apolo Ohno skating around the track inside. They learned they had to create a look for the opening ceremony for the summer Olympics. Apolo served as the episode's guest judge.

KENLEY VS. TIM (AND EVERYONE ELSE)

When Tim came to check on Kenley's progress for the Rock N' Runway challenge he told her he wasn't sure what she was making was hip hop. Kenley took issue with the fact that Tim asked her if hip hop was oversized. He told her that it would help if she removed the sarcasm and faceitousness. Her fellow designers were also irritated by her behavior. During the judging for the next challenge she argued with the judges. Nina called her defensive, Heidi said her attitude was annoying, and Michael said she came off flippant and smug. Kenley apologized to the judges.

MICHAEL KORS:

"A bad attitude is not something that will help them once they enter the real fashion world. It might make for interesting television but in the business you are going to be criticized. Not everyone is going to love everything you do. When we say that we're looking for the next great American designer, it's a combination of everything that's going to make someone succeed: they have to be talented, they have to know who they're designing for, they have to answer a question that's not answered already, they have to be smart, curious, articulate helps, and be good with people."

CLOTHING MADE FROM CAR PARTS

The designers were taken to a parking garage to meet with Chris Webb, the lead color designer for Saturn. For this unconventional materials challenge they had to make an outfit from parts of recycled Saturn Hybrids.

KENLEY'S HIP-HOP LOOK

For Episode 11's Rock N' Runway challenge the designers had to dress each other in outfits inspired by a musical genre. Kenley was given the job of designing a hip-hop outfit for Leanne. Kenley decided to make a pair of high-waisted pants and a leather jacket. The other designers didn't think her outfit looked hip-hop, but didn't say anything to her. The judges agreed. Guest judge LL Cool J was asked if her outfit read as hip-hop, to which he responded no. Kenley was obviously annoyed, and was mad at Leanne for not selling her outfit on the runway.

DVF

The designers were given the opportunity to create a look for Diane von Furstenberg's fall collection inspired by the movie *A Foreign Affair*. The winning look would be produced and sold to American Express Card members.

JENNIFER LOPEZ OUT SICK

Jennifer Lopez was scheduled to be the guest judge for the finale. She was unable to make it due to a foot injury and Tim Gunn filled in for her at the last minute.

LET'S START FROM THE BEGINNING (KELLI)   GRASS IS ALWAYS GREENER (SUEDE)

BRIGHT LIGHTS, BIG CITY (KENLEY)   RINGS OF GLORY (KORTO)   WELCOME TO THE JUNGLE (KEITH)

GOOD QUEEN FUN (JOE)

FASHION THAT DRIVES YOU (LEANNE)

DOUBLE O FASHION (LEANNE)

WHAT'S YOUR SIGN? (JERELL)

TRANSFORMATION (JERELL)

ROCK N' RUNWAY (KORTO)

NATURE CALLS (JERELL)

FINALE PART 2 (LEANNE)

MODELS

JANINE BELL

RUNA LUCIENNE

LESLIE MANZANO

ALEX ARACE

ELENA ABETE

SHANNONE HOLT

ALYSSA APARICIO

KENDALL HIGHTOWER

GERMAINE VOLORIOZ

KARALYN WEST

POLINA FRANTSENA

XAVIERA TYTLER

NICOLE ZAAGER

TOPACIO PEÑA

KATARINA MUÑEZ

TIA SHIPMAN

AUSTIN SCARLETT
CREATIVE DIRECTOR, KENNETH POOL

SANDRA BERNHARD
ACTRESS

APOLO ANTON OHNO
FIVE-TIME OLYMPIC MEDALIST

NATALIE PORTMAN
ACTRESS/ENVIRONMENTAL ACTIVIST

BROOKE SHIELDS
ACTRESS/FASHION ICON

RUPAUL
ENTERTAINER

LAURA BENNETT

RACHEL ZOE
CELEBRITY STYLIST

FERN MALLIS
SENIOR VP, IMG FASHION

DIANE VON FURSTENBERG
FASHION DESIGNER

FRANCISCO COSTA
WOMEN'S CREATIVE DIRECTOR, CALVIN KLEIN COLLECTION

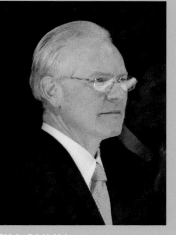

CYNTHIA ROWLEY
FASHION DESIGNER

LL COOL J
MUSICAL INNOVATOR/STYLE ICON

GEORGINA CHAPMAN
CO-FOUNDER/DESIGNER, MARCHESA

TIM GUNN
CHIEF CREATIVE OFFICER, LIZ CLAIBORNE, INC.

JERELL SCOTT

I really caught it the second season. Fell in love. Something about seeing the creative process from start to finish is kind of amazing.

HAD YOU ALWAYS WANTED TO BE A DESIGNER?

I've always been a very creative, visual kind of person and I found that through fashion you can help people express who they are, so in my own little way I feel like I'm giving back, one expensive garment at a time.

HOW DID YOU LEARN TO SEW?

I'm self-taught. On a modeling gig I met a girl who had a small line. I started designing with her and then I saw the money-making potential in it. She wasn't all that amazing, so I kind of ventured off and did my own thing. My mom bought me a sewing machine and then I started taking garments apart to understand how they were put together.

YOU WERE A MODEL. WHICH HAPPENED FIRST, MODELING OR DESIGN?

Modeling came first for me. I think it's kind of ridiculous to judge people solely on their appearance. We all have so much more to offer than that, so through modeling I finally discovered my love for fashion.

DID YOU AUDITION FOR THE SHOW BEFORE YOU ACTUALLY MADE IT ON?

I was part of a design duo during the first season. We tried to audition but didn't make it because there were two of us. The second time I went out for it I was so nervous. It's almost like they could do a show called *Getting on Project Runway*, because of the psych tests and all the back and forth once you've made the cut. It's crazy.

WHAT WAS YOUR FIRST DAY ON *PROJECT RUNWAY* LIKE?

It was intimidating. We all stood in the lobby and sized up the competition. It was interesting, too, getting introduced to the whole sequestered segment. You don't have your cell phone, you have to stay in this room—it's kind of weird.

WHO WAS THE FIRST PERSON YOU MET?

Korto. She had this big ass horn bag on her shoulder, and I was like, "What the fuck was that?" I thought she was going

to be a bitch and now she's like my sister. Love that girl.

I was with Blayne, who I came to love. At first it seemed as if he was a bit much but he's such a genuine, amazing guy. I was with him and Joe Faris, who was like the cool but kind of cheesy straight dad.

WHAT DO YOU THINK MADE YOU SUCCESSFUL IN THE SHOW?

I think I'm pretty good at time management. If you're too ambitious and you're not really aware of how long something is going to take it's really going to hurt you.

DID YOU HAVE ANY FAVORITE CHALLENGES?

The ones I won! The first was the What's Your Sign challenge. I got to work with Jennifer, who is a sweet girl. I think she's really talented but didn't get a chance to shine on the show, so it was cool to share that victory with her. I think that she over thought things a bit. I don't stress out. They would ask me in interviews why I don't get stressed? Well, stress doesn't get this shit sewn fast.

Looking back, I was really pleased with what I did throughout the course of the show, because you never know how you're going to be able to handle something as intense as the *Project Runway* experience. I loved what I was able to create and I am particularly proud of the way I played the game. I felt that in a situation like this your biggest competition is yourself. It's about keeping yourself on task and doing the best that you can do. Because fashion is subjective there's really nothing wrong or right. You have to trust yourself. This is my passion. I love design so getting an opportunity to not have to do anything else but design was amazing.

ANY FAVORITE GUEST JUDGES?

It's always fantastic to get to show your work to some of your idols like Diane von Furstenberg or Fern Mallis.

IS WHAT YOU WEAR ON THE SHOW IMPORTANT TO YOU?

It's crazy how my style has evolved since Season 5. I was all about plunging necklines—you could see my belly button. I would read the blogs and stuff and they can rip you apart so now I don't read blogs anymore.

HOW MINDFUL ARE YOU OF REAL WOMEN'S BODIES VERSUS A MODEL'S FIGURE WHEN YOU'RE DESIGNING?

What you make for runway is different from what you make for real clients. Even if it is a challenge for real people, it still has to have this element of excitement to it because it's for TV, and at the end of the day you're really not trying to sell that particular garment. It needs a wow factor.

WHAT IMPACT HAS THE SHOW HAD ON YOU?

To me one of the best parts of this is inspiring people, young people, especially. I believe that we can do anything that we want with our lives. Where I come from, South Central LA, it's like the kids are afraid to dream. For me this is a platform to show them it doesn't matter that your parents were broke or that your dad wasn't there for you when you were growing up. You can do whatever you want to do with your life if you believe you can. It's cute when celebrities want to wear your stuff, but for me it's about inspiring other people to do their thing.

THE DESIGNERS

ARI FISH

MALVIN VIEN
FROM: ENGLEWOOD, CO
STUDIED: PARSONS THE NEW
SCHOOL FOR DESIGN

MITCHELL HALL
FROM: MOSCOW, RUSSIA
STUDIED: SAVANNAH COLLEGE
OF ART AND DESIGN

QRISTYL FRAZIER
FROM: ST. LOUIS, MO
STUDIED: STEPHENS COLLEGE

JOHNNY SAKALIS
FROM: LONG BEACH, CA
STUDIED: FASHION
INSTITUTE OF DESIGN AND
MERCHANDISING

RA'MON LAWRENCE COLEMAN
FROM: CHICAGO, IL
STUDIED: SCHOOL OF THE ART
INSTITUTE OF CHICAGO

LOUISE BLACK
FROM: TEMPLE, TX
SELF-TAUGHT

RODNEY EPPERSON
FROM: ASTORIA, NY
SELF-TAUGHT

SHIRIN ASKARI
FROM: TULSA, OK
STUDIED: UNIVERSITY OF
NORTH TEXAS

NICOLAS PUTVINSKI
FROM: MOSCOW, RUSSIA
STUDIED: FASHION INSTITUTE
OF TECHNOLOGY

LOGAN NEITZEL
FROM: BLACKFOOT, ID
STUDIED: THE ART INSTITUTE
OF SEATTLE

CHRISTOPHER STRAUB
FROM: ST. LOUIS PARK, MN
SELF-TAUGHT

GORDANA GEHLHAUSEN
FROM: YUGOSLAVIA
SELF-TAUGHT

CAROL HANNAH WHITFIELD
FROM: ANDERSON, SC
STUDIED: COLLEGE OF
CHARLESTON

ALTHEA HARPER
FROM: DAYTON, OH
UNIVERSITY OF CINCINNATI,
CENTRAL SAINT MARTINS
COLLEGE OF ART AND DESIGN

IRINA SHABAYEVA
FROM: REPUBLIC OF GEORGIA
STUDIED: PARSONS THE NEW
SCHOOL FOR DESIGN

SEASON

MOVE TO LOS ANGELES AND LIFETIME

The show's sixth season made the move from New York to Los Angeles, and also switched TV networks, from Bravo to Lifetime.

JANE CHA:

"Besides the difficulty of that first season, which had a lot to do with relocating to Los Angeles when we're at heart a New York show, the transition was pretty seamless. Bravo was a great partner and absolutely helped make Runway what it was. Lifetime too has been a wonderful partner—enthusiastic, creative, and supportive."

MICHAEL KORS:

"I missed quite a few of the shows shot in Los Angeles. I commuted as often as I could. When we first started the show in New York things were very rudimentary, to say the least. The craft table was cheese doodles and a bucket with some ice and some drinks; then we go to LA, we're in the entertainment capital of the world, and suddenly we had dressing rooms and it was very, very high polish. But New York was and is such a huge character in itself on the show. So as talented as the group was that year, we were missing a character. I think that everyone realized that pretty quickly."

FASHION FROM NEWSPAPER

Tim took the designers to the *Los Angeles Times*, where he informed them they were to create a design using newspaper as fabric.

SARA REA:

"As a producer I was scared out of my mind that the designers were going to fail miserably and that we had put them in a tough position. When I saw the runway show and they just blew it out of the water I was ecstatic. It remains one of my favorite challenges for that fact. There is nothing better, for me or the audience, than to think there is no way that they can do this, and then see them create amazing dresses. It's priceless."

WEDDING GOWN TRANSFORMATION

The designers had to convert an old wedding dress into a fashionable new look for the challenge Til Dress Do Us Part. The models took a break as the former brides walked the runway wearing their updated outfits. The judges thought Gordana's look was the best and gave her the win.

GORDANA GEHLHAUSEN:

"Being divorced myself, I wanted to create something completely new, like a new life. It had more meaning for me; I wanted to transform the life this former bride had into something better and more exciting."

BOB MACKIE

The designers were thoroughly excited when Tim took them to meet Bob Mackie. The experience was extra meaningful for Nicolas, who said that Mackie was his idol. The designers were even more thrilled when they learned that they would be making an extravagant stage look for Christina Aguilera.

NICOLAS PUTVINSKI:

"When we were filming that episode I actually guessed who the guest judge was going to be. When we were at FIDM I saw posters about Bob Mackie's exhibition. When the producer said the guest was someone incredible and legendary I knew it was Bob Mackie. I had adored him for years. Three weeks after *Project Runway* ended I bumped into him in New York. It was the most awkward moment. We recognized each other, but couldn't say anything because the episode hadn't aired yet."

JOHNNY'S DAMAGED DRESS

When Tim came to check on the designers during the Paper Dresses challenge he told Johnny that he didn't like the way his dress was coming along. Not long after, Johnny scrapped the dress and started another. He told everyone, including the judges, that the dress got damaged while he was ironing it. The other designers didn't believe him, and on the runway Nicolas said that Johnny's first dress was a "red mess." Johnny responded by calling Nicolas a jerk. The judges didn't think that Johnny's second dress was successful either, and they eliminated him. Tim told the other designers that he was incredulous at that utterly preposterous spewing of fiction that Johnny did on the runway.

COPYING?

Close to the end of the competition the designers were given the challenge The Best of the Best, in which they had to create a companion piece for their best look from the season. First Althea thought that Logan was doing a collar very similar to one she did previously. Then Irina thought that Althea was copying her Aspen look. During the judging Heidi asked Irina and Althea who had the idea for the sweaters first. Althea insisted that her design was original, and seemed annoyed that Irina implied she had copied her. Althea was named the winner of the challenge.

RED CARPET READY (CHRISTOPHER)

MOMMY CHIC (SHIRIN)

SURFS UP (RA'MON)

MODELS AS CLIENTS (ALTHEA)

PAPER DRESSES (IRINA)

LIGHTS, CAMERA, SEW! (NICOLAS)

WORKING BLUE (IRINA)

TIL DRESS DO US PART (GORDANA)

SEQUINS, FEATHERS, AND FUR, OH MY!
(CAROL HANNAH)

A TALE OF SEVEN CITIES (IRINA)

THE BEST OF THE BEST (ALTHEA)

THE END OF THE ROAD (IRINA)

MODELS

YOSUZI SYLVESTER

ERIKA MACKE

ERICA MILDE

VALERIE ROY

EMARIE WILTZ

FATMA DABO

VANESSA FITZGERALD

TARA EGAN

EBONY JOINTER

CELINE CHUA

KOJII HELNWEIN

KATIE STICKSEL

MATAR COHEN

LISA BLADES

TANISHA HARPER

KALYN HEMPHILL

KALYN HEMPHILL

The audition was so packed with models that I almost left, but thank goodness I decided to wait it out. The first day I did my runway walk for the casting director, then they gave me a callback where I did an in-depth interview all about my life and experiences as a model.

WHO DID YOU BOND WITH MOST ON THE SHOW?

I was really close with Matar and of course my designer, Irina.

DID YOU WANT TO BE CHOSEN BY THE SAME DESIGNER CHALLENGE TO CHALLENGE OR WAS IT JUST IMPORTANT TO BE CHOSEN AT ALL?

It was of course vital to be chosen to stay in the competition, but I definitely wanted to stick with Irina once we started working together.

WHAT WAS YOUR FAVORITE CHALLENGE?

My favorite challenge was Around the World in Two Days. Irina designed a gorgeous outfit fit for Aspen. My least favorite challenge was probably the Paper Dress challenge simply because I couldn't sit or go to the bathroom that day—but I loved my newspaper dress!

WHAT WAS WINNING LIKE?

It felt so surreal. It will always be one of the highlights of my life. I was so proud of Irina, and to get to share that experience with her was incredible.

WHAT HAVE YOU BEEN DOING SINCE *PROJECT RUNWAY*?

I have been modeling tons and last year made the move from NYC to Los Angeles to do more acting projects. I am so grateful for *Project Runway*. It has opened so many doors.

We were filmed all the time.
We couldn't even take off our
microphones when we went to
the bathroom!

LINDSAY LOHAN
ACTRESS/SINGER/
FASHION DESIGNER, 6126

MONIQUE LHUILLIER
FASHION DESIGNER

REBECCA ROMIJN
ACTRESS

MAX AZRIA
FASHION DESIGNER

BOB MACKIE
FASHION DESIGNER

RACHEL BILSON
ACTRESS/FASHION DESIGNER

MARC BOUWER
FASHION DESIGNER

ZOE GLASSNER
EDITOR, *MARIE CLAIRE*

**CHRISTINA
AGUILERA**
SINGER/FASHION ICON

MILLA JOVOVICH
ACTRESS/FASHION DESIGNER

NICK VERREOS
PROJECT RUNWAY, SEASON 2

KERRY WASHINGTON
ACTRESS/L'ORÉAL SPOKESMODEL

JENNIFER RADE
COSTUME DESIGNER/
CELEBRITY STYLIST

TOMMY HILFIGER
FASHION DESIGNER

EVA LONGORIA
ACTRESS

JOHN VARVATOS
FASHION DESIGNER

ARIANNE PHILLIPS
COSTUME DESIGNER

ZANNA ROBERTS
SENIOR FASHION EDITOR,
MARIE CLAIRE

MARTINE REARDON
EVP, MACY'S INC
INTERNATIONAL CONCEPTS

TAMARA MELLON
BOARD MEMBER OF HALSTON

CYNTHIA ROWLEY
FASHION DESIGNER

CINDY CRAWFORD
SUPERMODEL/FASHION ICON

SUZY MENKES
FASHION EDITOR, *THE
INTERNATIONAL HERALD TRIBUNE*

ZANNA ROBERTS RASSI

HAVE YOU BEEN INVOLVED WITH *PROJECT RUNWAY* AS LONG AS *MARIE CLAIRE* HAS BEEN INVOLVED?

I have indeed. My first role with *Project Runway* was doing the castings with Tim Gunn. We went on the road, cross-country. We would see thirty to forty people a day with a rack of clothes that we would look through. Tim was always incredibly gracious, and always gave the most mentor-ish advice—very constructive criticism. He and I were never the mean judges. There would always be another person besides Tim and I who could fill that bill so there would always be a mixture of personalities, but Tim and I were the softies.

CAN YOU TELL FROM THE WAY SOMEONE IS DRESSED WHETHER OR NOT THEY MIGHT BE RIGHT FOR THE SHOW?

Yes. I think a designer should absolutely have style. It could be a uniform style. Look at Calvin Klein and Michael Kors. Many great designers have their own uniform, but they always have a style about them. I think a designer has to have an eye for style in so many arenas; you have music, popular culture, interior design. It absolutely matters what they look like when they walk in.

CAN YOU TELL ME ABOUT YOUR FIRST EXPERIENCE JUDGING ON THE SHOW?

Nina had recently started at *Marie Claire* and I filled in for her for a couple of episodes. I was petrified. It was when they were filming in Los Angeles. I flew out from New York to these massive studios. Luckily I had TV

experience, but nothing of this magnitude. This was when Lifetime had just taken over. They were delightful. They had flowers and a bottle of champagne waiting for me. I met Heidi and she was very lovely. I immediately noticed the banter between her and Michael. It's not an act—that was the first thing I realized. Heidi and Michael were so welcoming. They had me in stitches before the show started, I mean falling off my chair laughing, and that party, that fun friendship, continues through the show.

During judging you watch the contestants' models come out and you sit there scribbling. We give honest, straight off the runway remarks; whatever you see you write. There's no moment where we all shuffle off and discuss what's to come. We'd sit at lunch together, but chat about something completely different. It's almost an unspoken rule not to mention what we just saw. That's what I think gives the show integrity and that element of surprise. We don't know what somebody else is going to say. I think if we did it would ruin that banter and flow of the conversation we later have about the designs.

IS JUDGING ON *PROJECT RUNWAY* VERY DIFFERENT FROM WHAT YOU DO AS AN EDITOR OF A MAGAZINE?

I always have an editing eye. You have to be judgmental as an editor. I see new designers all the time and have to remember they usually don't have the finesse of a seasoned designer; they haven't the production house, marketing, PR, packing, and branding that goes with a designer that I go see on a regular basis. But I absolutely have to view designers with an editorial and commercial eye.

DOES YOUR OWN PERSONAL STYLE COME INTO PLAY?

I try to stop that, but I don't think you can completely help it. I know a well-made dress and I know when the craftsmanship, taste level, and the whole picture is there—including styling, hair, beauty, shoes, belt, necklace, bracelet, etc. If that's all in place then of course I'll say it's an amazing dress.

IN SEASON 8 THERE WAS AN EPISODE WHERE YOU HELPED THE DESIGNERS WITH A PHOTO SHOOT.

Yes, we showed them how to be on the shoot, how to direct the model, how to direct the hair and makeup. You're creating an image, you are creating a brand; the hair, the makeup, the accessories, the models (the face you choose for your brand)—it's all so important. It's great for these designers to watch and to know what makes a good photograph.

WHAT DO YOU THINK PEOPLE DON'T KNOW ABOUT *PROJECT RUNWAY*?

That it is absolutely real time. There is no leeway; there is no extra hour here or there. They barely sleep; they are exhausted by the end of it. They are in intense situations with cameras around them all the time. That's why you get all these breakdowns towards the end; they are just exhausted.

YOU'RE OFTEN INVOLVED IN CASTING. IS THERE ANYONE YOU ARE PARTICULARLY PROUD OF FINDING?

Olivier for Season 9. I think he has amazing talent. He showed me his designs and his jackets and his tailoring and I wanted to take every single piece off that rack and put it on my back. The quality, the craftsmanship that went into it all—I think at the end of the day that was part of his downfall on the show because he couldn't work quickly enough. Designers are always going to be working quickly, no matter if you're Michael Kors or Karl Lagerfeld—at that level a designer is creating at least four collections a year these days. Then you have accessories on top of that, and you may have a diffusion line on top of that, so you're constantly creating. The show is real in reflecting that aspect of a fashion designer's work.

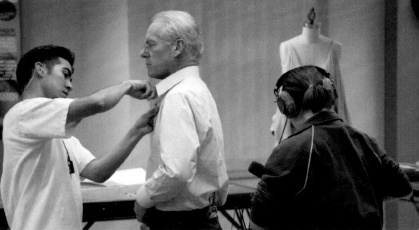

DAVID HILLMAN

FROM YOUR PERSPECTIVE AS A CREATIVE EXECUTIVE AT LIFETIME, WHAT WAS IT LIKE COMING ONTO *PROJECT RUNWAY* FOR SEASON 6?

It was exciting to be involved in a show that I had enjoyed watching, and to be part of the creative process in shaping what others see on the screen was thrilling.

WHAT IS YOUR DAY-TO-DAY ROLE WITH THE SHOW?

I provide input on show challenges, guest judges, notes for cuts of episodes, and serve as the voice of the network. I also try to push the creative envelope to provide the designers with a platform to allow their creativity to shine.

DOES THE CREW HAVE ANY INTERACTION WITH THE CAST WHILE FILMING?

Certain crew members are tasked with getting designers from point A to point B so they have to be involved with them. But since this is a competition, we don't want the judges to have any biases with the designers so they really only see each other on the runway. The producers also keep a distance from the designers so there is no favoritism or anything that could jeopardize the equal playing field.

WHAT WENT INTO THE DECISION TO EXPAND THE SHOW TO NINETY MINUTES?

Expanding the show gave us more opportunity to tell each story in a more robust way. We get to know the designers better, viewers get more of a chance to see the creative process and are exposed to more of the deliberations with the judges so they can determine how the judges came to the conclusion of who is in or out each week.

WHAT WOULD PEOPLE BE SURPRISED TO KNOW ABOUT *PROJECT RUNWAY*?

We set the designers up for success. Each challenge allows them to be as innovative as possible to celebrate their creativity. We never want to put them in impossible situations. The designers are chosen because we know they are talented, so giving them challenges is a way for them to push themselves further than they would normally.

I think the thing that surprises most people is that the time constraints for each challenge, is really true to life. If they have twenty-four hours, that is it. If its seven hours, that

is it. We don't "cut" and take breaks. Filming is continuous and while viewers at home may see a new challenge each week, the designers are getting challenges almost daily. It's no wonder that as we near the end, some designers run out of steam, while others rise to the occasion.

TO WHAT DO YOU ATTRIBUTE THE SUCCESS OF *PROJECT RUNWAY,* STILL STRONG AFTER NINE SEASONS?

Fans love this creative format and the chemistry of the judges. It's truly magical with Heidi's irreverent, wonderful sense of humor and work ethic; Tim's unique charm; Nina's editorial eye; and Michael's unique perspective from a designer standpoint. Not only are viewers fans of the creative process the talented crop of designers bring each season, it's television magic to see their hard work critiqued by an amazing panel week after week.

WHY DO YOU THINK FASHION MAKES SUCH COMPELLING TV?

Fashion is subjective and peeking into a creative process you can agree or disagree on their creative talents, so it really allows you to root for some designers and not others. You are oftentimes blown away by their creativity but at the end of the day it's a competition and to see those designers cut, sew, and sometime claw their way to victory is very compelling to watch week after week.

HOW HAS *PROJECT RUNWAY* CHANGED LIFETIME?

Project Runway has brought in a new audience to the network—a younger, more affluent demographic. It's allowed us to create new shows that appeal to today's contemporary woman. In many ways, I feel it's allowed Lifetime to make its brand hipper, bolder, and more relevant.

WHAT HAVE BEEN SOME OF YOUR FAVORITE MOMENTS FROM THE SHOW?

I personally love it when something surprising happens, like Maya quitting in Season 7 and Gretchen winning in Season 8. It polarized the audience, which again reinforces the authenticity of the show and its subjective nature. It's not produced drama. This stuff happens organically.

JONATHAN MURRAY

WHEN DID YOU BECOME INVOLVED WITH *PROJECT RUNWAY*?

Season 6, when it moved from Bravo to Lifetime. The original producers were Magical Elves. They stayed with Bravo/NBC. When the show went to Lifetime the Weinstein Company and Lifetime were looking for another company to take over the day-to-day production of the series. That's when they called us.

YOU'RE A PIONEER IN REALITY TELEVISION, GOING BACK TO CREATING *THE REAL WORLD* WITH MARY-ELLIS BUNIM IN 1992.

A lot of what you put into producing a reality show is the wisdom you gain from working on other shows, and quite honestly making mistakes with other shows. Coming into *Project Runway*, I had had twenty years of experience with reality television. It was incredible coming into an already great format, looking at it, and over time making small changes to hopefully make it even better.

SEASON 6 WAS SHOT IN LOS ANGELES. WHAT WENT INTO THE DECISION TO MOVE THE SHOW FROM NEW YORK?

Due to the fact that Lifetime wanted to get it on the air quickly and we would have to shoot it during the school year, the decision was made to shoot in LA. That presented a number of challenges, most significantly that

Michael and Nina, their daily businesses, were in New York. It wasn't like when we shot in New York, when they can just pop over for four hours. It meant they had to get on a plane. The show definitely suffered because we couldn't have them there on a consistent basis. That was hard on the designers because they look for that consistency in judging.

WHY WAS THE SHOW BROUGHT BACK TO NEW YORK THE NEXT SEASON?

We recognized that we needed consistency. But I do think that LA has a lot

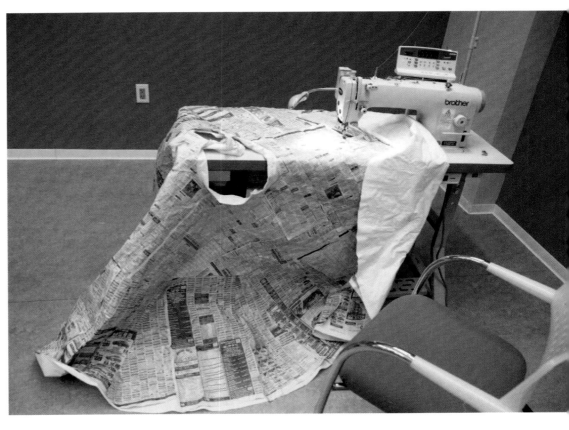

to offer. The challenges that season were a lot of fun, like when we went to the *Los Angeles Times* and they had to make dresses out of paper. We played with the movie industry a little. Tim came out for the season. We got him an apartment downtown across from the Ralph's supermarket. Tim was just amazed by Ralph's because it was so different from the grocery store he goes to in New York. I think he had fun. Ultimately, I think Los Angeles gave us some great challenges, but the most important thing is consistency in judging. Unless Michael and Nina could be there for the whole season it made more sense to do the show in New York.

WHAT OTHER CHANGES HAVE YOU INCORPORATED INTO THE FORMAT?

A lot of what a producer does happens before we ever start shooting. It involves looking at the previous seasons and deciding whether you want to make any changes to the show, to hopefully improve it. For instance, in Season 9 we decided to begin the show a little differently. We

had twenty designers come to New York and present themselves to Heidi, Michael, Nina, and Tim, and then they were going to choose the sixteen designers that were going to continue with the competition. We felt that would really give them an investment in these designers, because they had helped to choose the sixteen participants.

One of the things we really did was to encourage them to take ownership of the designers they liked and supported, and in the deliberations to really fight for the people they believed in. We wanted them to have a no-holds-barred discussion. I think the deliberations have been much more vociferous and much more entertaining because of that. We've had some deliberations go for an hour. We've had times when we've had to break for ten minutes for everybody to catch their breath. The judges are very passionate. They really want to get it right.

WHAT DO YOU LOOK FOR WHEN YOU'RE CASTING THE SHOW?

We start with talent when we do the casting. We have a

consultant involved who will vet people's portfolios before we get to them, so there's a basic level they have to be at. The big question when you look at that portfolio or what they bring in to the audition is always, how can you be sure that they've made it? How can you be sure exactly what they've put into it? It is challenging. We certainly rely on Tim Gunn. He's very generous in the casting process; taking a look at people, helping us decide if they have the talent.

Our designers also have to have a personality. Sometimes it can be a personality that you wouldn't

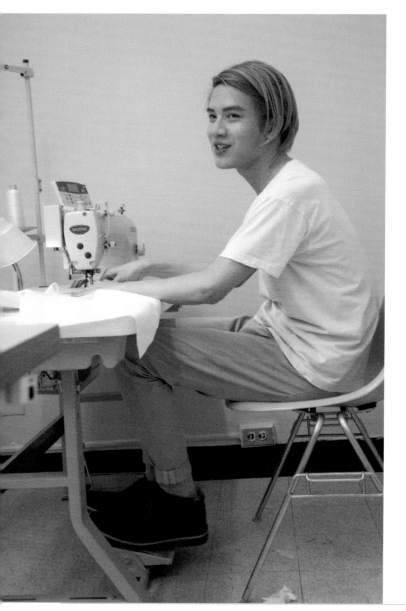

typically find on television. Olivier in Season 9, for instance, was a very withdrawn person but an interesting personality. That hilarious episode when he had to work with real women with real women's breasts. He would much rather work with a model. Someone like that you would not normally think of as a television personality. He was fascinating. Something I learned at the very beginning of *The Real World* is you need a diversity of personality types and backgrounds in the cast members.

ARE YOU LOOKING FOR PERSONALITIES THAT WILL CLASH?

My philosophy is that you find the most interesting cast, and you make sure there's diversity, and you see what happens. You do like those people who can be difficult. It's funny, sometimes at the end of the casting process I'll ask who were the most difficult people to deal with in terms of scheduling their flights, etc. Sometimes that can tell you a lot about someone, what they're going to be like in the workroom, and how they're going to relate to the other designers. You do want to have some difficult people in your cast, but you don't know where the conflict will come. We didn't know that Bert and Josh (Season 9) would have conflict and ultimately become friends. Even going back to *The Real World*, the basic belief was that, while we all come from different backgrounds, ultimately we'll discover that we have more in common than we don't. We will, through the conflict, become friends.

ALTHEA HARPER

WHAT WAS IT LIKE DOING THE SHOW IN LOS ANGELES INSTEAD OF NEW YORK?

There were definitely benefits as well as drawbacks. Since I live in New York I liked the experience of being in LA for two months, even though we didn't get to explore on our own. However, the Mood we went to was really far out, and we had to deal with LA traffic. It was a big ordeal. We probably missed out on work time.

DID YOU HAVE A FAVORITE GARMENT YOU MADE FOR THE SHOW?

The outfit I worked on with my model, Tanisha. The models were able to tell us what they wanted and we made a look based on that. That was my favorite. I thought Tanisha was by far the best model on the show. She had a great body type for the look I was going for.

I actually think she came off softer on TV. What happened that season was tenfold. When we came back for Bryant Park it was very awkward. One of her models actually quit because Irina was so rude. The model's agency called and complained.

YOU HAD CONCERNS THAT LOGAN WAS DOING SOMETHING SIMILAR TO A DESIGN OF YOURS.

I'm one of those people who gets over things. I have to say it and then I'm over it. I was frustrated with Logan because I had just done that collar for the Christina Aguilera challenge, and his was almost exactly the same. I said something mean and then I was over it. In the episode it seemed like I was seething, but it was really just ten minutes of me stressing out about it and then letting it go. It wasn't that big of a deal.

DO YOU THINK YOUR LOOKS HELPED YOU ON THE SHOW?

Definitely not! Watching yourself on TV when you've had

DID YOU HAVE A FAVORITE CHALLENGE?

It was not my favorite while I was doing it but I liked the Paper challenge, where we had to make a garment out of something that wasn't a traditional fabric. It was very frustrating but in the end it pushed me into thinking differently. I think that's what the show is about.

IT APPEARED ON THE SHOW THAT IRINA WAS VERY COMPETITIVE WITH YOU. DID YOU FEEL THAT AT THE TIME?

Absolutely. I think I was maybe a bit naïve to how cutthroat the industry can be. I went to the show directly from college. The thing they didn't show is that for most of the show I really considered Irina one of my closest friends. When she said I copied her I realized there could be backstabbing. It was hard for me, being away from family and friends. I felt like I didn't have anyone to talk to. The person I considered my friend turned out to be someone I couldn't trust. I was really surprised when she accused me of copying her. I had shown her my sketches from the get-go.

six hours of sleep, you've been stressed out, and you've been working so many hours with no breaks is hard. You're really watching yourself at your worst. Looking back, I wish I would have been a little more thoughtful about that. It may have made watching it a little less painful! At the time I felt like I didn't need to dress any special way to do what I was doing. I was not concerned with how I looked.

DO YOU CONSIDER WHAT SHOES YOU WEAR FOR THOSE LONG RUNWAY DAYS WHEN YOU'RE STANDING FOR HOURS?

Absolutely. The girls would take off their shoes when they filmed someone else. The critiques last a long time. Sometimes they'd spend up to an hour on one person. If you're in the bottom three it's really hard. The models have it the worst. In some garments they can't even sit down and wouldn't be able to go to the bathroom for a really long time. Plus they keep the studio super cold because they don't want the equipment to overheat. I remember we'd be thirsty, freezing, you'd have chapped lips!

WHEN YOU'RE CHOSEN TO STAY ON THE RUNWAY DO YOU KNOW WHETHER YOU'RE IN THE TOP OR THE BOTTOM?

No. You don't know until you start getting the criticism.

Usually after the first judge you can tell.

DO THE JUDGES HAVE DIFFERENT STYLES IN THEIR CRITIQUES?

Yes and no. I think Heidi thinks more about if she would wear the garment. A lot of the celebrity judges had the same approach. Michael Kors and Nina Garcia step back and look at it more as a design. I think that mix works. Michael can look at the construction, Nina at the editorial aspects, and Heidi can approach it from a customer's point of view.

HAVE YOU KEPT IN TOUCH WITH ANYONE FROM THE SHOW?

Christopher and I talk. Ra'mon was really helpful after the show. I actually lived with Carol Hannah and Malvin for a year after we filmed the show, but before it aired. We keep in touch a bit. Nick Verreos and I have gone to Europe twice for a project with Miami University. He's a great guy. I've also done a few things with Jay McCarroll, who is really funny. It's been a unique experience.

CAROL HANNAH WHITFIELD

WHAT WAS YOUR *PROJECT RUNWAY* AUDITION LIKE?

Like a first date with fifteen people.

HAD YOU EVER AUDITIONED BEFORE?

I made it to the next to last cut for Season 5, and hadn't intended to try out again, but when casting calls you, you really can't turn down that opportunity!

WHO DID YOU THINK WAS YOUR TOUGHEST COMPETITION?

Irina, both for her forcefulness and her range.

HOW HAS *PROJECT RUNWAY* CHANGED YOUR LIFE?

My mom likes to joke that the show changed everything about my life except my gender. I think it fast-forwarded my career five to ten years. It made me take myself and my work more seriously. Coming from a small city in South Carolina, the support and encouragement that came from *Project Runway* was really validating. It made me realize I have something unique to offer, and gave me the boldness to launch my line.

DID YOU FEEL THAT ANY ONE JUDGE WAS PARTICULARLY IN YOUR CORNER?

Heidi, I suppose. That's hard to say, since I was never in the bottom three and was spared the harsher words!

WHAT WAS IT LIKE WINNING THE BOB MACKIE/CHRISTINA AGUILERA CHALLENGE?

That was exciting, especially since I'd never used sequins or feathers before. I love them now and use them all the time!

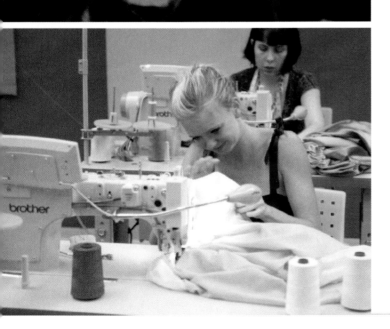

WHAT WAS IT LIKE HAVING TIM GUNN COME TO YOUR HOME?

I loved the home visit because I really wanted my family to be a part of the experience. They supported me so wholeheartedly, and I'm glad they were there when he came. I remember there was a big snowstorm the day of the visit, and the crew got stuck while out taking B-roll of the town. As a result, my family and I sat around a fire with coffee and cookies for several hours while Tim told us stories. I don't think I'll ever forget that.

DID YOU FEEL CONFIDENT YOU WOULD MAKE IT TO THE FINAL THREE?

I felt confident that I could, but you never know what's going to happen! There are so many factors involved, but I felt like I deserved to be there.

YOU WERE SO SICK DURING THE FINALE. DO YOU FEEL THAT HURT YOUR CHANCES OF WINNING?

That's not a question that I've ever really dwelled on. It was disheartening of course, but I have no regrets regarding the results. It was incredibly frustrating and disappointing to be so sick at the most important part, but everything has worked out wonderfully in the end.

WHAT HAVE YOU BEEN DOING SINCE *PROJECT RUNWAY*?

I launched my bridal line in April 2010 and we now sell to over fifty retailers in the U.S., Canada, Ireland, and Australia. My team and I work with brides directly out of our showroom in the heart of New York's fashion district, just one block from Mood, actually. I often travel to our stores to do trunk shows and events and host several charity or fashion events each year. I also have a smaller line of ready to wear, which is sold mainly on our website and in our studio. I spend every day doing what I love. I am eternally grateful to *Project Runway* and all of its fans!

THE DESIGNERS

CHRISTIANE KING
FROM: ABIDJAN, COTE D'LVOIRE
STUDIED: WOODBURY
UNIVERSITY

PAMELA PTAK
FROM: PITTSFIELD, MA
STUDIED: PRATT INSTITUTE,
MAISON SAPHO SCHOOL OF
DRESSMAKING AND DESIGN,
FASHION INSTITUTE OF
TECHNOLOGY

PING WU
FROM: CHENGDU, SICHUAN
PROVINCE, CHINA
STUDIED: NORTH CENTRAL
COLLEGE

JESUS ESTRADA
FROM: MAZATLAN, SINALOA,
MEXICO
STUDIED: FASHION CAREERS
COLLEGE

ANNA LYNETT
FROM: WHITEFISH BAY, WI
RHODE ISLAND SCHOOL OF
DESIGN

JANEANE MARIE CECCANTI
FROM: WILLOWS, CA
STUDIED: THE ART INSTITUTE
OF PORTLAND

JESSE LENOIR
FROM: PAINESVILLE, OH
SELF-TAUGHT

BEN CHMURA
FROM: SOUTH MERIDEN, CT
STUDIED: SAVANNAH COLLEGE
OF ART AND DESIGN

AMY SARABI
FROM: PLANO, TX
WON GENART FRESH FACES
IN FASHION

MAYA LUZ
FROM: SANTA FE, NM
STUDIED: MASSACHUSETTS
COLLEGE OF ART AND
DESIGN, FASHION INSTITUTE
OF TECHNOLOGY

JONATHAN PETERS
FROM: WOONSOCKET, RI
STUDIED: THE UNIVERSITY
OF RHODE ISLAND

ANTHONY WILLIAMS
FROM: BIRMINGHAM, AL
STUDIED: THE UNIVERSITY OF
ALABAMA

JAY NICOLAS SARIO
FROM: MANILA, PHILIPPINES
STUDIED: HONOLULU
COMMUNITY COLLEGE

MILA HERMANOVSKI
FROM: DALLAS, TX
STUDIED: RHODE ISLAND
SCHOOL OF DESIGN

EMILIO SOSA
FROM: SANTO DOMINGO,
DOMINICAN REPUBLIC
STUDIED: PRATT INSTITUTE

SETH AARON HENDERSON
FROM: SAN DIEGO, CA
SELF-TAUGHT

SEASON

BACK TO NEW YORK

Project Runway returned to New York for Season 7.

MICHAEL KORS:

"I think a lot of fashion comes from LA, but because LA is not a street life city, it doesn't have the mélange and the energy that you have when you take so many people of so many different backgrounds and cram them into a space as small as Manhattan, which makes for great fashion, great energy, and I think a sense of excitement from the designers. We were missing a character, she's a big character, NYC."

ANTHONY'S DRESS ON THE COVER OF *MARIE CLAIRE*

The designers went on a field trip to the Hearst building to visit Joanna Coles, the editor-in-chief of *Marie Claire*. They were told they would be designing an outfit to be worn by Heidi Klum on the cover of the magazine. Anthony won the challenge and Heidi wore his blue dress on the cover of the April 2010 issue.

JOANNA COLES:

"It was a beautiful blue that looked fantastic on Heidi. Anthony understood the crop that we used is really from the waist up, so he used a lot of effort and attention to detail in the top half of the dress, whereas some of the others had been messing around with the hemlines without any realization of what we actually wanted it for. I felt like he understood the challenge and he delivered."

EMILIO'S "SWIMSUIT"

For Episode 7's Hard Wear challenge the designers had to create an unconventional look using materials from a hardware store. Emilio had an especially hard time with the challenge, and sent his model Holly down the runway with almost nothing on.

EMILIO SOSA:

"I struggled with that challenge a great deal. I think by the time I got to the design of the bathing suit, I had already had many meltdowns. Even calling that a bathing suit is a stretch; I called it a bathing suit because it was basically all I could call it, but it was washers and twine."

JONATHAN INSULTED

Jonathan used polka dots in the textile he created for the Hey, That's My Fabric challenge. The judges were not thrilled with his look and let him know. Jonathan was very insulted when Michael Kors said that his jacket looked like a disco straightjacket and that his print was like a dirty tablecloth. Jonathan stood by his creation. Although he was in the bottom for that challenge, Jonathan was not eliminated; Anthony was instead.

CAMPBELL'S FASHION

The designers were asked to create a signature dress for the Campbell's AdDress Your Heart program. The looks had to feature the color red, as well as elements with Campbell's branding. The models for this challenge were women who had been affected by heart disease. The winner's look was to be produced and sold on projectrunway. com, with the profits going to the American Heart Association.

HIGHLIGHTS

ANTHONY IS QUIETED (TEMPORARILY)

Everyone made a bet on how long Anthony could go without talking. He went so far as to allow his mouth to be taped shut. He lasted fourteen minutes and fifty-six seconds.

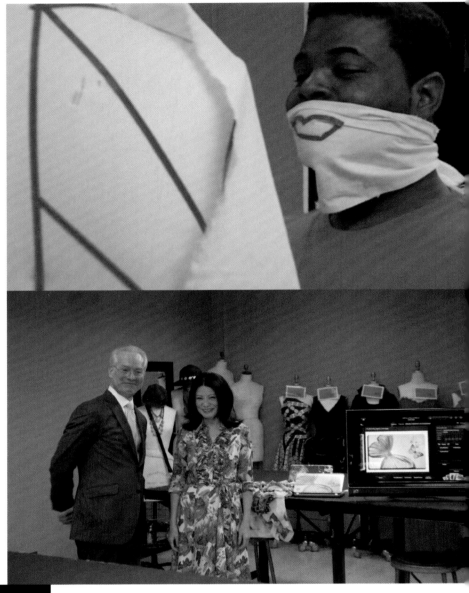

DESIGNING PRINTS WITH VIVIENNE TAM

Vivienne Tam visited the designers in the workroom to introduce the challenge called Hey, That's My Fabric. They were given the opportunity to design and create their own textiles. Emilio's design was influenced by graffiti and 1940s French fashion. He created a print using the text ESosa with hearts representing the Os. The judges flipped for his look, and gave him the win.

MAYA WITHDRAWS; ANTHONY RETURNS

Maya surprised everyone by making the decision to leave the competition. She felt that at twenty-one she was too young and not yet ready for the competition. Anthony was brought back to replace her.

EXPECTANT HEIDI

When the designers met Heidi they saw that she was visibly pregnant. Klum was pregnant three times during the run of the show: Season 2, Season 3 (finale), and Season 7.

HEIDI KLUM:

"I've been pregnant a lot on the show but everyone was always fine with it. Sometimes, before I told anyone, Michael and Nina would know just by the size of my boobs, and they would ask if I was pregnant again. For me, early on you just don't tell people yet because you never know how things might go, but they could always tell because my boobs would get so big. It was cool to show you can be stylish and pregnant at the same time. It was always a challenge for me to find interesting things to wear. I was never tired, I always enjoyed it."

JAY VS. MILA FOR THE FINALE

The judges couldn't decide between Jay and Mila to join Emilio and Seth Aaron to compete in the finale. They were both asked to make collections, but only one would be chosen. They came back and showed a portion of their collections to Heidi, Michael, and Nina. Michael thought Jay should continue, but Heidi disagreed and wanted Mila. The three judges eventually decided to give the third spot to Mila.

BACK TO NEW YORK (EMILIO)

THE FASHION FARM (JAY)

THE HIGHS AND LOWS OF FASHION
(MILA)

DESIGN YOUR HEART OUT (AMY)

RUN FOR COVER (ANTHONY)

A LITTLE BIT OF FASHION (SETH AARON)　　　　　HARD WEAR (JAY)

THE ELEMENTS OF FASHION
(JONATHAN)　　　　　TAKIN' IT TO THE STREETS (EMILIO AND SETH AARON)

HEY, THAT'S MY FABRIC (EMILIO)

SEW MUCH PRESSURE (ANTHONY)

SEW MUCH PRESSURE (EMILIO)

FINALE (SETH AARON)

MODELS

KELLY GERVAIS

ELIZAVETA MELNITCHENKO

SOPHIA LEE

SARAH BELL

KASEY ASHCRAFT

MEGAN DAVIS

ALEXIS BROKER

ALISON GINGERICH

HOLLY RIDINGS

VALERIA LEONOVA

CERRI MCQUILLAN

MONIQUE DARTON

BRITTANY OLDEHOFF

BRANDISE DANESEWICH

LORENA ANGJELI

KRISTINA SAJKO

GUEST JUDGES

LAUREN HUTTON
MODEL/ACTRESS

GEORGINA CHAPMAN
FASHION DESIGNER

TORY BURCH
FASHION DESIGNER

NICOLE RICHIE
TV PERSONALITY/
DESIGNER

MOLLY SIMS
MODEL/ACTRESS

FRANCISCO COSTA
WOMEN'S CREATIVE DIRECTOR,
CALVIN KLEIN COLLECTION

STEPHEN WEBSTER
JEWELRY DESIGNER

FAITH HILL
SINGER

JOANNA COLES
EDITOR-IN-CHIEF, MARIE CLAIRE

VIVIENNE TAM
FASHION DESIGNER

CYNTHIA ROWLEY
FASHION DESIGNER

JESSICA ALBA
ACTOR

ISABEL TOLEDO
FASHION DESIGNER

ROLAND MOURET
FASHION DESIGNER

MATTHEW WILLIAMSON
FASHION DESIGNER

JOANNA COLES

TELL ME HOW *MARIE CLAIRE* BECAME ASSOCIATED WITH *PROJECT RUNWAY.*

Well obviously we watched and we loved it and were fascinated by it, and we were really following the characters, but we knew there was another magazine sponsoring the show—*Elle*. We also knew that sponsoring was due to end, so we were ready to jump when it did. Coincidentally, Nina Garcia, who was working for *Elle*, left that magazine and we hired her. The two actually were completely coincidental and unrelated. We would have had Nina regardless of her connection with *Project Runway* but that made me even more inspired to try and make sure that *Marie Claire* carried on the sponsorship.

WHAT DOES IT MEAN FOR THE MAGAZINE TO SPONSOR THE SHOW?

That means that we have posters of the covers on the workroom walls. It means that we're thrilled to have a *Marie Claire* challenge every season. One of the challenges in the last season was to dress Nina. One time we did a challenge to design a dress for Heidi Klum that she then wore on the cover. It also means that the winner gets their work in *Marie Claire*, which is a fantastic thing for a young designer. It's incredibly difficult to get into a major magazine, and certainly not the amount of pages that we give the winner. It's a fantastic package from the winner's point of view because you really do begin a relationship with a professional magazine, and our fashion staff is on hand to give advice and to be engaged. More recently we've done *Project Runway: All Stars*, the spinoff, which was exciting and then the *After the Runway* show, so not only is Nina involved but our Senior Fashion Editor, Zanna Roberts Rassi, has been very involved and so have I. We've had Tim Gunn as a columnist. He's very popular in the magazine and people write to him asking for advice. I think he's one of the most loved characters on television and people adore him. Our readers always want to know about him and his viewers hold him in great esteem.

THERE ARE DESIGNERS WHO SPECIALIZE IN FANTASY, AND THEN THERE ARE OTHERS WHO SAY THEY MAKE CLOTHES, NOT ART. DO YOU THINK THE *PROJECT RUNWAY* DESIGNERS SHOULD BE ABLE TO DO A BIT OF BOTH?

I think the best designers are people like Marc Jacobs, who are able to go on extraordinary flights of fantasy but still bring it back to something very real that the customer can

wear. He just had an extraordinary show that he'd done that was inspired by *Oliver Twist* and that song "Who Will Buy?" It was a pastiche of Victorian Covent Garden flower girls, and yet when you took the looks apart, there were silver jackets, beautiful brocade skirts, and fantastic pilgrim/eighteenth-century buckled shoes. He's someone who is able to bridge that gap really nicely. Not everybody can. My dream for the designers, especially the winner of *All Stars*, is to be able to stay true to their vision as a designer but really make sales. That, to me, seems to be the perfect combination. No one really wants to be sitting in a garret spending two months designing a dress for one person because it would never get seen.

WHEN YOU COME ON *PROJECT RUNWAY* AS A GUEST JUDGE, YOU'RE REPRESENTING *MARIE CLAIRE*. ARE YOU EVER CONCERNED WHAT THEY'RE DESIGNING WON'T BE UP TO PAR FOR THE MAGAZINE?

What I've noticed is that any designer who isn't up to snuff gets voted off pretty quickly, so when I've been a judge in the beginning of the series, when you've had say twelve contestants, you see more variety in quality. As it gets down to the final five or six, the wheat has been separated from the chaff. I'm always astonished at how they're able to put something together in so little time with so little money; it's really extraordinary. A lot of established designers wouldn't be able to do that.

WOULD YOU SAY THAT THE *PROJECT RUNWAY* VIEWER IS A *MARIE CLAIRE* WOMAN?

Yes. I'm surprised at how many people are so engaged by *Project Runway*. They really feel it very strongly and want to take you to task for all the things that you've said. We have a lot of readers who tweet during the show or tweet me or tweet Nina or tweet my assistant and there's a sense of a real *Runway* community. I also think it's a thing that mothers and daughters do together and friends do together, so we have groups of girlfriends that I know read the magazine that watch the show together if they're in on a Thursday night. They watch and connect on social media, so they're on Twitter or a Facebook page giving

a rundown of what they think. Our digital editor loves *Project Runway*. She has been obsessed with it since the beginning, so she's a frantic Tweeter about it. The minute the episode goes up she's on there, so I feel there's a growing community of *Project Runway* fans and many of them are *Marie Claire* readers. I hope we brought new viewers to the show and I'm sure the show has brought us some new readers, too.

THE PRIZE OF ONE CHALLENGE WAS A BILLBOARD IN TIMES SQUARE. WHAT A GREAT OPPORTUNITY FOR GRETCHEN, WHO WON THAT CHALLENGE.

I think Gretchen was just thrilled with it. It was a fantastic prize. Many, many designers would never have that in their entire life. Initially it went up for the timing of the episode, and then it ended up staying there, I think an extra month longer than planned. It was fantastic for Gretchen. That was a really fun challenge. We had great fun coming up with it as an idea and we were really pleased with the outcome.

That's the kind of thing that we, as a magazine, can bring to the show. We can bring a top model (Coco Rocha), photographer, and a billboard in Times Square, which might be harder for a reality TV show to get on its own. I think the great thing for *Project Runway* being connected to *Marie Claire* is that we really are a fashion magazine with our feet on the ground, with a big readership and we know what we're talking about. Nina is a really good fashion director. People love her in the industry. She's taken seriously in the industry as well as by readers, and that's invaluable for the show.

HAVE YOU STAYED IN CONTACT WITH THE *PROJECT RUNWAY* WINNERS YOU WORKED WITH ON THE SHOW?

We've had all the winners into the office and we've asked what they're doing and if they've asked us for advice we try to give it. We've certainly stayed connected with them. We've always been very willing to keep the lines of communication open. It's a bit confusing I think for some of them, especially if they win and they're high profile and then suddenly the next day you wake up, the show's not on anymore, and you're terrified you're going to fade from memory.

WHAT IS COMING IN AS A GUEST JUDGE LIKE?

It's intimidating, partly because Nina and Michael are so knowledgeable and both very proper and articulate. But it's also enormous fun. There's much hilarity in the green room beforehand. Michael is very funny and Heidi Klum is always divulging the latest details of whatever diet she was on. I think when I was there she was pureeing vegetables and drinking them through a straw. I tried it but I didn't end up looking like Heidi Klum! When you're actually going on set, you try to be really clear about what you think works and what doesn't work and hope that just one or two words will stick with the designers.

YOU'VE BEEN A GUEST JUDGE A NUMBER OF TIMES. ARE THE EXPERIENCES DIFFERENT EACH TIME OR ARE THEY BASICALLY THE SAME?

They're very different because the contestants are different and the challenges are different and you're looking for different things. The Heidi cover dress was immense. I was anxious that we choose something that gave us real oomph on the cover and that was strong. We had a lot of really good outfits but we could only have one winner. Anthony won and he was delighted about it. We knew it was going to work and that issue sold really well.

I felt particularly judging that challenge that it was essential that I got the dress I knew I wanted because I didn't want someone else deciding for us. Nina and I both agreed, and it was nice listening to Michael and Heidi discuss what they felt would work for *Marie Claire*. They were so nice about the magazine and about the readers and what they thought the readers would expect on the cover; it was rather a good learning experience for me.

PROJECT RUNWAY OFFERS DESIGNERS INCREDIBLE OPPORTUNITIES. DO YOU THINK THE DESIGNERS CAN APPRECIATE THAT?

I think some of them do, not all of them understand how frankly amazing these opportunities really are. To have your own billboard in Times Square—unparalleled! To dress Heidi Klum for the cover of a magazine that will go on to sell 1.1 million covers—unbelievable. We have Dolce & Gabbana's bodysuit on the March cover and I've had two e-mails from Stefano Gabbana just saying thank you. Even at his stage, designers don't get blasé about having a cover.

WHAT WOULD PEOPLE BE SURPRISED TO KNOW ABOUT *PROJECT RUNWAY*?

I think they might be surprised by the level of support there is among the designers for each other, even though it is a competition. I think they would be surprised by the dedication and the things the designers were prepared to go without to follow their dream; witnessing that dedication and passion is very moving. You understand that this is what it takes to be Christian Siriano, or Gretchen, or Michael Kors when Michael Kors started.

WHAT DO YOU THINK HAS MADE THE SHOW THRIVE FOR TEN SEASONS?

It's about people following a dream. It's really a challenge of talent; it's not a challenge of personalities, which most reality shows are. The people on the show are not there to become reality stars; they're there to become big designers. Austin Scarlett, yes he's fantastic on television. He's a walking sound byte and a genius, but actually his real dream is to lock himself in his studio and create extraordinary flights of fantasy. These are real people trying to get a business off the ground.

SETH AARON HENDERSON

HAD YOU AUDITIONED FOR *PROJECT RUNWAY* PREVIOUSLY?

Yes, I had auditioned about three times before I received that magical "yes!" Each time Tim would say, "We have something here." He would give me some valuable advice and move me on to the producers, but somewhere along that long audition process I would be dropped. Tim always told me, "You do not want to get on this show just to bomb out. You want to win. Be patient and the time will come when you're ready."

DID YOU HAVE A FAVORITE GUEST JUDGE?

I really like Roland Mouret.

WHAT DID YOU LIKE ABOUT YOUR MODELS KRISTINA AND VALERIA?

I really worked well with them. I felt they were there to win, like I was, and while some of the other models were bitching about everything Kristina and Valeria were like, "Let's get the job done and win."

WHO HAVE BEEN SOME OF YOUR FAVORITE *PROJECT RUNWAY* DESIGNERS OVER THE YEARS?

Austin Scarlett, Santino Rice, Nick Verreos, Christian Siriano, Laura Bennett, Rami Kashou, Mondo Guerra, Leanne Marshall, Michael Costello.

WHO ARE SOME OF YOUR FAVORITE DESIGNERS?

Tom Ford, Alexander McQueen, Karl Lagerfeld, and Viktor & Rolf.

WHAT'S IT LIKE BEING A STRAIGHT GUY ON *PROJECT RUNWAY*?

Just like being a gay guy, minus liking dudes!

DID YOU HAVE A FEELING YOU WERE GOING TO WIN?

Absolutely, I came to win!

HOW HAS *PROJECT RUNWAY* CHANGED YOUR LIFE?

In every aspect possible. *Project Runway*, Bunim/Murray, Lifetime, and the Weinstein Company really have supported me, even today.

WHAT HAVE YOU BEEN DOING SINCE *PROJECT RUNWAY*?

I didn't waste any opportunities, that's for sure. I hit the media hard, as well as sponsors. We, as TV designers, can't sit on the davenport and wait for the telly to ring off the hook because it's not going to happen. We have an expectation for us to do well and we have to work thirty-one times as hard. I've done about three hundred TV, print, radio spots, and appearances throughout the U.S. with companies such as Macy's, Vitamin Water, and Rockstar, many fashion weeks, was asked by Nina herself to help out on a project for *Marie Claire*, went to the Oscars and other LA and NYC red carpet events and met numerous really cool celebs in the process. I was also named the "My TV Best Male Reality Star" of 2010. Nice! I was asked by Lifetime to be the head casting judge for *Project Runway* Season 9, because Tim was not available to do so. That was totally rad. I've had the chance to design dresses for award shows, ad campaigns, and so on. I launched an iPad accessory line with Maroo, and just signed with Earthtec for the Seth Aaron line, which is 100% sustainable.

EMILIO SOSA

TELL ME ABOUT THE PROCESS OF GETTING ONTO PROJECT RUNWAY, HAD YOU AUDITIONED BEFORE?

I never told anyone this, but I almost did a couple of years before. I waited in line. I had two clients to dress that same afternoon and the line was moving so slow I left. When Season 7 casting rolled around, I had just come off a world tour with Celine Dion, on her wardrobe team. I was then booked in Rochester, in the middle of nowhere doing a small show after being with Celine for ten months. I felt like, "Where is my life going?" I got an e-mail from a

friend in Los Angeles that said *Project Runway* is looking to audition people. You should try it. I said I'm too old to go on reality TV, I'm not a personality. I'm a more low-key kind of guy, but I gave it a try. I sent in my application, then a sample of my work and a video of myself. I got a call to do an on-camera interview. They still weren't sure, so I was called back two more times and finally made it.

YOU HAD A PRETTY HAPPENING CAREER BEFORE PROJECT RUNWAY. DO YOU THINK THAT THAT GAVE YOU AN ADVANTAGE ONCE YOU WERE ON THE SHOW?

I think in a sense it did, especially being a costume designer. I've had directors want a dress for that same night so you just have to not get caught up or fall in love with a piece. "Whatever is best for the show" has always been my theory and I carried that on to *Project Runway*. Whatever is going to give me the best dress, I have to do it regardless of what it is. I can't get caught up on one idea or one dress.

DID YOUR BROTHERS LIKE APPEARING ON THE SHOW?

I think that they enjoyed the process more than I did because I was so focused on winning. They didn't have to make a collection but they lived it with me. They would make dinners for me and came to my apartment while I was sewing. They took care of me during the process of making the collection.

DID YOU HAVE A FAVORITE GUEST JUDGE?

Isabel Toledo. She's an artist. I think in the U.S. the fashion industry doesn't really appreciate the artistic aspect of the business. It's more commerce driven. She was one of the judges on my infamous bathing suit (and I use that term loosely). Everyone was turning on me. It was really intense, but once she said, "Well it's not so bad," then I had a chance.

WHY DO YOU THINK YOU WERE CHOSEN TO STAY THAT WEEK?

I think I was able to stay that week because I went all out and really sold it. "I'm going down with the ship!" I told the hair people, I want all the blonde hair she has on her head as big as possible. At the end of the day I put together a look of sorts and I just went with it. I think that was part of my theatre experience—to wow them, even if it's all smoke and mirrors. It kept me in, but after that I dipped for a couple of episodes, because it was traumatic being that close to being sent home.

WHAT DOES BEING IN THE BOTTOM FEEL LIKE?

Like you let down so many people you know who wanted you there. I was so embarrassed that I let it get to that point.

WHEN YOU WORK WITH THE SAME MODEL OVER AND OVER DO YOU FIND THAT YOU DESIGN FOR HER?

I think you have to. A good model could sell a questionable design, but then a bad model could take down an amazing design, so it's 50/50. Model selection is really tough for me. Unfortunately I switched after that bathing suit, so Holly and I didn't work together again.

WHO WAS YOUR MODEL IN THE FINALE COLLECTION?

Lorena. I think she was closer to the high-fashion ideal. Holly is a beautiful girl, but she is more of a statuesque bathing suit type of model, and I think going forward I had to move away from that. Once I was with Lorena, it was just pure design.

WOULD YOU SAY A MODEL WHO IS AS CLOSE TO THE DRESS FORM AS POSSIBLE IS IDEAL?

It's ideal because you only have so much time, so you don't want to have to spend another two hours doing alterations.

DID YOU ENJOY WORKING WITH MILA?

Towards the end when we were the last two and we had to narrow down to one we had a chance to really speak. I like her a great deal; I think she's amazing.

WHO DID YOU BOND WITH MOST IN THE CAST?

Anthony and Jesse, most definitely.

YOU HAD A VERY GOOD COLLABORATION WITH SETH AARON.

I love Seth Aaron. He's a really talented, easy, and fun guy. We had so much fun together going up to Harlem. I got to go back to my old neighborhood, even if it was just for an hour. I feel like I owe Seth Aaron dinner there. I told him I was going to take him to Sylvia's, but now it's a Red Rooster.

DID YOU FEEL THAT ANY ONE JUDGE WAS PARTICULARLY IN YOUR CORNER?

I think I got really good feedback from all of them, but I think Nina was always positive towards my work. Nina was always sweet and positive, and so was Michael. They were great. Tim and I—everyone thinks that we had such a contentious relationship on screen and that I didn't like him, but I just saw him a couple of months ago at an event and we really came to an understanding. Looking back at it I realize that most of the problem was coming from me because I was so caught up in winning that I wasn't accepting of outside influences.

YOU GOT ONE OF THE BIGGEST COMPLIMENTS I'VE EVER SEEN ON THE SHOW, WHEN MICHAEL KORS SAID THAT YOUR CIRCUS DRESS WAS THE BEST THING HE HAD SEEN ALL SEASON.

That was great. You know why? Because he said that my bathing suit was one of the worst things, so I did both. I went from the lowest to the highest.

YOU WERE KNOWN MORE FOR YOUR WORK ON THE SHOW RATHER THAN ANY PERSONALITY TRAIT OR ISSUE.

I wanted my work to be what people remembered, not being the funniest or the sappiest or the mean one. I had fun when they would do the interviews, because that was the only time that I could talk everything out. It was very therapeutic.

HOW DOES THE ACCESSORIES WALL WORK? ARE THERE TEN PAIRS OF EACH SUNGLASSES, TWENTY PAIRS OF A SHOE?

It's just one of everything. At the beginning I got caught up in the whole accessories thing but towards the end it was about the shoe and then the dress, and then on the hair and the makeup.

DID YOU HAVE A FAVORITE GARMENT THAT YOU MADE THAT SEASON?

The ESosa print. That challenge was a favorite of mine. Then the finale, then the one that Heidi wore. Towards the end they were all my favorites because I was in the zone.

WHAT WAS IT LIKE HAVING HEIDI WEAR YOUR DRESS?

She's amazing. She's so supportive of all of us, and the fact that she wore it the day before the finale aired was also a great boost for my career. Heidi is like a goddess to American fashion. She put us in the public eye. It gave people an awareness of the craft.

HOW DO YOU USE THE EXPERIENCE OF BEING ON THE SHOW TO FURTHER YOUR CAREER?

Once the show ended I booked myself solid. I didn't give myself any chance to come down and worry what I'm going to do next. Some highlights: I was the costume designer for the Spike Lee film *Red Hook Summer*, I was the costume designer for *Porgy and Bess* on Broadway (and earned a Tony Award nomination!), and I launched my line, ESOSA.

MILA HERMANOVSKI

WHAT WAS YOUR *PROJECT RUNWAY* AUDITION LIKE?

Since I didn't have any recent work and was required to show up to six garments, I pulled a marathon week and only got a couple of hours of sleep each night. The judges were unanimous in putting me through.

WHAT WAS YOUR FAVORITE AND LEAST FAVORITE CHALLENGE?

Favorite: hardware store. Least Favorite: dress for Heidi's red carpet.

DID YOU HAVE A FAVORITE GUEST JUDGE?

Isabel Toledo and Stephen Webster were my favorites.

WHO ARE SOME OF YOUR FAVORITE DESIGNERS?

Phoebe Philo for Céline, Marni, Helmut Lang, Phillip Lim, Martin Margiela.

DID YOU FEEL CONFIDENT YOU WOULD MAKE IT TO THE FINAL THREE?

From the moment I was asked to apply to the moment I was called back before the judges (while I was standing in the Smithsonian Institute) to the moment I went from alternate to cast member and had to be on a plane in seventy-two hours to the moment presenting my final collection at Mercedes Benz Fashion Week, the entire *Project Runway* experience was a series of "why not" moments unfolding before me.

WHAT WAS IT LIKE HAVING TO FIGHT FOR YOUR SPOT IN THE FINALE?

While I was building my final collection, I wasn't thinking about the others. I just wanted to make the best collection I could. It wasn't until choosing the three looks to show the judges that the nerves took hold.

HOW WAS WORKING ON *ALL STARS* DIFFERENT FROM WORKING ON SEASON 7?

On the one hand, going into *All Stars* I knew what I was getting into psychologically (lack of communication to the outside world, long hours, no music, no books, etc.), but one can never be prepared for the mental and physical challenges presented. And one of the most stressful things about *All Stars* was dealing with the number of alpha personalities under one roof.

HOW HAS *PROJECT RUNWAY* CHANGED YOUR LIFE?

I started my career in fashion design and got swept away by the world of costuming for TV and film. Prior to being asked to apply for *Project Runway*, I had been feeling creatively unfulfilled by my work. The application process to *Project Runway* reignited my love for fashion and made me realize that I need to be designing again.

WHAT WOULD PEOPLE BE SURPRISED TO KNOW ABOUT *PROJECT RUNWAY*?

Being on *Project Runway* attracts a fair amount of media attention, but when it comes to the business of a contemporary women's sportswear collection it doesn't really open as many doors as one might think. I have to work as hard as any other emerging designer out there trying to get orders and in seeking funding.

WHAT HAVE YOU BEEN DOING SINCE *PROJECT RUNWAY*?

I've been working on my brand, making collections and trying to get into stores, but I have had to balance the hardships of my line currently being self-funded with the reality of having to continue to work in TV and film in order to fund it.

ANTHONY WILLIAMS

IT MUST'VE BEEN AMAZING WINNING THE CHALLENGE FOR YOUR FABULOUS BLUE DRESS.

It's interesting because at that point I had given up in the competition. I actually said a prayer to be eliminated, but I was reading, I think Psalms 138 and 8 and it said forsake not my own work. I thought at that moment, "If life is calling me for such a time as now, you just stick it out in this competition. I will continue to give it my best." Not only did I win that challenge, but that gave me the breath of fresh air I needed. It gave me that reassurance that I needed to be there and it was my job to press forward.

WHAT WAS IT LIKE HAVING HEIDI KLUM WEAR YOUR DRESS ON THE COVER OF *MARIE CLAIRE*?

It was amazing. I wasn't there when they did the photo shoot, but when I saw it, it was so interesting. It was my dress! And you want to tell everybody in the grocery store and everywhere you see the magazine. Maybe they don't care, but I've never felt so proud of myself. To see something you made in publication is absolutely phenomenal. If you come into my home, you would see how proud that moment still remains—I have huge posters of it framed.

DID YOU CARE THAT THEY CROPPED IT SO MUCH ON THE ACTUAL COVER?

I felt that they could have shown more of the dress, but they showed the best part. In the magazine they showed more of it. I think, how dare I be concerned with how much of the dress that they had shown? Anybody who looks at the cover and watched Season 7, they knew that it was my dress. It's like—you know what honey, just be grateful.

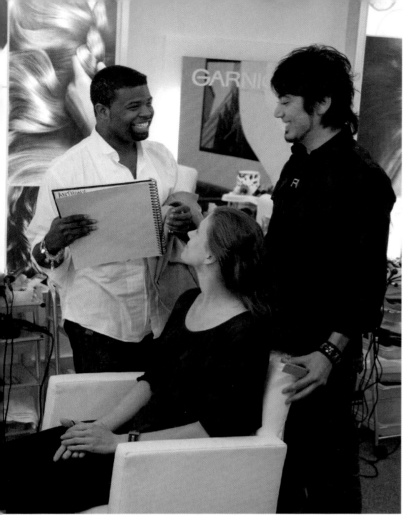

THERE WAS A MOMENT ON THE SHOW WHERE THEY TAPED YOUR MOUTH SHUT.

I talk a lot and I placed a bet with myself and my fellow designers to see how long I could stay quiet, so to give me some further insurance, they actually taped my mouth closed. I didn't even make it thirty minutes.

YOU WERE ELIMINATED AND THEN THEY ASKED YOU BACK. HAD YOU GONE HOME ALREADY?

No, I was still there at the host hotel, the Atlas. I was off one day and I was back on the next.

TO THE AUDIENCE, IT SEEMS LIKE AT LEAST A WEEK.

No, it's not like that at all. It was nice to be asked back. People always say they wouldn't have gone back or they can't believe that I went back. What else was I doing at that moment? I think that in order to survive the *Project Runway All Stars*, you need a little ego, but sometimes you need to move past your ego to navigate and do certain things.

YOU'RE SO GRACIOUS ON THE RUNWAY. EVEN WHEN THEY ELIMINATED YOU, YOU HANDLED IT SO WELL.

I don't think anyone is immune from the *Project Runway* process of life. You're going to have some ups, you're going to have some downs. I think it's a slap in the face for my mother, the people that have been supporting me, for me to act ugly and rude because things didn't work out in my favor. I don't think that even years from now I would feel good watching a tape of me acting out because something didn't go my way, looking like a two-year-old with a tantrum.

YOU'RE ONE OF THE MOST BELOVED CONTESTANTS. DO YOU STILL FEEL THAT ON THE STREET?

I do! I'm quite amazed that people talk to me in such a beautiful and warm capacity. That's a beautiful thing. I think that I represent something that people can connect to. I didn't put on a lot of airs, when I go to the grocery store, I'm still one of those people thinking, "Lord, please don't let me get embarrassed if my card is declined."

WAS DOING *ALL STARS* ANY DIFFERENT FROM DOING SEASON 7?

It was wonderful to be at *All Stars* and it was a bit different. It was more relaxed, believe it or not. I was more prepared for the *All Star* challenges than I was for Season 7. Well not only had I gone through it already in my season, but I was so much more comfortable with myself.

DID YOUR HUMOR HELP YOU GET THROUGH?

My humor is what gets me through everything. Some people think it gets in the way, but it gets me through. You have all these different personalities gathered. You have people who are away from their children and husbands. You have people away from their companies. All of us are suffering to some degree. I say I'm going to laugh through this process because it's not worth it—it's only a moment in time. I love *Project Runway*, but the reality is that it will go in the television history vault as another great show. It's the human connection that we make and the relationships

that we form that make the whole process worth it—including the sacrifices.

WHAT HAS BEEN THE BIGGEST SURPRISE ABOUT DOING THIS SHOW?

I think the biggest surprise about doing the show has been the way we connect with people in such a personal way. Going into the lives and the homes of people is a responsibility. When you have a platform such as *Project Runway* to show your creativity, you have a responsibility to also be intelligent. You have to be considerate of what you say and how you say it. I think that you have to understand that you are a hero to someone. It doesn't matter if you got eliminated from *Project Runway*, because who you are to the people watching the show has nothing to do with who you are on that runway in those moments. Those people see you as a hero, they see you as talented. I am very grateful for that.

THE DESIGNERS

MCKELL MADDOX
FROM: LAYTON, UT
STUDIED: ACADEMY OF ART
UNIVERSITY

JASON TROISI
FROM: GREENWICH, CT
STUDIED: PARSONS THE NEW
SCHOOL FOR DESIGN

NICHOLAS D'AURIZIO
FROM: HACKENSACK, NJ
STUDIED: THE CATHOLIC
UNIVERSITY OF AMERICA,
FASHION INSTITUTE OF
TECHNOLOGY

SARAH TROST
FROM: TOLUCA LAKE, CA
COSTUME DESIGNER

KRISTIN HASKINS-SIMMS
FROM: PHILADELPHIA, PA
STUDIED: RHODE ISLAND
SCHOOL OF DESIGN

A. J. THOUVENOT
FROM: ST. LOUIS, MO
STUDIED: LINDENWOOD
UNIVERSITY

PEACH CARR
FROM: WINFIELD, IL
SELF-TAUGHT

CARLOS CASANOVA
FROM: FAJARDO, PUERTO RICO
STUDIED: CARLOTA ALFARO
COLLEGE, LISA THON SCHOOL
OF DESIGN

MICHAEL DRUMMOND
FROM: ST. LOUIS, MO
STUDIED: THE ACADEMY OF
ART UNIVERSITY

IVY HIGA
FROM: KAILUA-KONA, HI
STUDIED: PARSONS THE NEW
SCHOOL FOR DESIGN

VALERIE MAYEN
FROM: CORPUS CHRISTI, TX
STUDIED: THE CLEVELAND
INSTITUTE OF ART

CHRISTOPHER COLLINS
FROM: ENCINITAS, CA
STUDIED: SAN FRANCISCO
STATE UNIVERSITY

APRIL JOHNSTON
FROM: MOORESVILLE, NC
STUDIED: SAVANNAH
COLLEGE OF ART AND
DESIGN

MICHAEL COSTELLO
FROM: LOS ANGELES, CA
SELF-TAUGHT

ANDY SOUTH
FROM: WAIPAHU, HI
STUDIED: HONOLULU
COMMUNITY COLLEGE

MONDO GUERRA
FROM: DENVER, CO
SELF-TAUGHT

GRETCHEN JONES
FROM: FAIRPLAY, CO
SELF-TAUGHT

SEASON

HIGHLIGHTS

MCKELL'S ELIMINATION

When the designers arrived they found out that they were not officially on the show yet. They had to compete in the And Sew It Begins challenge, and one designer would be eliminated. McKell lost the challenge and was sent home before becoming an official cast member.

EXPANDING TO 90 MINUTES

The show was expanded from sixty minutes to ninety minutes starting with Season 8.

JONATHAN MURRAY:

"That really opened up a lot of possibilities in terms having more time to get to know the designers, stronger character development, more opportunity to get to see what goes on behind the scenes when the designers are backstage waiting for the judges to make their decisions, more time to see how the judges come up with their decisions, and to let some of their arguments play out."

WOOLLY BALLS

The It's A Party innovation challenge took the designers to a party store to gather materials for an outfit. When Tim came to visit the designers in the workroom he asked Kristin what she was planning for her waistband. He couldn't control his laughter when she showed him a package of animal woolly balls. He and Kristin laughed even harder when she said if that didn't work she had real balls she could use. They were both hysterical when Tim told her he preferred the woolly balls.

CASANOVA'S DOLCE & GABBANA PANTS

The first challenge of Season 8 was called And Sew It Begins. The designers had just arrived with their suitcases at Lincoln Center. They were asked to take one item out of their suitcase to incorporate into the challenge. Then they had to pass their garments to the person to their right to use. Casanova was upset that the item he chose was a pair of $1,070 Dolce & Gabbana pants.

GRETCHEN'S BILLBOARD

For the Larger Than Life challenge the designers had to create a look that defines the *Marie Claire* woman. Gretchen won the challenge, and was awarded the incredible prize of having her look on a billboard in Times Square. As if that wasn't enough of a prize, the model used for the billboard was Coco Rocha.

GRETCHEN JONES:

"It was surreal to see that billboard in Times Square. Just a few weeks earlier I was a struggling designer from a town of four hundred in rural Colorado. To go from that to seeing my work plastered on a billboard in the fashion capital of the western world was unreal. Things like that don't happen very often. It really made me feel like I can achieve my goals; it was life-affirming."

COCO ROCHA:

"I've been a fan of *Project Runway* from the start. Not only is it entertaining but it presents some serious fashion talent. When I was asked to model one of the winners' outfits on a billboard in Times Square I didn't hesitate to accept the offer. The best part was the fact no one had any idea why the billboard was there for a good few months before the episode aired. I had so many people ask me about it but of course I was sworn to secrecy."

HIGHLIGHTS

PHILIP TREACY

The designers were greeted on the runway by the legendary milliner Philip Treacy. They were excited to learn that they were to create a look inspired by one of Treacy's hats, which their model would wear on the runway.

MOM

While working on creating their textiles the designers got a surprise visit from their mothers. Christopher was visited by his partner instead. Everyone was thrilled when they got the day off to spend with their loved ones.

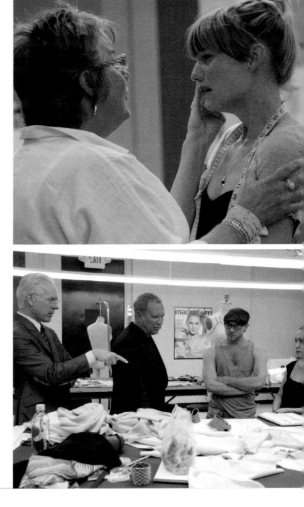

RESORT WEAR

Michael Kors met the designers at a boat dock to tell them they would be creating a resort wear look for their next challenge. He sent them on a boat ride to get into a relaxed state of mind, where they were treated to brunch and a pair of Michael Kors sunglasses. They later received an extra special treat when Kors showed up to the workroom and offered advice to each designer.

MICHAEL KORS:

"Well I could've stayed there for days. Designers, myself included, can get very myopic—either we fall in love with something we're working on when really it's not that great and we should move on, or we have something that's great and we don't even know it. Unless you're a designer it's kind of hard to understand that. So I was able to walk into the room and say things like, 'Seeing this detail is great! Your whole garment is in this detail.' I kept stressing to them about accessories, how you put the look together, and presentation. Just as when I was a critic at Parsons, my objective in that situation in the workroom was not to turn them into little mini Michael Kors, but to figure out how we take what they're working on and make it the best it can be. It was definitely fun, definitely interesting, hopefully informative for them."

DESIGNERS GANG UP ON MICHAEL COSTELLO

Episode 5 featured the challenge There IS an "I" in Team. The designers were split into two groups of six. The first group was called Team Military and Lace, and consisted of April, Mondo, Michael D, Valerie, Casanova, and Peach. The other team was Team Luxe and had Michael C., Gretchen, Christopher, Andy, Ivy, and AJ as its members. Team Luxe was deemed the losing team. When asked, each designer, except AJ, said that Michael C. was the weak link. The judges countered that it was easy to say Michael was weak because he had immunity. Michael was hurt by his fellow designers' words, and broke down afterwards.

MONDO'S EMOTIONAL PATTERN

The designers had the opportunity to create their own textile for the HP challenge, There's a Pattern Here. Mondo's print was extremely personal, and was based on his HIV positive status, which the other designer and judges knew nothing about. The judges loved his pattern, but Mondo didn't tell them the origin. Nina said she was sorry she didn't know what the story was. Before leaving the runway Mondo made the decision to address Nina's comment and told everyone his story. There were many tears on the runway from the other designers, but Mondo was happy he shared what he had previously been hiding.

INSPIRED BY JACQUELINE KENNEDY

The designers were given the task to create a look that was their take on classic American sportswear á la Jackie Kennedy. Tim's advice to Andy? Jackie Kennedy would not have camel toe.

HIGHLIGHTS

IVY ACCUSES MICHAEL COSTELLO OF CHEATING

The eliminated designers came back to help out with the A Look in the Line challenge, in which the designers had to create a look for Heidi's New Balance line. While they were sewing Ivy accused Michael C. of cheating by using Topstick tape in the Jackie Kennedy challenge. AJ let Michael know that the others also thought he cheated. Tim later came in to confront the group about the accusation. He said that he saw nothing wrong, the judges saw nothing wrong, and that their many cameras saw nothing wrong, and put an end to the controversy.

JONATHAN MURRAY:

"A lot of the Season 8 designers gave Michael Costello a hard time. Some of them were frustrated with his ability to—in their opinion—throw something together; the way he could drape something and win. I think they saw him as the idiot savant of designing. It was frustrating for them because they would put in all this thought and work, and he would do three or four dresses while they were still thinking it through. You also saw Gretchen and a number of the other designers ultimately embraced Michael and came to like him."

MICHAEL COSTELLO ELIMINATED

Michael C., Mondo, Andy, and April were all asked to make collections for the finale with the knowledge that only three would actually go on to compete at New York Fashion Week. Michael C. was the eliminated designer. He was extremely upset and broke down crying. He didn't know how he would tell his parents; he thought they would want him to give up designing.

MICHAEL COSTELLO:

"When I went home they told me they loved me no matter what. They were very disappointed that I came out on the show, though. I really didn't want to let my mom and dad down. I wanted to at least make it to Fashion Week. Of course I did with the decoy collection, which is still great, but my parents need so much validation that they would have to see it on television. But the next day I was on the cover of *The New York Times*. That instantly validated me. It was wonderful."

THE JUDGES BATTLE IT OUT

The final three designers competing at New York Fashion Week were Gretchen, Andy, and Mondo. The judges agreed that while Andy's collection was good, he was not the winner. However choosing between Gretchen and Mondo was no easy task. Guest judge Jessica Simpson and Heidi both thought Mondo should win, while Nina and Michael wanted Gretchen. After making what they called the toughest decision in *Project Runway* history, Gretchen was named the winner.

GRETCHEN JONES:

"For me it was such an honor to show at the tents in the inaugural year of New York Fashion Week's move to Lincoln Center—and to have my mother and sister there watching me was great. I was really proud of the collection I showed; I felt it was very representative of me as a designer. I believed in myself and felt that winning was meant to be for me. It was what I needed to keep moving forward with my creative dreams."

HEIDI KLUM:

"I really fought for Mondo. I always go for the person who is a little bit more out there, but that's also my personality. Nina and Michael are a little bit more conservative. When Mondo made that polka-dot dress they said, 'You're crazy, who can walk around with a gigantic polka dot dress?' I thought, you know what, I'm going to wear this damn polka-dot dress just to prove a point! Some people liked it and some didn't. It's easy when you wear clothes that are safe. I'm not one of those people."

WINNING LOOKS

AND SEW IT BEGINS (GRETCHEN)

LARGER THAN LIFE (GRETCHEN)

IT'S A PARTY (ANDY)

HATS OFF TO YOU (MICHAEL C.)

THERE IS AN "I" IN TEAM (CASANOVA)

YOU CAN TOTALLY WEAR THAT AGAIN (MICHAEL C.)

WHAT'S MINE IS YOURS (APRIL)

A ROUGH DAY ON THE RUNWAY (MONDO)

RACE TO THE FINISH (MONDO)

THERE'S A PATTERN HERE (MONDO)

A LOOK IN THE LINE (ANDY)

FINALE (GRETCHEN)

MODELS

VANESSA RATNAVICH

DRE DAVIS

JULIA RODRIGUEZ

SAMANTHA ZAJARIAS

KAVEN JO CAVEN

AMARE TK

IFEOMA "IFY" JONES

SARAE CART

ZHANNA VED

EKATERINA PY

ALEXANDRA PALMER

EYEN CHORM

ROSE COOK

CASSIE DZIENNY

LENKA DAYRIT

TINA MARIE CLARK

MILLANA SNOW

GUEST JUDGES

SELMA BLAIR
ACTRESS

JOANNA COLES
EDITOR-IN-CHIEF, *MARIE CLAIRE*

BETSEY JOHNSON
FASHION DESIGNER

PHILIP TREACY
HAT DESIGNER

GEORGINA CHAPMAN
DESIGNER/CO-FOUNDER,
MARCHESA

CYNTHIA ROWLEY
FASHION DESIGNER

KRISTEN BELL
ACTRESS

JANUARY JONES
ACTRESS

NAEEM KHAN
FASHION DESIGNER

RACHEL ROY
FASHION DESIGNER

NORMA KAMALI
FASHION DESIGNER

CHRISTIAN SIRIANO
PROJECT RUNWAY SEASON
4 WINNER

JESSICA SIMPSON
MUSICIAN/ACTRESS

RACHEL ROY

WHAT IS IT LIKE BEING A GUEST JUDGE ON *PROJECT RUNWAY* LIKE?

Project Runway is probably one of the most professional television environments I've ever worked on. It is a well-oiled machine. Very classy, very well scripted in terms of knowing what they need, very organized. They all treated me so well. I was very happy with my experience. Michael Kors is one of the most generous people I've ever worked with. He is engaging. He is someone that wants you to be in on the joke, and wants you to feel like you're part of the family. I was so impressed by him; his nature, his spirit and who he is as an individual—and he's one of the funniest people that I've ever met. I felt like I had just come out of an abs workout class after I was done. He literally made me laugh until it hurt.

Michael's point of view is right on. He teases and can make a joke out of a flaw in a garment, and yet he doesn't hurt people's feelings. I have such great respect for Nina. I admire Heidi's sweetness and her beauty. She's so happy and upbeat and brings that energy to everything she does.

HOW DOES THE JUDGING WORK?

It's like what I do at work. I do four collections with my designer label, so I'm constantly in the

position of judging collections—only I don't usually have to do it in hair and makeup and I don't have to watch what I say when I'm at work. But the process of judging on *Project Runway* and the process of judging/finalizing my collections is very similar. It's just your point of view. This is not a black-and-white industry. It's an industry based on emotion. Michael Kors' customers believe in and rely on his point of view. My customers do the same. That's the beauty of working in art. There should be different opinions because there are so many customers out there, so many people you can sell to.

I try to give the designers on *Project Runway* as much advice as I can, based on my ten years in the industry, but at the end of the day they still have to go through that experience themselves and have their own failures. If you learn from your failures it's really a success. If I offered something that might have been unpleasant for a designer to hear I also tried to offer ways to work around it next time. Or if I thought something was lacking I tried to explain why it was lacking, and how they could possibly look at it differently next time. It's how I approach my company. If any of my employees have an issue they also have to bring up a solution.

DO YOU THINK YOU BRING A FRESH POINT OF VIEW AS A GUEST JUDGE?

It can be considered an advantage or a disadvantage. Someone may know that for the last few weeks this person has been copying other people or this person hasn't actually been sewing their own stuff, or whatever it is. When I'm looking at a beautiful jacket, I don't care who sewed it. The final element is beauty. If you created a piece and you gathered people more skilled than you in certain areas to help execute it there's absolutely nothing wrong with that to me.

DO SEWING SKILLS MATTER?

For *Project Runway* sewing skills matter because they're required to do everything from the thought to the execution. In real life you're not going from point A to Z unless you're just starting out. I don't sew. I pay someone who sews very, very well to sew. But if I understand the construction of a garment it will only help me relate to the sewer if I am displeased with something. Instead of just saying this looks awful, I can suggest solutions.

DO YOU DESIGN WITH YOURSELF IN MIND?

I have the woman that I aspire to be for my designer line, and for my secondary line it's the younger sister to that woman. So it's the girl I used to be, and the options I would have liked to have had when I was that girl.

MONDO GUERRA

I remember the first season my mom cut out this little article from the newspaper saying Heidi Klum plans to launch a new show and it gave a brief summary of what this is. It was very exciting to see how it has developed through the seasons. The beautiful thing about *Project Runway* is that you never know what to expect. You tune in to see what's next. I was hooked and watched every season. From Season 1 I also became a huge fan of Austin. He set the tone for the show in such a creative and artistic way.

HAD YOU AUDITIONED BEFORE MAKING IT ON TO THE SHOW?

I auditioned for Season 7 and I made the short list. Then they called me on my birthday and said, "Sorry, we're taking 15 and you're number 16." So I didn't get in. I'm a firm believer that everything happens for a reason, and looking back I don't think I was ready yet.

WAS THE EXPERIENCE WHAT YOU IMAGINED IT WOULD BE?

I really didn't have any expectations except to use it as a platform to grow as a designer, hone my skills, and learn from the other contestants, and that's what I got from it in the long run.

ON THE SHOW YOU SEEMED SO LONELY FOR A LONG TIME. WHAT CHANGED THINGS FOR YOU?

I woke up one day and realized this is an opportunity, and either you choose to do it to your fullest or throw in the towel. That's when I really started talking myself out of my self-doubt. As an artist you always go into something thinking that you're not good enough. With me it's always a process of getting out of that head space. When I got there my initial reaction to the energy in the room was flashbacks of high school, being very lonely and just not fitting in, so I would go to bed and didn't

really want to socialize with the other designers. I would go into the room and shut the door, and of course people wondered why I was being so standoffish and acting the way I was. Then it was a matter of kicking myself in the ass and saying, "Why don't you show them that you can be personable, so they'll know that you're not just this jerk who doesn't want to hang out?" My work is really inspired by my family and my culture, so that came into play as well in my decision to really get into the game.

I jumped on the bandwagon, like I was one of the popular kids. He was winning challenges and people did not understand why he was winning because Michael has a different process than everyone else. He didn't even have a ruler. When I was paired with him I felt that this was my ticket home. I not only disrespected him, I really underestimated what he could accomplish, not only in his design and skill set but in his persona. Once we started working together, I thought he might not have the skill set to accomplish certain tasks but he would listen and communicate and I could see that he wanted to learn and grow in his technical abilities. That really impressed me and I feel that's where our friendship started—on a foundation of mutual respect. Once I started saying "Michael's not a bad guy" people started to notice. I think if we didn't have that connection the other designers wouldn't have had an opportunity to see Michael at his best. I think we both had similar journeys through the season and that's another reason we became such good friends. I'm getting a little teary because he's a good buddy.

WAS IT A HARD DECISION TO DO THE POSITIVITY PRINT?

It wasn't a hard decision for me because it was doing something that I loved, that I was very passionate about. I had done two textiles and I asked April Johnston to come over and take a look at my prints. One of them was inspired by the view from a plane looking down over the buildings in New York the first time I ever came. It was a really cool cubist, modern design, and then I had my positivity print. Without filling her in on the background I asked April which one she liked better. Automatically she said, "I like this one. This one is more you." That connected with me and I realized yes, that was me and there is a story behind it—so much love, so much pain, and so much passion. Then our mothers were there for that challenge so it really came full circle. When Tim came in and asked about the design

I said I really love color, I really love construction paper, I love shapes. I danced around the topic. Then when I had the one-on-one interview with the producers I let go. Art has always been my motivation and to work on something so personal and then lie about it would have been deceptive and disrespectful to who I am, so I had to let go.

Later when we were on the runway I wasn't ready to talk about it again even when Nina said specifically that she wanted to know the story behind my print. I heard everybody else's stories and they were really passionate about what they were communicating. Leaving the stage I stopped and said, "Nina you asked me what my story was . . ." I'm a very spiritual person and I carried a picture of my grandmother in my pocket every single episode, even on *All Stars*, and I touch it to give me strength. I felt that she was there with me in that moment, telling me this is your time. When I started talking about it, I didn't know that it was going to be so easy, so revealing, and so much weight off my shoulders. I think my grandmother was taking that pain, and it happened in a really organic and beautiful way. You could see physically that I was happy and glowing. Everybody else on the runway was crying. I only saw the episode when it aired, and I think I saw a clip of it at an event, and now it's difficult for me to watch. I'm not sure why and so I'm still working on that.

For anybody who is HIV positive, it's an issue. Before I

would say that I was HIV positive. Now I say I'm living with HIV. Before I wasn't taking responsibility for the disease and I was letting that plus sign define who I was. I've really had to change the way I think about it because it is a responsibility, checking in with the doctor all the time, taking your meds on time. I didn't talk about it because being Latino, being gay, and then being HIV positive too, I felt like it was so disrespectful to my family that they would disown me. What's amazed me is that my family has opened up the dialogue about HIV with me and they ask questions. My family that has lived in the same neighborhood for five generations is talking about it and I know it's making a difference out there and that's why we need more people to talk about it.

Oh yeah. After that episode I got so many e-mails from people. When you're living with HIV you get closed into this idea of it being a gay man's disease. I got stories from people who were drug users and got infected, and stories about having it passed down, like a mom was HIV positive and her fourteen-year-old has HIV. Even one of my best friends contacted me and said I didn't know this about you and I have to share something . . . both of my parents are HIV positive. It really opened my eyes, and that support has motivated me to be an advocate and combat the stigma that's associated with HIV. The lack of dialogue and the stigma is really the disease itself.

Yes they did.

I told four days before the show aired while we were having dinner. There was no easy way to say it. I said, "There's something I have to tell you. I'm HIV positive." I don't think they were shocked because I had been very, very sick and had been in the hospital twice with PCP pneumonia. My numbers were down to fourteen, and I was on a respirator for Christmas the year before I got on the show. *Project Runway* really did change my life because I don't think I would have ever talked about it if I never got that opportunity that day. When I told my parents, my dad didn't really say anything but my mom looked at me and said, "I'm proud of you." That was a relief because she understood. That's all I've needed from them for the past ten years. I really underestimated them. I think that they would've understood this much earlier. I was really happy when they knew, and now they're really participating in my health and in my journey.

To have the support of Heidi meant so much. I went to the finale not only with the pressure of the shows already starting to air on TV and developing a fan base, but with these blogs and interviews all saying they think Mondo is going to win. Meanwhile you don't even know what's going to happen. That was a lot of pressure and that was scary for me, but I got to a place where I was very confident about what I was going to show, how it would look, the hair, the makeup, the music. I listened to that runway music over and over in my studio before I even got to Fashion Week. I have to visualize what I want to accomplish to really get to that point.

I think Michael Kors felt I wasn't listening to him and in some way disrespecting his opinion. I think they appreciated what I did though and I understand that. Michael felt they needed a sportswear designer. I feel like I can do sportswear but that was not what I was showing in the finale so it's okay. I'm happy for Gretchen, I'm happy about how everything went down. I don't think I would have had the opportunities to do advocacy work had I won, and that has fulfilled my life and really taken charge. I was shocked when I lost but I got over it really quickly, especially with the support from my amazing friends and family. People always ask when my line is coming out, but there are other things to do. There are bigger issues to be addressed. You're not going to be able to wear fashion if you're not alive, so there are bigger issues to tackle.

MICHAEL COSTELLO

WHAT WAS THE PROCESS OF GETTING ON THE SHOW LIKE?

It was really tough because I'd tried out a few times before. I was asked to come back, but I ran into difficulty because my dad was sick. One day my mom told me, "Just do it. God's with you." My partner told me just go; he'd handle everything. I called my friend Suwana Perry, who went with me to the previous auditions. We told each other we're going to make it this time. I got a flat tire one mile away from the audition. I said, "Please God, just get me there." I actually drove one mile on that flat tire and made it. The casting director told me to be ready, be smart, be you. I get in there with my samples. They're pressed and bedazzled, they look good, and I'm really feeling it. I walk in and I see Nick Verreos, Zoe Glassner, and Tim Gunn in the middle. The first thing Tim said was, "Michael, you've tried out before." Nick said, "Michael, I just disclosed with Tim and Zoe that you and I have been friends for a really long time. It's not going to affect anything." I gave them the rundown of how I made my dress. I bought the fabric from Walmart for $8. I made the dress the night before. Of course I put beads on it, sparkles, glamour. I gave it a ninety-foot train because it's me. Zoe asked me if I could do tailoring. I thought she meant hemming pants and cinching in a waist. I said, yeah I can do After Six. I was so embarrassed by that. When Tim said we're going to move you forward I knew right there life was changed forever.

HOW LONG HAVE YOU BEEN DESIGNING?

I've been designing as far back as I can remember. I was drawing on the walls, paper, whatever I could find, from age two. I would play with clothes. I used to cut my sister's things. My parents never got upset with me. They always knew I would do something with my obsession with clothes later.

YOU WERE ELIMINATED RIGHT BEFORE THE FINALE, BUT YOU STILL SHOWED AT FASHION WEEK WITH YOUR DECOY COLLECTION. WHAT WAS THAT LIKE?

I was one of the finalists. In fourth place you get to make a collection that's shown on television. It's wonderful that the eliminated designers are allowed to do decoy collections and show at Fashion Week so no one at the show knows which ones actually are being judged. A lot

of people don't realize that we do that. It's a wonderful opportunity for us. We can't be thankful enough because it allows us to still live our dream. Normally Fashion Week falls around the second week of September. On TV we're only eight or nine episodes in, so the public doesn't know who's been eliminated. There's another secret about the big day though. There are two episodes filmed: one with a full audience and one with a select group that gets to know who the finalists are and they all have to sign a waiver. The producers come backstage to all the designers and say we're going to draw a name out of a hat and you will be the fourth designer so they still don't exactly know who the final three are. In my season April was the person who got picked out of the hat.

THE OTHER DESIGNERS ON THE SHOW WERE VERY HARD ON YOU—YOUR SEWING SKILLS WERE QUESTIONED AND YOU WERE ACCUSED OF CHEATING. WHAT WAS THAT LIKE FOR YOU?

It was tough. It took me a while to process and figure out why they all had a problem with me. Some of the designers were self-taught, but they had some formal training or graduated from Parsons, the Fashion Institute of Technology. You have to respect what they went through in their career paths and what they've learned. But you also have to appreciate and respect the aesthetic and process of other designers. I never went to school. I've just always loved fashion. I've always done things in my own way and learned how to work with the fabrics to make them do what I wanted them to do. The way they saw it, they worked so hard and this guy with no formal training is winning challenges. It upset them, and I can see how the animosity comes in. But they all acted like assholes, and they'll each say it—except Ivy; she'd say I was mean to everyone else. What happened was actually beneficial to me though because it made more people want to know about me. Why are they targeting him? Is he really doing manipulative things behind people's backs or is he really this decent, cool, humble guy?

What viewers don't understand (and I don't understand why the cast didn't) is that we have cameras everywhere, even underneath the tables. When you're watching you don't think about it, but there are about a dozen camera people and hidden cameras. If we need to go to the bathroom we have to wave so that we don't ruin a shot. You can't just walk out those double doors because that's where the whole production crew is. If there was any kind of cheating it would have been caught. I can't just run with the model and tape her in the toilet, put tape here and there. Being accused of cheating hurt me. When my look came down the runway I told everybody if you want me to make the dress again give me forty minutes and fabric and watch me work my magic. I also said the only reason the dress was holding up is because I made a blue belt to hold it in place. It's a TV show. You have to make stuff fast.

YOU AND IVY CERTAINLY CLASHED. HOW IS YOUR RELATIONSHIP TODAY?

Right now Ivy and I are fine but she put me through misery.

WHAT'S YOUR SCHEDULE LIKE AS A CONTESTANT?

There's a challenge every other day. The audience at home thinks we have a week because they see the show once a week but we don't. Sometimes the way it works is when we're done with a challenge and the winner is announced, we instantly have to go upstairs and change into our next outfit so it looks like it's another day. Then we go back downstairs and meet Heidi Klum on the runway to get a hint of what the next challenge is going to be. We never know until the next day when Tim or Heidi actually presents the challenge. When you're doing a challenge you don't have twenty four hours. We get into the workroom about 9:30–10:00 a.m. and we have until midnight. There are fifty or sixty production people and they all have a time limit. Everybody has to go home at some point. Some of the designers try to sew built-in corset lining with French seams. You don't have time for that. You have to be able to use your time well to be "*Project Runway* good." That's the term a lot of designers use. It is a television show and you have to be able to execute your best work in a timely manner to make it look runway ready. Some can do it, some can't.

I have severe commitment issues with my garments. That's why people always tell me not to second guess myself. I am capable of working really quickly because I have been sewing since I was eleven years old. I've had businesses where people would need custom-made things. Those were by no means the first dresses I ever made. I know what I can do and what I can't do. I never recreated anything on the show that I had done before. A lot of designers did. That was disappointing to find out. Mondo, April, and I are the only ones that used only the inspiration from the challenges given to create something beautiful.

The group challenge was a mess. I was so blindsided because you don't know what they're saying about you in their personal interviews. You think these people really are your friends. We didn't have a group leader. It was up to me to put that group together. The reason I chose Gretchen was because I loved what she did for the Philip Treacy challenge. I thought the look was beautiful, and she'd bring that to whatever we were going to do. When Tim told Gretchen she was bullying everyone Gretchen broke down for two days. We didn't see her for two days. She said it was because of some personal problems at home, but I think it was what Tim said to her. I don't blame him for saying it because she did take on the role of a team leader. It was a rough day for her.

When we had the New Balance challenge, Heidi Klum's line, we didn't know we were going to get critiqued by Heidi in the workroom. She came up to my stuff and asked if it was her fabric. I said some of it's yours but the rest I bought at Mood. She said, "Who's that designer who said you can't sew? Oh, she's not here anymore." I loved it. The judges were always wonderful towards me. Michael Kors was always a fan of what I did. Nina was the hard one. She's a tough critic. Look at her position. She's a fashion editor of a magazine. She's seen everything, and not just from *Project Runway* designers. She's seen things from Marc Jacobs, Alexander McQueen, etc. It's really tough to impress her. To have the judges in your corner feels good. You're still scared for deliberations. You never really know whether they're going to like it or not. My model Lenka gave me a little heads-up. She told me Heidi comes in the back really quick to get her hair and makeup touched up. She gets to see the model lineup. She talks to them and secretly lets them know she likes something. So Lenka would say, "You're okay. Heidi likes your outfit." It instantly takes the stress down a little bit. I made short things on the show so Heidi would want to wear them!

It was a thrill to win the Phillip Treacy challenge. The hat I got resembled some kind of sea creature. I wanted to create something like a mermaid or an octopus. I found what I was doing was a tortured mess. There are times when you need Tim's validation in the workroom. I wasn't feeling it and I told him. He said, "You have all this fabric. Can you do something?" I did and turned it out in about two hours. Yes, it was very simple, but that's me. People know that I love simplicity. I can't do structured pieces. I like simple things because I think they look great on women. I picked up the fabric, sewed it together, and whipped it up really quickly. It draped beautifully. It didn't take away from the hat. We were told to make something inspired by the hat and complement the hat. When it came down the runway I was really happy with it. I thought they might say it was too safe, but when it came down to deliberations Michael Kors started first and he said, "This is what harmony looks like. When I saw this coming down the runway it was harmonious. It is beautiful." Nina said, "It looked effortless, beautiful. The nude shoe made her leg look longer. You couldn't have done it more perfectly." I really thought Michael Drummond was going to take it because his was really beautiful too. When I won that one it was so great because it was Philip Treacy.

THE DESIGNERS ON THE SHOW TEND TO GET UPSET WHEN THEY HAVE TO DESIGN FOR NON-MODELS. WHY IS THIS?

When the designers get challenges for women who are not a size 2 they are devastated because most of them are either just out of school or only used to working with small sizes. I have to say I was one of those devastated people. I was afraid I was going to get a size 22 bridesmaid with a crazy dress to alter into a denim jacket or a cocktail dress. I was terrified. The fear is about the fit and making them happy. A lot of size 12–14 women are insecure about their bodies. When they get something custom made they feel like its instantly going to make them thinner. Like there's some trick we can do to make them into a size 4. We can build corsets into the dress to give you a beautiful shape, but it's not going to shed pounds.

WHO WERE YOUR ROOMMATES?

My original roommates were Nick, Andy and AJ. Nick and AJ left kind of early. It was just Andy and I for a long time. When Mondo and Christopher moved in it was great. We weren't ready for Mondo's wardrobe! There were so manny suitcases everywhere. We would find scarves on the sink, studded boots in the bathroom, chaps on the dresser. We got used to it.

YOU AND MONDO WERE PAIRED UP FOR THE WHAT'S MINE IS YOURS CHALLENGE. HE TOLD YOU RIGHT OFF THE BAT HE WASN'T HAPPY TO WORK WITH YOU. DID THAT SURPRISE YOU?

I was not surprised to hear that Mondo didn't want to work with me. He and I had some tension early on. He is the most creative genius in the room, Ivy was the best seamstress, and I was labeled as the guy who can't sew. When I was paired with Mondo in this challenge he was completely devastated. Everyone's jaws just dropped. We actually stopped production for about three minutes because he had a fit. The cards just worked out perfect. If I hadn't been paired with him I would never have been validated as a sewer on the show. That is the best challenge for me. He let everyone know that I did know how to sew. I got paired with the most creative guy in the room who does the most fabulous things when it comes to sewing. I was able to execute his look. It was a reversible jacket with a built in hoodie, exposed zipper, French cuff sleeves, double hem. The look was in the bottom, but what you didn't see was that Michael, Nina, and Heidi said it was sewn very well for someone who can't sew. That was great for me. I said, "I'm sorry that Mondo's in the bottom but getting paired with him was so wonderful." I came out of that with a real friend. That was the beginning of our very close friendship.

AS A DESIGNER, IT MUST BE INCREDIBLE TO GET ADVICE FROM MICHAEL KORS ON A REGULAR BASIS.

You never know what Michael Kors is going to say. You can't wait to hear. It's your own personal moments in history with Michael Kors.

WHAT HAS THE PUBLIC'S REACTION TO YOU BEEN LIKE?

When people approach me on the street they tell me they just want to hug me because I was so lovable. One guy told me he loves me so much because I'm so fluffy. That was the sweetest, weirdest thing. It's shocking to see what the show can do to people. I heard that there was a woman in Minnesota who was dying of cancer. From her hospital bed she told every nurse she needed Lifetime on, "I can't miss my show." Her sister wrote me a letter after she passed away. She said she had to watch to see if I made it to the next episode. I cried. To hear that you have that kind of effect on somebody . . . there's nothing greater.

APRIL JOHNSTON

WHAT WAS THE PROCESS OF GETTING ON *PROJECT RUNWAY* LIKE?

The process for me getting on *Project Runway* was pretty spectacular because I actually was approached by one of the casting directors. They contacted me because they saw my website and my portfolio and told me that I should try out. I was getting ready to graduate and I didn't have anything lined up. I had my senior fashion show coming up at Savannah College of Art and Design. It's a huge deal to get into that, and I had the opportunity to go to Atlanta and to do the casting. So I went to my fashion show and then I left the next morning at 5 a.m. to drive to Atlanta to try out for the show. When I left the audition Tim Gunn said that he thought that I might be too one-note for the show, so I was a maybe at first. I went back home to Savannah and that night I got the call to come back, so I drove back the next day. Then in the middle of my graduation I got the call that I got the show. It was pretty crazy but it was easy for me to transition into the show format after working on my senior collection every day.

DID YOU HAVE ANY FAVORITE CHALLENGES THROUGHOUT YOUR SEASON?

I loved the resort wear challenge. I thought that was really cool because I don't do resort wear, so for me to make it my own was really cool. I also enjoyed doing the print challenge. Now I have a line of fabrics at Jo-Ann stores and we do a lot of prints.

SO YOU EXECUTED THE INFAMOUS "DIAPER" LOOK . . .

Well I knew it was bad when I sent it out there. That's the thing with *Project Runway*, you could know when something's horrible but what are you going to do? Not send anything out? You really can't. I didn't want to throw in the towel so I just sent out the look and I was ready to take whatever came.

HOW MUCH OF YOUR PERSONAL STYLE AFFECTED WHAT YOU DESIGNED FOR THE SHOW?

My personal style is exactly what I make. I'm like Goth punk rock, but it's so funny because Anthony Williams would tell you I'm so conservative. My personality is not a hardcore punk rock party queen, but I dress like I would be. He says it throws a lot of people off.

DOES IT HURT YOU WHEN YOUR POINT OF VIEW AS A DESIGNER IS DIFFERENT THAN THE JUDGES'?

It totally hinders me. Kristen Bell was the guest judge for the resort wear challenge I won. She has a similar style to me so I think that helped, whereas through *All Stars* nobody saw what I was going for and it does hurt me. It's disappointing, but I also don't have the time to execute the looks and really get the point across. I feel like the Miss Piggy challenge was a pretty good one, and the opera and the 99-cent store, I feel like my looks for these challenges were almost there but if I had more time to execute them I would've gone the extra mile.

IS IT HARD TO EDIT YOURSELF AS YOU'RE CREATING?

Yes, because I have only so much time to make something, and then to edit myself too—and style? For the Gelato challenge I really tried to be something I wasn't just to please the judges. Not the garment but the styling, and it resulted in me being kicked off. That taught me to stick with who I am.

IS WHAT YOU WEAR WHILE YOU'RE ON THE SHOW A REFLECTION OF YOU AS A DESIGNER?

It is. I tried to look good but it's so hard because when I'm designing, I'm wearing old grandpa sweaters that cost about three dollars at Goodwill and leggings and maybe some Uggs because they're comfortable and no one is going to see me, but when I'm out mingling with people or going to galas or events or meeting people for consultations I dress up. But designing dressed up is hard. You want to be comfortable and worry about what you're designing, not about breaking an ankle in the studio. But it's TV and I try to keep the image I portray very true to who I am as a designer.

A LOT OF TIMES DURING SEASON 8 YOU WOULD STYLE YOUR MODELS VERY SIMILAR TO HOW YOU STYLE YOURSELF.

Yes, because I am my own client. I had a mentorship with Zac Posen my senior year and the first thing he said to me when I came in with my portfolio that had all my inspiration, was, "Did you make what you're wearing?" I said no, and he said, "Well it looks like your style, so that's why I'm asking. You should always make what you're wearing or have a really true reflection of what you design because that's very important in fashion. People are always going to ask, 'Is that yours?'"

CAN YOU TELL ME SOME OF YOUR FAVORITE MOMENTS FROM BEING ON THE SHOW?

I think watching the montage of me cussing was rather funny to watch. It's a little embarrassing too but that's who I am. Then also seeing me evolve was great. I was in the bottom the first challenge and it was devastating. Then to make it to the top five in Season 8 and going into *All Stars*, I felt like I had made a place for myself and I was one of the designers that stood apart from the rest. That was really important to me.

DO YOU LIKE THE UNCONVENTIONAL MATERIALS CHALLENGES OR DO YOU LIKE THE MORE REALISTIC CHALLENGES?

I like the challenges that are unconventional because they spark creativity. You have to be creative to take materials that are not fabric and turn them into something that is avant-garde and fashion forward.

WHAT DO YOU LOOK FOR IN A MODEL?

I like my models to look kind of vampirish, but also really ethereal. White hair—kind of like me but even more pale. I liked Rose, who was Christopher Collins' model. I love Lara Stone. I wish she could be my model.

IS IT HARD TO FIND INSPIRATION WHEN YOU'RE CUT OFF FROM THE WORLD?

It's very hard, but when I was on the show I would get inspiration from my nightmares. I get inspiration from things that are weird and distorted and eerie because I have a curiosity for those things. That worked for me throughout the competition.

IVY HIGA

YOU CAME TO *PROJECT RUNWAY* HAVING ALREADY SHOWED AT FASHION WEEK. DID YOU FEEL THAT GAVE YOU AN ADVANTAGE?

Not at all. We all have our idiosyncrasies and experiences, good and bad, which could've been an advantage one way or another on the show. Having shown during NYFW made no difference in the competition.

WHO ARE SOME OF YOUR FAVORITE DESIGNERS?

I have so many favorites; it's too difficult to have only a handful. But, here are a few I love: Stella McCartney, Consuelo Castiglioni, Donna Karan, Calvin Klein, Vivienne Westwood, Junya Watanabe, Alexander Wang, Jil Sander. The list could go on and on.

WHAT WAS YOUR *PROJECT RUNWAY* AUDITION LIKE?

My audition was very nerve-wracking. I remember showing my collection to Tim, Irina, and Zanna Roberts Rassi, and feeling incredibly nervous. You just never know whether you have what they're looking for. It was so refreshing, and a huge relief to know they responded well to my pieces.

HAD YOU EVER AUDITIONED BEFORE?

Yes, this was my second audition. I remember almost getting in the first time, and being incredibly disappointed. I truly believe that if you want something bad enough in life, and work hard, it happens. Sometimes not exactly the way you want or expected. Be careful what you ask for—you just might get it.

WHO DID YOU BOND WITH MOST ON THE SHOW?

I bonded most with Valerie Mayen. She's a sweetheart. She came up to me at one point and said, "You're my new best friend." I thought, "What? Are we in kindergarten?" But we really bonded and laughed a lot together.

WHAT WAS YOUR FAVORITE AND LEAST FAVORITE CHALLENGE?

My absolute favorite was the Philip Treacy challenge. How amazing is it to be in the presence of such an amazing

artist? I just admire him very much. You can truly see his love and passion in his work. To have the opportunity to create a look inspired by one of his amazing pieces was truly the best experience of the show for me. What an honor.

My least favorite challenge was the resort wear challenge. Having another contestant make your design meant compromising your design based on their abilities, or lack thereof. If the show was based solely on design then that would've been the challenge I should've been sent home.

WHO DID YOU THINK WAS YOUR TOUGHEST COMPETITION?

Honestly, I always believe your toughest competition is yourself. You're your best and worst critic. The importance was staying centered and trying to do well, regardless of any outside factors.

DID YOU HAVE A FAVORITE GARMENT YOU MADE FOR THE SHOW?

My favorite was the Jackie O look. I really loved how clean, fresh, and modern it looked. It was definitely chic and classic.

WHY DO YOU THINK YOU GOT SO SICK ON THE SHOW?

I think the temperature that day we were filming was 103 degrees. I didn't drink enough water that day and got dehydrated. They have to turn the A/C off as it interferes with the mics, so it was very hot. I was running on a lot of caffeine, which also wasn't helpful. It made me learn that taking care of your health is always the most important.

HOW LONG WERE YOU AT THE HOSPITAL? DID YOU MISS ANY WORK BECAUSE OF IT?

I remember not even wanting to go to the hospital because I'd miss work, or the challenge, and would be forced home by default. Fortunately I was only there overnight. The producers were nice enough to offer to give me extra time to work for the missed time, but I declined. I didn't want any special treatment as it was my fault I wasn't responsible

enough in taking care of my health.

WHY DID YOU HAVE SUCH A PROBLEM WITH MICHAEL COSTELLO?

Some people acted differently when cameras were on and off. I don't like two-faced, inauthentic people. Michael antagonized most of us on the show, and what you saw was the result of that on my behalf. People thought I bullied Michael and turned others against him. That's absurd.

Michael and I have discussed this several times and I've apologized for how I approached the situation, but I am not sorry for what I said. I have no tolerance for someone who continues to play the victim when they were the cause.

DO YOU FEEL YOU WERE PORTRAYED FAIRLY ON THE SHOW?

Fair is a matter of perspective. I'm headstrong, opinionated, matter of fact, and have very high standards. I believe that was portrayed fairly. Where it appears that I'm picking on others, that was untrue. I try to be respectful of others, but also speak up when disrespected or lied to. Perhaps my execution and delivery may be coarse, but my intentions are always good.

GRETCHEN WAS CALLED OUT FOR TAKING OVER THE GROUP CHALLENGE YOU PARTICIPATED IN. WHAT'S YOUR TAKE ON THAT SITUATION?

I agree with parts of what Tim said, however didn't agree with how he handled the situation. Gretchen definitely has a strong personality, but to imply she bullied and manipulated everyone was unjust. We all had a choice to partake and input ideas.

WHAT WAS IT LIKE WORKING WITH MICHAEL DRUMMOND ON THE RESORT WEAR CHALLENGE?

Challenging. Michael Drummond and I have very different ways of executing things. When you're working with time constraints, and not knowing the other person's abilities, you can't help but micro-manage. It's like asking someone to babysit your child, without knowing much about the babysitter.

HAVE YOU KEPT IN TOUCH WITH ANYONE FROM THE SHOW?

Yes, a lot actually. Casanova, Christopher, Mondo, and believe it or not, Michael Drummond, more frequently than others. I also keep in touch with Andy, Valerie, April, Peach, and AJ from time to time.

HOW HAS *PROJECT RUNWAY* CHANGED YOUR LIFE?

It changed my life by connecting me with such amazing people. Realizing that we're all going through some kind of struggle to fight for a love called fashion was, and is,

amazing. It was refreshing meeting so many talented people with so many commonalities. It makes you aware that you're not the only one going through challenges to follow your dream. I appreciate that very much.

WHAT WOULD PEOPLE BE SURPRISED TO KNOW ABOUT *PROJECT RUNWAY*?

We actually have less time than is portrayed on the show to create something. As a viewer, I always thought the designers had additional time to give direction and inspiration for hair, makeup, and styling. That's farce. All of those aspects have to be done inclusive of the time that's allotted to us. So imagine having to come up with a creative concept for the challenge, and having it executed well, while trying to figure out the right accessories (if what you have in mind hasn't already been taken by another contestant), and figuring out hair and makeup that goes with your look all in a matter of hours. It's pretty insane.

WHAT HAVE YOU BEEN DOING SINCE *PROJECT RUNWAY?*

I've been fortunate enough to have been commissioned to design and create a dress for Lifetime's President, Nancy Dubuc, for the Primetime Emmys, and a private client for a Philippines political wedding. I had taken a break from my label to build capital, and had opportunities to work at Zac Posen, Diane von Furstenberg, and Theory. I dressed Olivia Munn for an MTV appearance. I'm debuting a capsule collection, Chic & Sheer by Ivy h. Proceeds from every purchase will be going towards an organization I've been honored to be a part of, Nomi Network, a leading nonprofit organization that bridges the private, public, and nonprofit sectors through enterprise and education to end human trafficking. It's important to me to try and help rebuild hope in women. I am grateful to help with such an amazing cause.

CASANOVA

WHAT WAS IT LIKE COMING TO NEW YORK FROM PUERTO RICO?

It was the experience of my life because for about three years I'd been thinking about moving to New York or Miami. It was scary; I was so comfortable in my country. I had my own huge couturier, my employees, my dream apartment, dream car, and just to quit and start over at thirty is kind of crazy. I had nobody here, no family, no friends. I had no job opportunities, but I just did it. I never spoke in English in Puerto Rico so I was in English classes for three months. I thought I'd probably have to work in a grocery store or in retail. I gave myself a timetable of three or four years to make contacts with stores, models, photographers, everything. I got everything and beyond in less than five months. Everyone knows me from the show, and everything becomes so easy. I know it's not everyone's story. I've been so lucky, so blessed. The show divided my life in two—there was before the show and after the show.

WAS THE SHOW WHAT YOU EXPECTED?

During filming the show I would say that it's not what I was expecting, that I would never do that again, probably I would say that I regret it. But after the show, I would do it over again a hundred times.

WAS IT HELPFUL FOR YOU TO HAVE NINA THERE BECAUSE IF YOU NEEDED TO SPEAK SPANISH YOU ALWAYS COULD?

No. When I brought the contract to my lawyer, she made it clear that one of the bullets of the contracts is that you must speak in English because the show is designed for an English-speaking audience. I accepted the challenge to do everything in English so even when I saw Nina after the show I told her everything will be in English. I'm good with my English.

DID YOU GO IN THINKING I'M GOING TO USE THIS AS A PLATFORM TO PROPEL MY CAREER?

Probably, but when I did decide to do the casting, I was

sure they would never pick me because I could not handle an interview in English, but I would try because I have nothing to lose. Another shock was the fashion sense. I've been on a Caribbean island for thirty-three years, ten years designing for that market, so when I came to New York, it was a shock. This is very cosmopolitan city with people from everywhere around the world. I was so traditional,

and then I lost my virginity in New York, talking about fashion! So many shocks, but everything was so cool.

DID YOU HAVE A FAVORITE GUEST JUDGE?

Georgina Chapman. First of all, I just get melted by her beauty. I believe she was expecting a baby and she was impeccable. I like also the crazy designer Betsey Johnson, but the rest of the designers I had no idea.

DID YOU KNOW MICHAEL KORS WHEN YOU GOT ON THE SHOW?

I knew Michael Kors. Once they called to say that I got on the show, I just went to YouTube, trying to see as much as I could two weeks before. I had never seen the show. That's why I picked my pants.

YES, WHY WOULD YOU GIVE UP THOSE EXPENSIVE PANTS?!

We are on TV, you have to look fabulous. I expected some producer would say, "Don't worry, we're going to replace your pants." I was totally lost, I had no idea. I'd been like a ball in a pinball machine like going from here to there until the point that I just got eliminated, and then I just take a deep breath, like I'm not bouncing wall to wall anymore.

IT WAS SO HARD TO WATCH THEM CUT UP THOSE PANTS.

Oh yeah, and I was worried—what about if I go home right now and I go without my pants? Every one of the other designers had an idea of what was going on and probably after the third challenge some of them gave me a hint.

DID YOU HAVE A FAVORITE GARMENT THAT YOU MADE ON THE SHOW?

The lace blouse. I didn't make it again because when I looked for that kind of lace it's sold out, even at Mood.

WHEN YOU WERE ELIMINATED, DID YOU FEEL IT COMING?

Since the beginning I was so nervous. The show is like musical chairs, it's not about you it's about when the music stops and you are not sitting—you go home. I remember I would mention that to Gretchen a lot. I was so close to Gretchen during the show. I was expecting to go home any moment. The only time that I was relaxed was after the team challenge when I had immunity, I just took a break.

DO YOU KEEP IN TOUCH WITH ANYONE FROM THE SHOW?

Andy—he's in Hawaii and we talk on the phone almost daily. Ivy, she lives in New York so it's easy for me. We used to hang out at least once a month and go to restaurants. She has a lot more experience being in New York than me so sometimes I need her advice. I keep in touch with Michael Drummond, too.

WHAT HAS YOUR LIFE BEEN LIKE SINCE THE SHOW?

Totally busy. I did not stop working. This is what you dream about.

PEACH CARR

WHAT WAS YOUR AUDITION FOR THE SHOW LIKE?

My audition for *Project Runway* was such a surreal experience; I will never forget it. I was nervous when I arrived with my daughter Molly and my husband Wayne. I didn't think I could do this alone, right? The nerves continued to build until I walked into the audition room and was greeted so warmly by Tim Gunn and Zanna Roberts Rassi. I didn't notice the other people in the room, including the cameraman. I must have done a fairly decent tap dance, defending my garments and dodging the rocks the judges threw in my direction. At one point, Tim asked for my Look Book. That's when he and Zanna, upon seeing the two tennis looks, told me that tennis was my niche and gave me the invaluable advice to go home and start a tennis line along the vein of those two looks. My nerves melted into calm at that moment. Tim told me that I would be moving on to the next round, and asked me to leave out the door from which I came. So, I headed straight into the closet. At that moment, laughter erupted and I was aware of the cameraman and the others in the room. I imagine that it was the first time someone came out of the closet during an interview.

HAD YOU EVER AUDITIONED FOR THE SHOW BEFORE?

I had auditioned the year before, and Tim Gunn, Korto Momolu, and Zoe Glassner were my judges. Yikes, was I intimidated! I was blown away by Tim's warmth and Korto's beauty. Really, you have to see her in person—gorgeous! I was immensely intimidated, to say the least. At the end of the audition, Tim made me promise to apply again if I wasn't selected. I wasn't ready to be on Season 7 and Tim knew it. So did I.

WHO DID YOU BOND WITH MOST?

We had such a batch of dynamic and warm designers on Season 8 and I became close to so many. I immediately bonded with April and Mondo. I love them both dearly. Mondo and I met during the first few seconds of the show, and I said to him, "You are real and I know it," and we have been close ever since. He is the one who gave me the nickname "Fairy Dragmother" because I took care of the boys . . . and did their nails. In February I was in Denver hosting an AIDS benefit with Mondo; I have a very strong connection with the LGBT community, who have been so supportive of me.

The first night in our apartment April and I discovered that I was married on her second birthday, and that we are the same person separated by twenty-nine pesky little years. She is honest, loyal, very talented, and wicked-funny! April and I were in Paris together for Fashion Week and I recently attended her fabulous wedding. She calls me "GangstaFace" and it cracks me up every time. I am so blessed to have April and Mondo as my dear friends.

TELL ME ABOUT YOUR FAVORITE AND LEAST FAVORITE CHALLENGES.

My least favorite challenge of Season 8 was (for obvious reasons) the bridesmaid episode. What a disaster! I tried to send that poor beautiful girl a Peach Carr Designs dress but she hasn't responded. Scarred for life, I imagine.

My favorite challenge was the Party Glitters throw down. It was exciting to see what treasures everyone dragged out of that shop. The workroom looked like a cross between Bourbon Street the morning after Mardi Gras and the bottom of a hamster cage. It was a fun runway because the non-fabric materials made crazy noises as the models walked down the runway. That was also the challenge in which April and I were finished with our designs early and helped Andy, who won instead of going home for having a very unfinished garment. Other designers were upset about the assist and even called it cheating but I stand by my decision.

WHO DID YOU THINK WAS YOUR TOUGHEST COMPETITION?

I felt that my toughest competitors were April, Mondo, and Andy, who, after the second challenge, I saw making it to the finale. I was close!

DID YOU HAVE A FAVORITE GUEST JUDGE?

I was excited to see Betsey Johnson as a guest judge; she is a little bundle of talent and positive energy. However, I was safe for that challenge and didn't get a chance to speak to her until we chatted at the finale. The sight of Philip Treacy was a moment I will never forget, and when I saw that we would be designing for his hats, my knees buckled. I am in awe of his immense talent and grace. I was excited about the challenge but just was afraid I would blaspheme his art with a poor design. My *favorite* guest judge, however, is Joanna Coles, hands down. It was the second episode, in which I made what we call the "Barbie Sofa Dress." Joanna thought it looked like an animal was crawling down the back of the sofa, and by the time my critique was over, I was calling it the "Dead Raccoon Dress." Joanna gave me the most valuable advice concerning my designs; advice which, to this day, rolls around in my mind as I design: stay youthful, fashion forward, tasteful—and please lower my necklines! Thank you, Joanna.

HOW HAS *PROJECT RUNWAY* CHANGED YOUR LIFE?

I was a fifty-year-old, self-taught children's wear designer who wasn't confident enough to dip my toe into women's wear. Now I have my own label, Peach Carr Designs: tennis wear which transforms into day wear with a shoe change. I went from questioning every design decision I made to trusting my instincts. I have had the privilege of meeting so many wonderful people who are also hoping for a second chance to live their dream.

I saw the Jean Paul Gaultier fashion show in Paris during Fashion Week. Who gets to do that? I cried upon entering his building, and was overwhelmed when he started his show with gorgeous plus-sized models, sending a message to the industry about size and beauty.

Every reporter has included my daughter, Molly, in the interviews, which, as a future journalism major, has been fun for her. She is always asked to recount how she downloaded the application, forcing me to audition. This whole chapter in my life has been a wonderful experience for Molly as well. How many teenagers get to meet the cast of *Glee* at an LA party? My husband Wayne has always been my backbone and this all has made me even more aware of how fortunate I am to have had such an amazing man beside be for the last twenty-three years.

I am a new person because of the experience: confident and happy, I no longer flinch when someone uses the words talent and Peach in the same sentence. Doors have been opened and new opportunities are around every corner, and I could not be more grateful.

WHICH JUDGE DID YOU FEEL GAVE YOU THE BEST ADVICE?

My time in front of the judges is such a blur. I believe they all gave me great advice. It was this bundle of advice which helped me find my voice as a designer. Michael Kors was the one who kept stressing the importance of taste, and his words are emblazoned in my brain. He encouraged me to push myself out of my comfort zone. Michael wanted me to take tasteful risks, which I did with the group challenge; the result was the military/lace dress. I almost won with that one.

DID YOU FEEL ANY ONE JUDGE WAS PARTICULARLY IN YOUR CORNER?

If I were going to say that one particular judge had my back, I would say Michael Kors. When I made the "Barbie Sofa" dress Michael stressed that not only was it the third garment I had made that day, it was well sewn in an hour and a half. He made it a point to vocalize that my garments were well made and well finished. Heck, I matched up the polka dots on that thing. Besides, I found his barbs amusing and not the least offensive.

DO YOU HAVE A FAVORITE GARMENT YOU MADE FOR THE SHOW?

My favorite garment would have to be the dress I made for the Team Military/Lace challenge. I was thrilled with the finished product. We had a few shortages with fabric. April saved my bacon by giving me the remnants of her lace, which I used for the top of the dress. She also gave me the belt template so that the cohesion of the collection was strong. April and Mondo were such leaders during that challenge. Nina Garcia loved my dress, as did Michael and Heidi, which was a high point for me.

DO YOU THINK CASANOVA'S ENGLISH WAS BETTER THAN HE LET ON?

Casanova had interesting language issues. It was very clear to me that he did not understand the details of the first challenge; no way would he have willingly sacrificed his Dolce & Gabbana pants. I think that when he was worked up Casanova could only think in Spanish. One day I came into the workroom in a skirt with attached leggings. Casanova said, "Peach your butt looks hilarious" Everyone roared and Michael Drummond told him that his comment was rude. Puzzled, Casanova said that people were telling him he was hilarious and he was sure hilarious meant fabulous. When told the true meaning of the word, Casanova blushed and apologized through a devilish grin. From then on, AJ and I started a section of his sketchbook for "Casanova's English Lessons."

WHAT WAS THE PHOTO SHOOT FOR THE BILLBOARD CHALLENGE LIKE?

The photo shoot for the billboard challenge was a complete nightmare for me. First I had this beautiful model in a Barbie sofa dress with a dead raccoon crawling down the back. Add to this a famous fashion photographer shooting my tragedy and Zanna Roberts Rassi coaching the shoot. Then my model, Ify, told the photographer that no one tells her how to pose. I was mortified. I knew I would be on the chopping block for the "Dead Raccoon-Barbie Sofa Dress," and feared I would be sent packing. Zanna was quite gracious about the whole disaster, assisting me in selecting the most acceptable of the photos with a straight face. That's when I started using the rosary beads on my wrist. I prayed that if I was sent home that I would leave with grace.

WHAT HAVE YOU BEEN DOING SINCE *PROJECT RUNWAY*?

I have shown three collections for my label, Peach Carr Designs. I am producing a line of fashion-forward sportswear which takes a woman from the tennis courts to lunch to cocktails. I have shown my collections on numerous runways all over the country; the latest was in Rhode Island at StyleWeek Providence, where I showed with Jonathan Peters and Ben Chmura from Season 7. I have an online shop and am represented in various stores in the U.S. I also have had the pleasure of mentoring a lovely thirteen-year-old future fashion designer, Caroline. This has been such a joy for me, and I hope to do more of this.

So much of my time is spent traveling all over the United States speaking, hosting, and showing my line in conjunction with a wide array of events and charity functions. Upon arriving back in Chicago after filming, I created a "Good China" T-shirt, which raised funds for amfAR and we recently held an event benefiting the Lynn Sage Breast Cancer Foundation in honor of a friend of mine. We sold scarves and skirts made from a fabric I designed for the event.

I cannot thank the Weinsteins enough for giving me, at fifty years old, the true opportunity of a lifetime, no pun intended. My life has been enriched in an unimaginable way. I always say that life begins when you say, "Now." This is my "Now." For this I will be forever grateful.

THE DESIGNERS

DAVID CHUM
FROM: MERONG, BATTAAN,
PHILLIPPINES
SELF-TAUGHT

GUNNAR DEATHERAGE
FROM: LA GRANGE, KY
SELF-TAUGHT

AMANDA PERNA
FROM: FT. LAUDERDALE, FL
STUDIED: UNIVERSITY OF
ALABAMA

SERENA DA CONCEICAO
FROM: KINGSTON, NY
STUDIED: FASHION
INSTITUTE OF DESIGN AND
MERCHANDISING

RAFAEL COX
FROM: ALAMOGORDO, NM
STUDIED: AMERICAN
INTERCONTINTAL UNIVERSITY

FALLENE WELLS
FROM: LAS VEGAS, NV
SELF-TAUGHT

JULIE TIERNEY
FROM: BATON ROUGE, LA
MT. HOOD COMMUNITY
COLLEGE, SAVANNAH
COLLEGE OF ART AND DESIGN

CECILIA MOTWANI
FROM: CORDOBA, ARGENTINA
SELF-TAUGHT

DANIELLE EVERINE
MINNEAPOLIS, MN
INTIMATES DESIGNER FOR
TARGET CORP.

JOSHUA CHRISTENSEN
FROM: SNOHOMISH, WA
STUDIED: FASHION INSTITUTE
OF DESIGN & MERCHANDISING

BECKY ROSS
FROM: CALUMET, MI
STUDIED INTERIOR DESIGN
AND SET DESIGN

BRYCE BLACK
FROM: TWIN FALLS, ID
STUDIED: THE ART INSTITUTE
OF PORTLAND

OLIVIER GREEN
FROM: NEW YORK, NY
STUDIED IN LONDON AND
MILAN

ANTHONY RYAN AULD
FROM: LINDEN, TX
STUDIED: LOUISIANA STATE
UNIVERSITY

BERT KEETER
FROM: WASHINGTON, D.C.
STUDIED: PARSONS THE NEW
SCHOOL FOR DESIGN

LAURA KATHLEEN
FROM: ST. LOUIS, MO
STUDIED: WESTERN KENTUCKY
UNIVERSITY, ACCADEMIA ITALIANA

KIMBERLY GOLDSON
FROM: BROOKLYN, NY
SELF-TAUGHT

VIKTOR LUNA
FROM: GUADALAJARA, MEXICO
STUDIED: FASHION INSTITUTE
OF TECHNOLOGY

JOSHUA MCKINLEY
FROM: CLEVELAND, OH
STUDIED: FASHION INSTITUTE
OF TECHNOLOGY, POLIMODA
INSTITUTE OF FASHION
DESIGN AND MARKETING

ANYA AYOUNG-CHEE
FROM: PORT OF SPAIN, TRINIDAD
AND TOBAGO
STUDIED: PARSONS THE NEW
SCHOOL FOR DESIGN, CENTRAL
SAINT MARTINS COLLEGE OF ART
AND DESIGN

SEASON 9

HIGHLIGHTS

LAST ROUND OF AUDITIONS

Twenty designers arrived for the ninth season of *Project Runway*. They were vying for sixteen spots on the show. Each designer had to present their garments to Heidi, Michael, Nina, and Tim, who made the final cuts.

JONATHAN MURRAY:

"We ended up having a big discussion over Anya—whether she could sew or not. Heidi really stuck up for her, and so Heidi was on the line. That played out through the season, and ultimately Michael and Nina admitted Anya could sew. Our feeling was she was very talented, but she was very new to fashion and sewing. It was going to be interesting because the question was could that eye of hers, that ability, that amazing personality, and beautiful face, all somehow persuade the judges to keep her around long enough for her to prove herself?"

PET STORE CHALLENGE

The designers met Tim at Petland Discounts to gather materials for the My Pet Project challenge. The designers had to create a look from items they bought at the store. Although the judges loved Anthony Ryan's dress made out of birdseed, they gave the win to Olivier, who made a top out of a dog bed and a skirt from pine wood shavings from hamster and rabbit bedding with a belt he made out of the piping from a fish tank.

THE SHEEPDOGS

The designers had to create a look for the band The Sheepdogs. The winning look would be featured in *Marie Claire*, *Rolling Stone*, and at a *Rolling Stone* live event. Instead of a runway show the band wore the designers' looks to perform on the show.

INITIALS CARVED ON A TREE

Joshua McKinley made a skirt and painted it to look like wood. He honored his beloved mother, whom he had recently lost to ovarian cancer, by drawing his and her initials with a heart on the skirt, as if they were carved into a tree.

STILTS

Heidi came out on stilts to announce to the designers their next challenge would be to create a look for stilt walkers. In a *Project Runway* first the runway show was outdoors in front of a live audience as well as the press.

SARA REA:

"The main challenge with the outdoor runway was that we were in New York in June—rainy season. It rained off and on during our prep day and it rained the morning of the show. We were standing by watching the rain and hoping for a quick break. When it finally did stop raining, which we knew was temporary, I called on walkie for everyone to get going and let's shoot this while we can. Everyone moved into position and we started the runway show. We were able to get the show done and keep everyone dry—mostly."

HEIDI KLUM:

"I really wanted to do something on stilts. Did it turn out the way I had it in my head? Not really, because I thought that the clothes could have looked more like real clothes and not so much like a Mardi Gras parade. I always fought for us getting out of Parsons. I always wanted to bring it outside, where fans could stop by and watch how it happens. I would've also done the judging there, so people can see how that process goes, but they didn't go for that, so we did just the fashion show outside."

HIGHLIGHTS

CECILIA WITHDRAWS; JOSH C. RETURNS

Cecilia and Julie were the bottom two designers for the All About Nina challenge. Cecilia was upset when Julie was eliminated; she said she wouldn't have minded going home. Soon after she spoke to Tim and Heidi saying that she was unhappy being on the show. Not wanting to take someone else's opportunity, she made the decision to leave. At that point the designers were in teams of three to start the Off the Track challenge. Without Cecilia, Viktor and Olivier were short a team member. They were given the opportunity to choose an eliminated designer to come back. They chose Joshua Christensen.

CECILIA MOTWANI:

"I had a hard time being there. I guess I can't create under pressure as I thought. It's really hard given the parameters they give you; the time frame, the challenge itself. I didn't feel happy about what I was doing. I saw the drive the other people had. It was a self-discovery process. Interacting with other designers who are so talented was a little overwhelming. It just made you think about yourself. It was really a very personal decision to leave."

JOSHUA CHRISTENSEN:

"It was the most exciting, crazy moment because I never thought it would be possible at that point in the contest. To know that my friends on the show had voted me back was pretty incredible. I was ecstatic!"

JOSHUA MCKINLEY ROUND ONE: BECKY

Joshua M., Anya, and Becky worked as a team for the challenge in which they had to create three looks for Heidi's New Balance line. Joshua and Becky clashed; he told her not to design, just to sew, and that she made dowdy dresses. Becky went into the bathroom and cried, but Joshua followed her in. He later apologized to Becky and stood up for her on the runway.

JONATHAN MURRAY:

"It was great when they went into the restroom. We were yelling to follow them in, to get the camera in there! We were so excited in the control room. We're in that workroom a lot, anytime the drama explodes into some other location is always fun for us."

LAURA AND NINA

During the Sew '70s challenge Tim warned Laura that Nina thought her taste level was iffy.

LAURA KATHLEEN:

"I feel that Tim was right that Nina was questioning my taste but I had already said something to Anya about it. Anya thought I was paranoid and then she heard Tim and finally said my suspicions were correct! I think I have taste but I appreciate Nina's critiques."

FABRIC LICKING

While shopping at Mood Joshua McKinley licked some fabric.

JOSHUA MCKINKLEY:

"I was trying to see if it was fusible. It was shiny, but I wanted to see if it would become tacky."

HIGHLIGHTS

JOSHUA MCKINLEY ROUND TWO: BERT

Joshua M. and Bert were on the same team for the challenge in which they had to design their own fabric. Joshua took issue with something Bert said (not to him), and started bickering with him. He continued to argue with Bert, while the rest of the team appeared frustrated. Joshua apologized to everyone, and explained that he was missing his mom.

JONATHAN MURRAY:

"I think as adults—and most of us who watch the show are probably older than the younger designers—we're fairly forgiving, and we believe when you're talented you have the right to be a little eccentric. We know they're under a lot of pressure. Most of them are in their twenties and they're figuring it out. If they're in their forties or fifties it becomes something different. Though he is young, Joshua has had a hard life. He had recently lost his mother. He usually apologized. He tried to make it better, but sometimes he couldn't help himself. As a producer, for audiences you want that kind of person who is unfiltered and says whatever they're feeling."

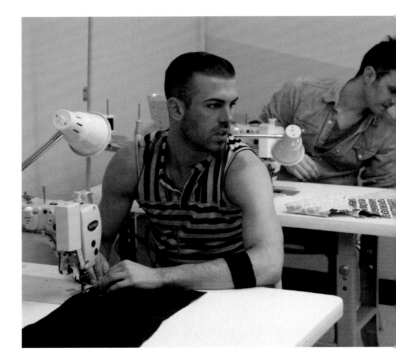

NINA THE CLIENT

The designers were given the task of designing an outfit for Nina Garcia. The winning look would be featured in a *Marie Claire* ad, and would also be on a New York City taxicab.

NINA GARCIA:

"Is it okay to say the Nina challenge is my favorite? It's always fun to have someone specially design something for you."

KIMBERLY GOLDSON:

"Winning the Nina challenge in my eyes was the biggest prize of the entire season aside from taking the title. Nina is tough when it comes to fashion. That's apparent. So, I was a bit intimidated when she asked me to change up my design but flattered because she specifically asked for my pants, which she loved! So at that point, I just decided to do what I do best and let it be. Going to her office and seeing her in it was the best and the taxi just took it over the top. It was a great moment, one that I'll never forget."

OLIVIER AND BOOBS

The designers had to design for real women for the challenge What Women Want. Olivier was unhappy to learn that his client had big boobs. He said that he didn't like women having boobs; it destroys the whole line of his looks. He asked Tim what "Double D" meant. Tim told him he had no personal experience with boobs, so Olivier went to the female cashier at Mood for help.

MICHAEL KORS:

"The challenges when the designers have to design for real women and not their usual models are interesting because it lets you see whether or not they will be commercially successful. I don't think you're going to have a lot of twenty-year-old customers who wear a size 2 and are 5'10". When I see them able to deal with someone who's curvier, more petite, or older and they do it well, it tells me that they're going to be able to deal with the real world."

ALL FOUR DESIGNERS ADVANCE TO THE FINALE

Joshua McKinley, Viktor, Kimberly, and Anya were all asked to make collections for the finale. However, only three would be selected to go on. The first designer Heidi said was in was Joshua. Then Viktor. It came down to Kimberly and Anya. Kimberly was told she was in. Anya remained on the runway by herself. Heidi finally told her she was also in. Anya was surprised and relieved that the judges were allowing all of them to advance.

MICHAEL KORS:

"Anya was a mystery to us at first. Knowing she had only been sewing for four months, at first Tim and I both thought that she couldn't have sewn her own clothes. Nina thought it seemed unlikely, and Heidi felt, well why not? I looked at the polish of the clothes and thought to myself, it's truly impossible. Heidi was really Anya's champion. She thought Nina, Tim, and I were just being negative. But I certainly liked what I saw. I liked Anya's point of view, I liked the vibe of her designs, and I thought she was bright so let's give her a shot and if she's disastrous she's going to sink quickly. Then when the show started I realized that she is one of those people who are truly great under pressure. A lot of fashion people are that way. A lot of designers literally wait until the night before their show and they're up all night. I'm not at all one of those designers; I'm very methodical and organized. Anya, I quickly realized, is a quick learner and a problem solver. But when I first saw the clothes I said come on, I don't believe you."

COME AS YOU ARE (BERT)

MY PET PROJECT (OLIVIER)

GO BIG OR GO HOME (LAURA)

ALL ABOUT NINA (KIMBERLY)

OFF THE TRACK (VIKTOR AND JOSHUA M.)

CAN'T WE JUST ALL GET ALONG? (ANYA)   WHAT WOMEN WANT (JOSHUA M.)

SEW '70S (ANYA)

THIS IS FOR THE BIRDS (ANYA)

FINALE (ANYA)

MODELS

KENZIE GALLO

ASHLEY LACAMP

TATJANA SINKEVICA

THAIS MAGALHAES

MICHEL ANN LIENHARD-O'MALLEY

KARIN AGSTAM

ALYSSA PASEK

HANNAH GOTTESMAN

CARLA BARRUCCI

CHELSEA BLACKBURN

KERSTIN LECHNER

MEGHAN GIFFIN

BOJANA DRASKOVIC

ERIKA KIMBERLY JONES

SONIA NIEKRASZ

SVETA GLEBOVA

GUEST JUDGES

CHRISTINA RICCI
ACTRESS

STACEY BENDET
FASHION DESIGNER

KIM KARDASHIAN
FASHION ENTREPRENEUR

JOANNA COLES
EDITOR-IN-CHIEF, *MARIE CLAIRE*

KERRY WASHINGTON
ACTRESS

ERIN WASSON
MODEL/FASHION DESIGNER

KENNETH COLE
FASHION DESIGNER

ZANNA ROBERTS RASSI
SENIOR FASHION EDITOR,
MARIE CLAIRE

RACHEL ROY
FASHION DESIGNER

ROSE BYRNE
ACTRESS

MALIN AKERMAN
ACTRESS

ADAM LAMBERT
MUSICIAN

OLIVIA PALERMO
GUEST EDITOR, PIPERLIME.COM

FRANCISCO COSTA
WOMEN'S CREATIVE DIRECTOR,
CALVIN KLEIN COLLECTION

ZOE SALDANA
ACTRESS

L'WREN SCOTT
FASHION DESIGNER

KENNETH COLE:

"I wasn't really sure what to expect as a judge on *Project Runway*. I had been asked to do it years prior, but it didn't make sense at the time. I at first thought it was far more about the broadcast than the contestants, but I came to realize it was very much about the contestants. It's very interesting to be in a place where you truly got to offer advice, and at the same time you wanted to make sure you remained encouraging and supportive, because you reflect back on when you were at that stage in your career and what you wished somebody had told you. At the same time you need to be firm and have a very distinct point of view. You need to tell it the way it is.

I think *Project Runway* has been great for the industry. It's absolutely to their credit because I did not in any way believe it could be what it's turned out to be. It has become an extraordinary platform for young, aspiring, talented designers. I think it's brought the industry's attention to this invaluable resource, which is a talent pool that would have otherwise had a very hard time breaking through.

I've watched and enjoyed shows throughout the seasons. I was intrigued and inspired by the impact the show had on Mondo Guerra. The fact that it brought out not only the ability for him to reach deep down and be the designer he thought he could be, but it also got him to address the person he was. Talking for the first time about his HIV status was pretty impressive. He exposed all of himself on that show, the creative as well as the personal. The following week I rang the bell at the New York Stock Exchange with him and Liza Minnelli as we celebrated World AIDS Day."

ANYA AYOUNG-CHEE

WHAT WAS YOUR *PROJECT RUNWAY* AUDITION LIKE?

I was very nervous for my audition and arrived at the lunch break for the crew, so I had to wait extra long in an empty room. Talk about nerves! Seth Aaron was very engaged with me and I remember feeling reassured by his response to my work. I have Mondo to thank for saying, "Yes, send her to the next round." The second audition, with the real judges, was much more intense. Tim was so mortified by my lack of sewing skills! But I was again fortified by Heidi's positive response. Having such high level experts like my work was enough for me to feel great at that point. It was icing on the cake that they agreed to accept me into the final sixteen designers.

WHO DID YOU BOND WITH MOST ON THE SHOW?

I bonded most strongly with Laura Kathleen; I adore her! I also am close to Anthony Ryan and Joshua. Bert and I had a great relationship, especially toward the end of the season. Our whole cast had a great camaraderie. I think we were very blessed.

WHAT WAS YOUR FAVORITE AND LEAST FAVORITE CHALLENGE?

I loved the L'Oréal bird challenge because it pushed me to new heights in my design process. I also loved the HP/Intel challenge because it allowed me to create my own prints and use my graphic design and motion graphics skills. It was incredibly enjoyable! I seriously disliked the Sheepdogs challenge. That made me want to run away!

WHO DID YOU THINK WAS YOUR TOUGHEST COMPETITION?

I think Viktor was my major competition. He had such impeccable construction skills, he was super fast, and has a sophisticated eye.

DID YOU HAVE A FAVORITE GUEST JUDGE?

I loved having Francisco Costa as a judge. Wow! I felt so honored when he praised my piece for the L'Oréal Raven challenge. He's so incredibly talented.

DID YOU FEEL ALLEGIANCE TO A PARTICULAR MODEL, OR DID YOU LIKE TO CHOOSE YOUR MODEL DEPENDING ON THE CHALLENGE?

I loved my original model, Sveta, #1 because she was a fabulous model with the ability to transform into many different looks and #2 because she is a wonderful person and so easy to work with. She'd check on me all the time to make sure I was eating during the day!

WHICH JUDGE DID YOU FEEL GAVE YOU THE BEST ADVICE?

Michael Kors gave me great advice, especially towards the end regarding my path forward as a brand. Nina gave me crucial advice at a point when I was losing my vision: she reminded me to be myself, and stay true to my aesthetic as a designer from the Caribbean.

DID YOU FEEL THAT ANY ONE JUDGE WAS PARTICULARLY IN YOUR CORNER?

Sometimes I felt like Heidi really stood up for me but she was always very honest as well, so I didn't feel like she treated me any differently from anyone else. I think Nina supported my vision and even though she was also very honest with me, I felt a strong sense of support from her.

DID YOU HAVE A FAVORITE GARMENT YOU MADE FOR THE SHOW?

The "Raven" dress was my favorite. I'd never designed anything so modern and streamlined. I was surprised even when it walked down the runway and I realized I made it!

YOU WERE CAUGHT IN THE MIDDLE OF JOSHUA'S FIGHT WITH BECKY. WHAT WAS THAT LIKE?

I grew up the first of six kids and the only girl so I am very accustomed to being the mediator! I felt that it was my role in that moment to bring everyone back together and I am happy it actually worked, at least for a while.

THE SHEEPDOGS CHALLENGE SEEMED TO BE ESPECIALLY DIFFICULT FOR YOU. WERE YOU WORRIED YOU MIGHT BE ELIMINATED?

I was sure I was going home. I was *so* embarrassed about what I made. It was terrible! I think I got intimidated by the idea of making menswear, when really I didn't have to be so scared.

HOW DID YOU LOSE YOUR MONEY AT MOOD?

To be honest I tripped on my mic that was attached to my ankle! I fell slightly and the envelope must have fallen out of my top then.

YOURS IS TRULY THE CINDERELLA STORY. DID YOU EVER THINK THAT ANYONE WITH FOUR MONTHS OF SEWING EXPERIENCE COULD WIN *PROJECT RUNWAY*?

I never imagined I could win, and probably I wouldn't believe anyone with as little sewing experience as I had could win either! This experience has taught me so much about life and the beauty of believing in something magical, something bigger than us. This is what it took for me to win. I really believe many small miracles added up to the big magical moment of winning the whole show.

WHAT WAS WINNING LIKE?

I was so shocked that I won! I had no idea that was even possible. My mind went blank and I was frozen in time for what seemed like ages. It was surreal.

WHO HAVE BEEN SOME OF YOUR FAVORITE *PROJECT RUNWAY* DESIGNERS OVER THE YEARS?

Mondo is by far my favorite!

WHO ARE SOME OF YOUR FAVORITE DESIGNERS?

I adore Alexander McQueen, of course. Who doesn't? Love Francisco Costa, Issey Miyake, Yohji Yamamoto, Haider Ackermann, Stella McCartney, Roberto Cavalli, Mara Hoffman, Thom Browne.

WHAT WOULD PEOPLE BE SURPRISED TO LEARN ABOUT *PROJECT RUNWAY*?

It's even harder than it looks! Hard to believe but true.

JOSHUA MCKINLEY

DID YOU KNOW ANYONE FROM THE SHOW BEFORE YOU BECAME A CAST MEMBER?

Daniel Vosovic was an RA in my dorm. I was a freshman; I remember meeting him. I asked him what his plans were for the summer. He just got this big smile. I asked, "Are you doing *Project Runway?*" He said, "I can't really say." I said, "You totally are!" It was so exciting to see him on it and see how well he did. I was so new to school that I wondered how these people do patterns right out of their heads so quickly. It's amazing to watch the seasons and then to eventually join that family of people.

HAD YOU AUDITIONED FOR THE SHOW PREVIOUSLY?

I tried to get on a couple of times before. I went to open calls, but they found out I was still a student. They said they're not interested in having students on the show. I just persisted. If at first you don't succeed . . . It was definitely a dream come true to be on it.

WHAT WAS YOUR AUDITION FOR SEASON 9 LIKE?

Seth Aaron and Leanne were part of the panel. I brought menswear. They told me I should try again next year. I just looked at them and said, "Listen, three times is the charm. This is the last time you will ever see me before you're competing to get that same spot at the tents with me." I took off my shirt and said, "You have to see this stuff on." I was really just selling myself and my product. I felt it was the right time for it to happen. It was really just me putting myself extremely out there to have them give me the shot.

I brought menswear to show a complete cohesion, really. I saw what a lot of people brought, and it was just pieces that were their best work. I felt I didn't need to show them my best work; I wanted to show them something you could see potential in, development of a line. Menswear was something I was passionate about.

FOR SEASON 9 THERE WAS AN EXTRA AUDITION THAT WAS SHOWN ON THE FIRST EPISODE. DID YOU KNOW WHAT TO EXPECT?

I knew there would be twenty designers narrowed down to sixteen. When you walked in and saw the panel of Heidi Klum, Michael Kors, Nina Garcia, and Tim Gunn, you knew it was that first moment of do or die. I was so nervous. My clothing rack was shaking as I rolled it in. It was quite an amazing moment.

A NUMBER OF TIMES ON THE SHOW YOU EXPRESSED FRUSTRATION THAT ANYA WAS DOING SO WELL IN SPITE OF HER LIMITED SEWING ABILITY.

I was just stating factual information. I wasn't trying to throw anybody under the bus. She can't sew that well. She doesn't say she can. We're extremely close. People think we're enemies. From the first casting day we really hit it off. Everything I did could be put on a hanger and sold as is. It became extremely frustrating to lose to a garment that the model had to be sewn into.

YOU HAD SOME TROUBLE DURING THE SEW '70S CHALLENGE.

Those plaid pants I did were fabulous, and the fit was fine. The problem was the way I did the darts. You couldn't see it. On TV it becomes one dimensional—flat. But when Tom Ford does them they fly out of the store, and everyone wants a pair of large plaid pants. I loved that outfit down to the styling of it. I loved the leopard boots, the belt. That was just a frustrating challenge and I was vocal about it. I was honest about not knowing about the '70s in that regard.

YOU AND BECKY HAD PROBLEMS WORKING TOGETHER. YOU SEEMED TO BE VERY HARD ON HER.

It was really coming from a place of honesty. I was saying, "If you're tired, take a nap." She was making mistakes. I know how it is when I get tired. Heidi had just said we had another six hours, so I told Becky to rest. She was making silly, amateur sewing mistakes. She was using grosgrain ribbon, which has no give, and trying to make a waistband out of it. I had to cut it off and replace it. So I told her if she was tired to take a nap and I would finish. I wasn't trying to be mean or critical. I guess I was a little dramatic. I laugh at myself.

WHAT WAS IT LIKE DESIGNING FOR HEIDI'S NEW BALANCE LINE? YOU HAD TO WIN A RACE TO BECOME TEAM CAPTAIN FOR THAT CHALLENGE.

I looked at this challenge as Heidi was my boss, and I was my team's boss. Heidi came into the workroom and didn't see anything she liked. She was putting her name on whatever the winning look was. There was nothing she was basically willing to sacrifice herself for, so we were given six extra hours and worked until 4 a.m.

YOU DIDN'T ALWAYS GET ALONG WITH BERT ON THE SHOW EITHER.

I had seen how Bert treated others. He could be grumpy. There was a moment when I was extremely irritated, but Bert and I are extremely friendly.

WAS THERE ANY ONE JUDGE YOU FELT WAS PARTICULARLY IN YOUR CORNER?

Nina and I both think from an editorial standpoint. Nina is so fabulous. She really is lovely. She always went to bat for me. She'll say the negative, but finds the positive as well. She can see true talent. She was always able to give an amazing critique.

DID YOU HAVE ANY FAVORITE CHALLENGES?

I loved the Pet Store challenge. I love unconventional materials. To think on your feet like that is quite interesting and fun. I loved my avant-garde look. A lot of work went into it. It had a constructed jacket underneath, with all these pieces on top. I think clothing should have stories, and there was definitely a narrative and a story to that look. The clothes are there to speak. The touch of the tulle. Daphne Guinness could rock that look.

YOU HAVE A THEATRICAL BACKGROUND. DID THAT HELP YOU ON THE SHOW?

My theatrical background completely helped me on the show. My athletic background helped. My collection on the show was athletic based. Having acting training, you learn to express. I like to make myself laugh, so I hope other people laugh with me.

WHAT DID YOU THINK ABOUT CECILIA LEAVING THE SHOW?

That should show people this is not easy.

DO YOU FEEL LIKE YOU LEARNED A LOT FROM THE JUDGES?

I felt like I really grew as a person. Normally I would be a spitfire, but I bit my tongue and smiled. I really wish we would have had more interaction with the judges. We were shuffled in and out.

YOU WON THE WHAT WOMEN WANT CHALLENGE, WHERE MEN HAD TO CHOOSE LOOKS FOR THEIR WIVES AND GIRLFRIENDS.

I made that dress in four hours. I picked the guy because he looked so sweet; so excited to be there. The girl was cool. I met them the day the episode aired. They're a cool couple. She got to keep the dress.

WHAT WAS IT LIKE WORKING WITH HEIDI?

People always want to know if she's that beautiful in person. Of course she is. Sometimes she made me laugh. One time she was criticizing me for bedazzling. And she's sitting there in this sequined mini! I think she would be the perfect client for me.

WHAT WAS IT LIKE WORKING ON YOUR COLLECTION FOR THE FINALE?

I did my collection in two weeks. Tim came for his visit,

and I really didn't have much done. All the talk of over bedazzling had gotten to me. Then I finally realized this wasn't about them anymore. This was about me doing what I do best.

VIKTOR LUNA

WHAT WAS YOUR AUDITION FOR THE SHOW LIKE?

I was hesitant to go on the show. I didn't want to be a TV celebrity. But at the last minute I picked up my garments and decided to try out. You go there, they judge you. If they're uncertain they tell you they'll give you a call. I left pretty confident that day. I felt like they liked it.

WHAT HAPPENED NEXT?

There's a process. I came back the next day and did a video audition. They want to see your character, and how you perform on camera. After that I waited about two weeks. I was in a restaurant when they called to say congratulations. Obviously I was screaming! I had to get out of the restaurant I was so excited. You have to fill out all this paperwork. It's a giant contract.

WHAT WAS IT LIKE MAKING IT ALL THE WAY TO THE FINALE?

I was thrilled to make it to the finale. It was like a dream to me. Secretly, I always wanted to be in the spotlight.

DID YOU HAVE A GAME PLAN GOING INTO THE SHOW?

From the beginning I knew this wasn't going to be a field trip to have fun. This was for me to make a name for myself. I'm very serious about this. I haven't stopped since *Project Runway*. I've been sewing and sewing.

DID YOU HAVE A FAVORITE JUDGE?

Nina. I admire her. Her criticism was always constructive. It was very on point. She dresses impeccably. This is the woman I want to dress.

WHAT WAS IT LIKE PRESENTING YOUR DESIGNS TO MICHAEL KORS?

Michael Kors is a legend. His clothing and talent are absolutely impeccable. I was mesmerized by how funny he is.

YOU WON THE SHEEPDOGS CHALLENGE. HAD YOU DONE MENSWEAR BEFORE?

I'd done menswear for myself, but not for anyone else. Menswear is way harder to make than women's wear.

With women's wear if something is crooked you can call it asymmetrical. With menswear there is no margin for error. You have to do it straight, it has to be crisp or else it looks awful. You can be experimental, but it has to be precise. Nobody had that experience.

WHO WERE YOUR FAVORITE GUEST JUDGES?

Definitely Christina Ricci. I grew up watching her movies. I'm that Goth boy that loved her. I loved Adam Lambert. I'm a huge fan. I'm doing a jacket for him. He's so cool and inspiring. Francisco Costa is amazing. He's a genius and a visionary. Zoe Saldana was stunning. She was wearing Michael Kors. It's nice when you meet the guest judges. You see them on TV or in pictures and then you're there with them in person. It's amazing.

DO THE HAIR AND MAKEUP PEOPLE GUIDE YOU?

It's your vision, but they do give you pointers. For my final collection I wanted to give the models thick eyebrows. They started looking very Frida Kahlo. It was distracting. One of the head makeup artists told me to pull it back a bit. When he did it—gorgeous. You have to listen to them.

DID YOU LIKE THE PET STORE CHALLENGE?

It was good to be out of my comfort zone, but I was caught off guard. It was difficult. When I saw Anthony doing the birdseed dress I wondered why I didn't think of that. That was genius.

WHO WERE YOUR ROOMMATES?

I roomed with Anthony, Olivier, and Bert. We got up at 6 a.m., got ready, filmed, and then got back by 11 p.m. or midnight, usually. Anthony and me, we were the gossip girls. We would stay up late and talk and analyze. He analyzes everything. We would talk about everything; who was going to be in the top, the bottom. We were strategizing the whole system. When he was eliminated I was very shocked.

WHAT IS TIM GUNN LIKE?

He is a ray of light. As soon as he comes into a room the energy transforms to positive. He's such a great person. It's a soothing feeling when you get to meet him and talk with him. He listens to you, really pays attention. He gives you the right answer.

DID YOU HAVE A FAVORITE CONTESTANT OVER THE YEARS?

I love Christian Siriano. I identify with him. He went there with a lot of talent. Now he's a household name. I'd like to mimic his career path.

WHAT HAS YOUR FAMILY'S REACTION TO THE SHOW BEEN?

My family is very proud. You can tell in my mom's eyes. Her first trip to New York was when she came for the finale. We toured the city afterwards. She was mesmerized that fans kept coming up to her son. I came to New York with very little money, not knowing anyone, to succeed; to make something of myself. It was proof to my family I can do this. I feel like *Project Runway* gave me a huge push—now I have to do it!

KIMBERLY GOLDSON

I stumbled upon the casting notice a week before the deadline. So I made a video of myself, shot photos of my garments and sent off the lengthy application all in one day! Almost a month had passed and I had forgotten about it, so I figured they weren't interested but I figured I would call the next day. I forgot to and then they called me the day after that. I was thrilled and on my way.

HAD YOU EVER AUDITIONED BEFORE?

I auditioned for Season 6, which was right after I had begun sewing. The process then was just show up at the closest open casting call, which was Miami for me. Tim Gunn and Jillian Lewis were on the panel. They both like my aesthetic but thought I needed more experience. They were right.

WHAT WAS YOUR FAVORITE AND LEAST FAVORITE CHALLENGE?

My favorite was the Avant-garde challenge. I was in my groove during that challenge, I was able to show something that I was proud of, really fulfilled the requirements, and pushed my design boundaries.

My least favorite challenge could go without saying: the menswear challenge. I may have psyched myself out going into it, knowing that I hated to do menswear, but the truth of the matter is, I had never done menswear. It was a disaster nonetheless and I wish to never do menswear again. Thank you.

WHO DID YOU THINK WAS YOUR TOUGHEST COMPETITION?

Viktor Luna. He was truly talented, original, phenomenal at tailoring, and he was quick.

259

Whereas, I was always struggling to get my garments finished down to the wire. I mean I was always last getting out the door. Every time!

YOU HAD A ROUGH TIME DURING THE BIRD CHALLENGE. WHAT HAPPENED, AND WHAT ULTIMATELY TURNED IT AROUND FOR YOU?

The Bird challenge came very close to the end and I was spent at that point. In a nutshell, everything that could go wrong, went wrong all in one day. I sewed through my finger, my dresses were not living up to my visions, they got stained and burnt by the glue gun. I thought I was done! Then, I relied on the pep talk and hug Tim gave me, had a cry in the bathroom, and pulled myself together to create a new dress with the time I had remaining.

HOW GREAT DID IT FEEL TO HAVE THE JUDGES LOVE YOUR THREE-HOUR DRESS?

It was amazing to have the judges love the dress! And I was up against Viktor so that was the icing on the cake for me. But the true lesson learned from that episode was one I have been through all of my life: even when everything is going wrong and seems to be stacked against you, keep pushing through. Victory is on the other side!

WAS IT A SHOCK THE JUDGES CHOSE ALL FOUR OF YOU TO COMPETE IN THE FINALE?

I thought I would make the final cut. I didn't think they gave me such a bad critique on my garments; it was mainly the styling, which they didn't relate to. I wasn't shocked at all that Anya made it too. The judges' decisions no longer shocked me at that point.

DO YOU FEEL ALLEGIANCE TO A PARTICULAR MODEL, OR DO YOU LIKE TO CHOOSE YOUR MODEL DEPENDING ON THE CHALLENGE?

I was (and still am) absolutely in love with my model Bojana. I am a loyal person by nature and she was my rock when things were getting intense for me. So not only was she tall, gorgeous, and had rocking curves, she was great support. The thought of switching from her was blasphemous.

WHO HAVE BEEN SOME OF YOUR FAVORITE *PROJECT RUNWAY* DESIGNERS OVER THE YEARS?

Christian Siriano is by far my favorite! His career post *Runway* is one to be applauded and respected. I love Mychael Knight (who I have a secret crush on), Michael Costello (my new favorite) and all of the Season 9 designers (in one way or another).

HOW HAS *PROJECT RUNWAY* CHANGED YOUR LIFE?

More people know who I am and what I do. My work and presence is now requested. The doors open just a little easier now, but not much. In some ways it's harder because people are now looking out for what I'm going to do next, which adds an extra layer of pressure to an already intense career path. However, I love it all and wouldn't trade it for anything.

WHICH JUDGE DID YOU FEEL GAVE YOU THE BEST ADVICE?

Nina hands down gave me the best advice when I sat with her after winning her challenge. She simply said to stay true to the simple, tailored pieces that I do. The separates and pants are what they especially loved from me. That revolutionized who I thought I was as a designer. I came onto *Project Runway* thinking I was all about cute dresses and now I'm totally rocking a separates business! Thanks, Nina.

LAURA KATHLEEN

WHO DID YOU BOND WITH MOST ON THE SHOW?

I would have to say it's a close tie between Anya and Viktor. Both were there for me during emotional times off-camera. I really appreciate their friendship. Both are talented and genuine people. I feel like most of the designers from my season were really great. I still speak to Bert about every month.

WHAT WAS YOUR FAVORITE CHALLENGE?

My favorite challenge was probably the Rocker/'70s challenge. I loved doing menswear since it isn't an everyday thing for me. I also love the style of the '70s, so that was really fun for me.

WHO DID YOU THINK WAS YOUR TOUGHEST COMPETITION?

I always thought Viktor was my toughest competition. He knows how to tailor and has a really sharp eye for dressing a woman of luxury.

WHICH JUDGE DID YOU FEEL GAVE YOU THE BEST ADVICE?

Believe it or not, Nina. She may have been extra critical with me at times but I appreciate every point of view. She is very well respected in the fashion community and had something valuable to say about what I was doing. I was and am absolutely taking into consideration her opinions.

DID YOU FEEL THAT ANY ONE JUDGE WAS PARTICULARLY IN YOUR CORNER?

I think Heidi was in my corner. I think she appreciated that I like to make women look pretty sometimes without so much edge. I also think she recognized my work ethic, which I really appreciated.

DID YOU HAVE A FAVORITE GARMENT YOU MADE FOR THE SHOW?

I loved my avant-garde gown. I thought it fulfilled what my student wanted and was a hell of a lot of work, in a short period of time.

WHAT WAS THAT LAST ROUND OF AUDITIONS LIKE WHEN THEY NARROWED IT DOWN FROM TWENTY TO SIXTEEN?

It was probably the most nervous elimination. It's the first one so we don't know what to expect and it was four at one time! We had gone through a lot already to get there and the thought of going home before it began was horrible.

YOU WON THE STILTS CHALLENGE. WHAT WAS WORKING ON THAT LIKE?

Awesome! I love Anthony Ryan and I loved being able to dress a walking fashion illustration. That's how I looked at it and that is why I think we had a successful outcome.

WHO HAVE BEEN SOME OF YOUR FAVORITE *PROJECT RUNWAY* DESIGNERS OVER THE YEARS?

Everyone loves Christian Siriano, but I really admire him for winning and making a name for himself. In two years his business generated $1.2 million in sales. Really impressive. I'd love to sit and chat with him about business.

WHAT HAVE YOU BEEN DOING SINCE *PROJECT RUNWAY*?

I have a new jewelry line called Love Armour. I also have a nine-piece fall collection that we are selling to independent boutiques. I designed the prints and all the clothing is made in the U.S. I'm also hosting a lot of events while advertising all the new products.

BECKY ROSS

WHAT WAS YOUR *PROJECT RUNWAY* AUDITION LIKE?

When people found out I was in fashion school, they often asked when I was going to be on *Project Runway.* I always laughed and said I'd never do it. I got an e-mail from the casting department inviting me to apply. I was looking over my shoulders thinking, "Who, me?!" I took two days to think about it, decided to go for it, and the rest is history.

The initial audition in Seattle was quite surreal. I felt like I had no idea what I was doing or what they were expecting. I had to drag my collection in on this gigantic clothing rack, wearing my 5-inch heels it felt like I was hauling a bus into the room. I didn't expect so many people to be there, and they were all so quiet. I was terrified but tried not to show it. The audition lasted all of seven minutes and Seth Aaron told me I was through to the next round. I'm pretty sure I jumped up and down and clapped my hands like a six-year-old.

WHAT WAS YOUR FAVORITE AND LEAST FAVORITE CHALLENGE?

My favorite was the Pet Store challenge. I love using unusual materials and I'm an artist at heart. My least favorite was the New Balance challenge because of all the drama, and because my name got stuck on a look that was *not* a representation of me.

WHO DID YOU THINK WAS YOUR TOUGHEST COMPETITION?

My toughest competition on the show was Viktor. He can make great clothing fast, and with all the details in place.

DID YOU FEEL THAT ANY ONE JUDGE WAS PARTICULARLY IN YOUR CORNER?

Well, even though Michael Kors had some choice

was in plain view leaning up against the wall in the wool section. I have no idea who had it cut first, but a few other designers tried to make a big deal out of it. I wasn't worried about it since Anthony Ryan and I have different aesthetics.

YOU AND JOSHUA MCKINLEY CERTAINLY CLASHED DURING THE NEW BALANCE CHALLENGE. WHAT HAPPENED?

He figured out how to push my buttons and did so repeatedly. I didn't attack back because I realized that the whole country would be watching . . . and judging. Anya wasn't exactly nice to me either. When Tim Gunn mentioned that I hadn't designed any part of that collection during the workroom critique I realized I might be on the chopping block if I was only sewing and being Josh and Anya's lackey, so I asked for a piece of the pie. His team leader status was being stepped on and he went to pieces over that. Being attacked like that killed my creativity, drive, and spirit; and that cost me a higher placement in the competition.

DID YOU FORGIVE JOSHUA?

I accepted Joshua's apology at the *After the Runway* show because he was sincere when he said it. I don't know if we'll ever be friends but I wish him the best . . . therapist.

WHAT WOULD PEOPLE BE SURPRISED TO KNOW ABOUT *PROJECT RUNWAY*?

We all have to stay for six weeks no matter when we get voted off. We don't get paid to do the show. And we actually have less time than it looks like to get it all done—we have to eat lunch, no?

WHO HAVE BEEN SOME OF YOUR FAVORITE *PROJECT RUNWAY* DESIGNERS OVER THE YEARS?

My favorites over the years are: Laura Bennett, Uli Herzner, Seth Aaron, and Mondo Guerra.

HOW HAS *PROJECT RUNWAY* CHANGED YOUR LIFE?

Wow, where do I start? I get recognized almost every day

comedic comments about some of my garments, he still called me a kick-ass tailor and the queen of sewing. You'll never hear me complain about that!

DID YOU HAVE A FAVORITE GARMENT YOU MADE FOR THE SHOW?

I really have a soft spot for the Avant-garde challenge. That dress fit like a glove. I never sent anything ill-fitting down that runway the whole competition.

YOU AND ANTHONY RYAN CHOSE THE SAME FABRIC FOR THE NINA CHALLENGE. DID YOU HAVE A PROBLEM WITH THAT?

That happened totally by accident. That bolt of fabric

when I leave the house. Going to the grocery store in my PJs isn't an option, not that I ever did that before but I have to be mindful of what I look like in public now. Being on TV means complete strangers feel like they know you. It's still strange when fans introduce themselves and act all giddy and nervous. I have to be gracious about it because I felt a bit like that when I've met cast members from past seasons myself.

HAVE YOU KEPT IN TOUCH WITH ANYONE FROM THE SHOW?

I'm still in touch with Fallene, Bryce, Cecilia, and Rafael.

Those of us who've been through it need each other once in a while to commiserate.

WHAT HAVE YOU BEEN DOING SINCE *PROJECT RUNWAY*?

I graduated with my BFA in Apparel Design from The Art Institute of Portland, showed a collection at Portland Fashion Week with Wicked Quick, I've done presentations and public speaking engagements, taught classes, and now I'm working at LAIKA making teeny tiny clothes for stop-motion puppets for their feature film due out in 2014.

PART 3:

BEYOND THE RUNWAY: THE SPIN-OFFS

(2009-2010)

Models of the Runway was the first *Project Runway* spin-off. The show aired immediately after *Project Runway* during Seasons 6 and 7, and picked up where the show left off, with the designer eliminations. *Models of the Runway* focused on the *Project Runway* models and their eliminations. Kalyn Hemphill was the first season's winner, while the second season was won by Kristina Sajko. The show was hosted by Heidi Klum.

(2009)

This two-hour special featured eight former *Project Runway* designers in a head-to-head challenge to win $100,000. The special aired right before the launch of Season 6. The contestants were:

Uli Herzner (Season 3)

Mychael Knight (Season 3)

Chris March (Season 4)

Korto Momolu (Season 5)

Santino Rice (Season 2)

Jeffrey Sebelia (Season 3)

Kathleen "Sweet P" Vaughn (Season 4)

Daniel Vosovic (Season 2)

Daniel Vosovic won, with Korto Momolu in second place, Sweet P Vaughn in third place, and Chris March in fourth.

JANE CHA:

"We'd wanted to do an all-star special for a while. We didn't quite know what to expect, but I was very impressed with how many of the designers had grown and how they kept their cool under stress in ways they probably would not have done so on their own seasons. All the designers put out pretty great stuff, and Daniel Vosovic deserved to win with a really professional, impeccable, modern American sportswear collection."

BARBARA SCHNEEWEIS:

"Going into Season 6 we wanted to launch with a big bang that represented a culmination of our first five seasons."

AFTER THE RUNWAY

(2011)

After the Runway was a companion series for the end of *Project Runway*'s ninth season. Zanna Roberts Rassi hosted the talk show, and her guests were the designers featured on the episode that had just aired. The series provided viewers with an in-depth conversation with the designers about what happened on that week's episode.

JANE CHA:

"Zanna is a talented stylist and editor, and a great camera presence. And as a judge who often helps us during the casting phase, she comes to know some of the designers and has insight of her own or knows how to channel the interactions in a natural way."

NICK VERREOS:

"I had a blast being on the *After the Runway* shows with the gorgeous Zanna Roberts Rassi. I was a bit nervous because I knew that the designers were still very fresh off their season and their emotions and psyche might be fragile. I only had to remind myself of how I felt months after we finished filming and the show was airing and when we were brought back for the reunion. The

contestants were very fragile, so I realized I had to tread lightly yet honestly. Most were very kind to me, and on that note, one person stood out to me for how classy and generous she was and that was the eventual winner (I didn't know it then): Anya Ayoung-Chee. After we shot one of the *After the Runway* shows, she approached me, shook my hand, and thanked me for being so kind and then said something to the effect of, 'Thank you for being a great ambassador to *Project Runway*.' That was class."

ZANNA ROBERTS RASSI

HOW DID YOU BECOME THE HOST OF *AFTER THE RUNWAY*?

I spoke to the producers at Bunim/Murray and they said, "We're talking about doing this show. Your name keeps coming up, would you be interested?" I told them absolutely! They said it would be quite quick; if it happened I would be in LA the next week. In the next few days I actually had to go to LA for other meetings. I was at Lifetime in a meeting with Scott Sassa, who is the head of Hearst Entertainment & Syndication. I walked past producers Rob Sharenow and David Hillman, who I know. Rob came in and said, "I'm watching you on a tape next door and you just walked past my office. You're one of the three people we're looking into as the potential host for this." He turned around and said, "Well, I never get the chance to do this, but congratulations, we want you to host it!"

WHAT WAS IT LIKE SHOOTING?

It was so intense. We did four episodes in two days. It was very much filmed to time; there was not a lot of editing. It was a great challenge. It was fun being with the designers and listening to them rehash it from their side. Sometimes it got nasty, and that was genuine. I just sat back and let it go!

WHEN DID YOU SEE THE EPISODES THAT YOU WERE GOING TO BE DISCUSSING?

They were still being edited while we were filming. I got two of them before I even left, but the other two I was watching in between takes of *After the Runway*. I watched while in hair and makeup, thinking of questions and speaking with the producers. One person is putting eyelashes on me and the other one is tugging on my hair and we're trying to decide what angle we're going to take.

DID YOU HAVE FREE REIGN AS TO WHAT YOU WANT TO ASK OR WAS THERE A SCRIPT?

There were suggested questions, which keep it flowing. I've done millions of TV segments but I'd never hosted a show before. It's great to have a guideline to follow, but you have to react to the moment if someone is going somewhere really interesting.

DID YOU STYLE YOURSELF FOR THE SHOW?

I did. I have some lovely contacts in the industry who are more than willing to lend me clothes, which is really nice. The more and more television I'm doing, the more my closet has changed because I need to have so much more color. It's only so often I can do the all-black editor thing. I notice when I watch myself on TV, if you're wearing color the difference is dramatic. I usually dress quite oversized and boyfriendish, but TV is not forgiving. If I wear black and oversized I look ridiculous. You need a belt; you need tight fitting. You need low cut here but not too much; its clavicle you want, not cleavage. I did put too much fake tan on. That's one thing I'll happily admit. Joanna [Coles] told me I looked very colorful. That's a lesson learned—no more spray tan on TV.

HAVE YOU HAD ANY FAVORITE CONTESTANTS OVER THE YEARS?

Mondo is a big favorite of mine. I love his style; the way he dresses, his attitude. To me he is absolutely a superstar.

(2011)

This spin-off was similar to *Project Runway* in format. However, these designers were making accessories. Each week the designers had to make at least three pieces for the runway show. Molly Sims was the host, Eva Jeanbart-Lorenzotti was the mentor, and the judges were Kenneth Cole and Ariel Foxman. Brian Burkhardt was the winner.

EVA JEANBART-LORENZOTTI

WHAT MAKES A GOOD CONTESTANT?

There are three components that I think are really important. The first is knowledge, or know how. When you're doing accessories, it's a bit different from fashion. It's kind of like architecture. You cannot go and build that door if you don't understand how to build that door. Then there's natural ability, and then there's passion. A lot of people get confused and think passion can compensate for the other two things. Passion gets you through, and makes you do things better than other people, but if you don't have the other components it's not going to work.

IS IT BETTER TO FAIL BIG OR SUCCEED SAFELY?

I don't believe that you can succeed safely. You can get by, but unless you take a risk you're never going to get anywhere. No risk, no reward. I think you can't play it safe. When people have immunity it's an opportunity to go for it. Don't play it safe. That's completely unacceptable.

KENNETH COLE

HOW IS BEING A CAST MEMBER DIFFERENT FROM BEING A GUEST JUDGE?

When you go in and you do it once you have no context for the body of work these individuals may have created before, so it's a lot harder, I think. When you do it week after week you experience with them and you watch their various efforts. Addressing the various challenges you really get a sense of not just execution but potential. You tend to not just judge what you're looking at but what you might one day see.

YOU'VE MASTERED THE CREATIVE AND THE BUSINESS SIDE OF THE INDUSTRY. DO YOU THINK THAT'S SOMETHING THE DESIGNERS HAVE IN MIND?

I don't know that it's emphasized enough in the show, but it is something that plays an important role in the ability for someone to be successful in this business—or any business. You have to understand the business of the product that you sell, not just the aesthetic of it. It's about the ability to conceive a product and ultimately bring it to market. To impact it from conception to consumption is the creative challenge. There are not that many people that have truly trained and/or have the instinct to do that. A lot of that comes with time.

DID YOU TAKE BUSINESS CLASSES OR IS THAT SOMETHING YOU HAVE A NATURAL INSTINCT FOR?

A lot of it was intuitive for me, and I was lucky in that regard. But I've always had a plan to make a plan. My plan is always to figure it out as we go along, because unlike many industries, having a long-term plan doesn't always work for you in fashion. You need to reassess and reevaluate the circumstances almost every day, because in this global industry the circumstances and the variables seem to adjust themselves on a constant basis. In a world of social media we speak to customers differently, we service them differently, and we address their needs and their passions far differently than we ever did.

ARIEL FOXMAN

WHAT WOULD PEOPLE BE SURPRISED TO KNOW ABOUT PROJECT ACCESSORY?

While it was never really featured on the show, as judges we were able to examine each accessory up close and in detail. We did not evaluate work based simply on how it looked on a model coming down a runway.

HOW DOES YOUR JOB AS MANAGING EDITOR OF *INSTYLE* IMPACT THE CHOICES YOU MAKE AS A JUDGE?

I am always evaluating pieces as an editor, not as a designer. That means I am most concerned with not only what's fresh and new, but also what's relevant and would work in the real world for real women.

WHAT'S BEEN THE MOST ENJOYABLE ASPECT OF THE SHOW?

Watching the episodes air and being able to see all the workroom drama. While we are taping as judges, we aren't privy to anything that happens before the work hits the runway, so it's fun to see all the detail filled in.

PROJECT RUNWAY: ALL STARS

(2012)

"My life is fashion, the runway is my reality. *Project Runway: All Stars* is my dream!"

—Ken Downing, Neiman Marcus Fashion Director and *All Stars* finale judge

This series featured thirteen designers from Seasons 1–8. Angela Lindvall was the host, while Joanna Coles was the mentor. Georgina Chapman and Isaac Mizrahi rounded out the cast as the judges. The designers were:

Elisa Jiminez (Season 4)
Kathleen "Sweet P" Vaughn (Season 4)
Gordana Gehlhausen (Season 6)
April Johnston (Season 8)
Anthony Williams (Season 7)
Rami Kashou (Season 4)
Kara Janx (Season 2)
Mila Hermanovski (Season 7)
Jerell Scott (Season 5)
Kenley Collins (Season 5)
Michael Costello (Season 8)
Austin Scarlett (Season 1)
Mondo Guerra (Season 8)

Mondo Guerra won, Austin Scarlett came in second place, and Michael Costello ranked third in the finale.

AUSTIN SCARLETT

When first invited to participate my immediate reaction was, "No way, why torture myself? Then I began to reconsider all the potential advantages of being involved. I think a return to the runway was different for each designer. After showing a more realistic, client-focused design touch in *On the Road with Austin and Santino*, I thought it would be fun to participate in something that had more opportunity for fantasy, like back to the runway. Also, when approached to participate in the show, I was already in the initial phases of planning the launch of my new collection, so the timing was ideal for me.

The real name of the game is projecting and maintaining a strong signature point of view. I saw it simply as an amazing platform for creativity, an opportunity to preach my glamour gospel to the world. It was sort of like summer art camp, another way to exercise my creative muscles. I may be one of the few people who actually enjoys the challenges, the frantic pace—it's all a delirious, hysterical game! If it's not the most dangerous game, it's definitely the most glamorous, the way I play it.

Coming from the original season, I felt the others looked up to me in some honorary way. Even thought I am younger than Mondo and some of the later season designers, I felt like I was sort of the big brother—the big brother of the most marvelous fraternity in the universe. Going through an intense experience like *Runway*, of course, you bond closely with the others. We all had the double degree of understanding having lived through it once, as alumni, then together again on *All Stars*. The friendships were the best part. No common cash prize could ever compare to the value of the lifelong relationships formed; these are precious beyond measure.

KARA JANX

WHAT WAS IT LIKE WORKING WITH MISS PIGGY?

I didn't grow up with Miss Piggy. We don't have Miss Piggy in South Africa. But my daughter said, "Miss Piggy is talking to Mommy!" Miss Piggy has a resume of phenomenal designers: Balenciaga, Marc Jacobs, Burberry. We took it very seriously. You have to take each client and each challenge very seriously. I heard some thought it was ridiculous, but it's not. If someone asked me to do a *Muppet* movie I would be honored. It is a massive

opportunity. You have to be diverse enough to do the job.

WHAT WAS IT LIKE HAVING JOANNA COLES AS A MENTOR?

I really wanted to hang on to what she had to say. You're speaking to an editor-in-chief; it's a massive big deal. *All Stars* is a very mature environment and her point of view is very important to us. She sees it from an editorial perspective, she sees it from a woman's perspective, and she sees it from a customer's perspective, so there are three sides that we're covering with her. She calls a spade a spade; she isn't trying to protect us. She's trying to get us to the next level. Tim is a professor and we were sort of the undergraduates. In *All Stars* Joanna's given us our post-graduate degrees. We definitely have respect for both and just to have someone who could give us an opinion was invaluable. You're so vulnerable in that environment and I don't think people understand. You really put yourself out there. This is your life. I design as my life. I have a family; I want to protect myself, my integrity. I don't go on this so I can be recognized in the street. I go on so I can be recognized in the stores.

ANTHONY SEEMS LIKE A HOOT!

He has such a great perspective on life. He's hilarious. I want a show just about Anthony. I'd watch it. He's lovable, he's smart. He's had a lot of adversity in his life and he's overcome so much. He can really just put a humorous spin on it and at the same time you can talk to him about it and be open. He's very special.

MICHAEL COSTELLO

I got a call asking if I wanted to do *All Stars*. I tried to do a cartwheel. I was in bed. I told my partner Richard. When we get good news the first thing we do is go celebrate, so we went to the buffet! I asked who some of the other contestants would be but they would not tell me anything. Mondo and I are so close. We kind of figured we would both be on it, but we couldn't tell. We signed contracts. I sent him a text message saying I'm having something on July 5, can you come. He said he's already booked for something. I looked at Rich and said, "You see, he's going to be there." When I finally got there I saw Mondo. I went and swung him around. He is my best friend.

I was secretly hoping that Rami would be there so I could spend time with him. I knew who one person was going to be—Jerell Scott. We just so happened to be booked on the same flight. We saw each other at the airport at LAX. We were getting ready to board. He asked me where I was going. I said, "The Bahamas. Where are you going?" He said, "I think I'm going to the Bahamas too." I said, "It's good to know you're here." He and I were friends before we both did *Project Runway*. Mondo and I were shocked that April didn't get further. She is like Ann Demeulemeester, Comme des Garcons, Jil Sander. She's really phenomenal and very fashion forward.

GEORGINA CHAPMAN

YOU HAD BEEN A GUEST JUDGE ON *PROJECT RUNWAY*; WHAT WAS IT LIKE COMING TO ALL STARS AS A PERMANENT JUDGE?

I really enjoyed being a guest judge on *Project Runway*. However, on those occasions I only critiqued the designers on what they presented to me on that particular challenge. As a permanent judge on *All Stars*, I was able to see the designers' progression and really get to understand their aesthetic. This I particularly loved.

WERE YOU ROOTING FOR ANY PARTICULAR DESIGNER?

I highly respected each contestant and truly enjoyed mentoring each and every one of them. As a fellow designer, I understood the amount of skill and hard work that goes into designing a collection, especially under the time constraints that the designers faced on the show, so I was rooting for all of them.

JONATHAN MURRAY

WHAT WENT INTO THE DECISION TO HAVE A DIFFERENT HOST, MENTOR, AND JUDGES?

It struck us that it might be more interesting for these designers to have new judges judging them. Another part of it was scheduling. Ultimately the decision was made between the Weinstein Company, Lifetime, and ourselves that it made the most sense to try and do it this way, and I'm glad we did. I thought the judges really came together well. I thought Isaac, Georgina, Angela, and our guest judges were smart. Their questions and comments were perceptive and I thought they were fun to watch.

I'm a huge fan of Georgina. She's always been such a good judge for us and she's just so incredibly beautiful. In

fact, in trying to put that together there were people who said they didn't know if they wanted to sit next to her, she's so beautiful. Isaac, meanwhile, is not only a fascinating designer who's had great successes, he's a wonderful personality, as we first saw in the movie *Unzipped*. When we knew we had Isaac and Georgina we started to feel really good about where we were going.

In general we wanted to shake things up. We didn't want to put on another person who was an academic from Parsons to be the mentor. It would be so unfair for them to have to be compared to Tim, who is so wonderful at what he does. He's really the soul of *Project Runway*. Plus, the *All Star* designers are at a different place in their careers than the young designers who come on to *Project Runway* as their first real exposure. We didn't think the all stars needed the same kind of handholding. They needed a fresh perspective, and who better to give it to them than Joanna Coles?

HOW DID ANGELA LINDVALL BECOME INVOLVED?

We arranged a meeting and she came in all glammed up. She lives a quarter mile away from me. I've seen her lots of times. Normally she dresses more like a hippie—no high heels, she wears her hair curly and topped with big floppy hats. When she came in to meet me she dressed like she was going to be walking that runway for the show. I had her read some of the copy from the show and worked with her. Everyone just fell in love with Angela. She grew up in Kansas City. We were trying to find someone who would be different from Heidi so people wouldn't draw comparisons. She's not afraid to have a point of view and at the same time she's very respectful of Georgina and Isaac's opinions. We felt it was important to have the perspective of someone who has to wear the clothes on the runway.

MERYL POSTER

I worked with Harvey Weinstein at Miramax for sixteen years on the film side. The company had just started producing *Project Runway* as I was leaving. I went to the finale shows but that was about it. Then I became a tremendous fan of the show—as did my young daughter. Part of the reason I wanted to come back and run TV for The Weinstein Company was to be a part of it, because it was something that my daughter and I really enjoyed together. It's completely entertaining, sophisticated, and relatable. It's a real pleasure to watch, so to be a part of it was very exciting. When I came back over to Weinstein to run TV my first job was to get *Project Runway: All Stars* into shape. The first thing that I did was get Isaac Mizrahi on board. At first Isaac wasn't going to be available because he had all these dates with QVC, but I kept on it and we eventually got him. That made the whole show really work and come together. It's hard to find a male designer that has charisma, appeal, and name recognition all at the same time. We were supposed to have Vera Wang be the mentor.

INSTEAD OF JOANNA?

Instead of Joanna; Joanna was going to be the other judge. Then Vera Wang fell out and we then decided to make Joanna Coles the mentor and ask Georgina Chapman to be a judge. You have to think on your feet when you're making these kinds of shows. We're thrilled by the way it worked out. Angela Lindvall was cast just a couple of days before we were supposed to begin. Models' schedules are very difficult. They have modeling commitments that make them a lot of money.

HAD YOU BEEN CONSIDERING ONLY MODELS FOR HER POSITION?

It didn't necessarily have to be a model but you like the panel to have that mix. They have the experience of actually wearing clothes and they have experience with all different kinds of designers. No one has as much experience with designers as a model does, so they bring that to the equation.

WAS IT EASY TO GET THE DESIGNERS TO COME BACK FOR *ALL STARS*?

It's not as easy as you might think. Some of them have family commitments, some have work commitments, some might not want to face the possibility of rejection again.

ARE YOU ABLE TO WATCH THE SHOW AND FORGET THAT YOU WORK ON IT?

Yes, I have been able to. I don't know how long it'll last, but I have been. Usually when I make a movie I can't separate myself at all; I can't take it in as an experience rather than as a process. When I'm working I'm not watching when they film the workroom, so I can appreciate the runway show. I'm really seeing it for the first time.

JOANNA COLES

HOW DOES YOUR JOB ON THE SHOW COMPARE TO WHAT YOU DO AS EDITOR-IN-CHIEF OF *MARIE CLAIRE*?

It's different in terms of advising designers as opposed to advising editorial staff, but it's the same in terms of dealing with creative people and trying to advise them and squeeze the best work out of them. At *Marie Claire* we all have to work on deadlines so we're very familiar with that rhythm and we're very familiar with working under pressure. We're also very familiar with working on a budget, so in those ways the jobs are similar.

TAKING ON THE TIM GUNN ROLE ON *ALL STARS,* INEVITABLY YOU WOULD BE COMPARED TO HIM. HOW DID YOU HANDLE THAT?

Well we are both blonde, that's why they're comparing us! It was daunting. A few days into shooting I realized I had just taken over the role of the most loved character on television. What was I thinking? But he brings something different and with the all-stars it's a different conversation. They need less mentoring and more wake up to the real world, so when they're dreaming around in the studio, and I remind them one of the prizes is a boutique in Neiman Marcus and you are not going to get there if you make this because nobody's going to buy this. I'm a sort of reality call. I think that designers, especially young designers, need a wakeup call about what actually sells and what women want to wear. We have millions of readers telling us that so I can be very helpful in terms of explaining to them what sells and what doesn't sell.

WERE YOU FAMILIAR WITH THE DESIGNERS GOING INTO ALL STARS?

Yes.

IS IT HARD NOT TO PLAY FAVORITES?

It's quite hard not to play favorites. There were two designers that got knocked out of *All Stars* that I was surprised by and I wished that one of them in particular stayed longer because I thought their work

was really exceptional. I felt like Rami was unlucky. He didn't do great work the week he was kicked out, but he's a super-talented designer. Two weeks later his garments were on display at the Super Bowl because he designed the gladiator costumes for the Madonna halftime show. He's gone on to be the bridal designer at Bebe. I was sorry that he didn't stay in the show longer because he is unusually serious about his art and he also gets the commercial thing.

WHEN DOING *ALL STARS,* WHAT WAS THE TYPICAL WEEK LIKE FOR YOU?

I shot every other day. I'd go in for two hours and spend time in the workroom listening to the designers and asking them where they think they were in the process. Some clearly needed more help than others, some just knew what they were doing that week, and others would be confused and actually want to talk about something and ask you, "Is this the right direction?" Sometimes I would see people just driving off down a lane that they were never going to come back from; it was too late. The hard thing was going in and not knowing who got voted off the episode before.

Sometimes I knew. I usually tried to get to the runway show but I couldn't always because I was doing the magazine as well, so there were some episodes where I didn't know who had been voted off. I would open the door and say hello to the designers and be scanning the room to look for who wasn't at their desk. That was always a little upsetting. You're rooting for everybody in a way. The prize was astonishing—$100,000 in cash, a proper contributing editorship with *Marie Claire*, the boutique in Neiman Marcus. It's totally life changing.

COULD YOU TELL WHEN YOU GO INTO THE WORKROOM WHO WAS GOING TO GO AND WHO WAS GOING TO STAY?

No, because you can't always tell what something's going to be like when it hasn't been finished. Some people pull it together in the last couple of hours and other people are really organized and get it all done up front and then there are some last-minute wonders who sort of whip it all together. I think I would know who might not last, but it was difficult. It's more difficult to tell who's going to win than who's going to be in the bottom three.

TO WHAT DEGREE COULD YOU GUIDE THEM?

What I tried to do is ask them questions that would force them to figure out what the answer was. There were times when I tried to ask a very pointed question to make sure they were going the right way. Sometimes it might be a styling issue. I would say that the biggest challenge for some of them was actually putting things together from the Neiman Marcus accessories wall. They might overdo the accessories, or they would get into a battle for the accessories and end up using the accessories because they want to stop someone else from using them. For the most part I tried to ask them the questions that made them feel uncomfortable and that would make them ask themselves honestly, "Is this the right thing for this challenge?"

WHEN YOU'RE ON THE SHOW DO YOU STYLE YOURSELF?

I do although I had someone help me for *Project Runway:*

All Stars because I had to get together fourteen outfits in two days. I didn't have the time and that really is a lot of outfits, and I didn't want to wear the same thing twice. I remember one weekend there were boxes from Net-A-Porter arriving one after another. It was like every girl's fantasy. I ended up buying nearly everything I wore on the show because I loved it all. I needed a great wardrobe on the show. It's intimidating walking into the workroom every week with twelve designers looking at you thinking, "What the hell is she wearing?"

THEY PROBABLY THINK THE SAME OF YOU THOUGH.

They probably do, but they all wanted to talk about what I was wearing. Jerell and Mondo in particular wanted to discuss it. Kenley would always want to know where I got things from. They were very involved. You feel pressure to make sure that you look the part. That was where Tim and I differ. Tim always looks magnificent, but he always has a uniform. He wears a suit and he always looks chic. I don't have a uniform and so it was more challenging.

WHAT WAS THE MOST FUN PART OF DOING THE SHOW?

I think the fun part was getting to know the crew and getting to know the designers. They're really good people, and it was fun to work with people that were smart and creative and really wanted this prize. A couple of them told me that the most exciting part of the prize was to have a regular slot working alongside Nina Garcia. It's very good because you have access to all the sorts of things that you really don't when you're working on your own at home. It's very isolated being a creative person—or it can be—because it's your vision. Being able to have a connection to something like a magazine is really helpful because it makes you feel less isolated and you have a place to come and ask people about things. I think some of them were really looking forward to that opportunity.

WHAT HAS BEEN THE BEST PART OF WINNING *PROJECT RUNWAY?*

JAY MCCARROLL, SEASON 1 WINNER:

The exposure—not only on the national but international level. It's fascinating to realize that your image and your work has been broadcast all over the planet. It's really surreal yet amazing to receive correspondence from folks in Europe and Asia congratulating me. Who knew that when I was a weird little boy in Podunk, Pennsylvania, one day I would be affecting someone's life in some way. It's super cool!

CHLOE DAO, SEASON 2 WINNER:

The best part of winning is the opportunities that are given to you, but also the recognition and respect of fans and real people in the fashion industry. I know there's an inclination to look down on a reality show contestant, but *Project Runway* is special. It's a show about real talent and skills and I will forever be happy to be associated with Project Runway.

JEFFREY SEBELIA, SEASON 3 WINNER:

Winning *Project Runway* changed my life completely. It helped to improve it in every way. I've been able to carve out a whole other career path that I might not have otherwise found. I never anticipated I'd be designing for kids, but I now have a line called La Miniatura Kids. I was on a good trajectory before the show, but now I am able to reach a whole new demographic.

CHRISTIAN SIRIANO, SEASON 4 WINNER:

After the show ended I was on Ellen. I also was on Oprah a year later. I showed my whole collection on Oprah. There was media behind it that just seemed excited for someone and it happened to work out for me.

LEANNE MARSHALL, SEASON 5 WINNER:

For me the best part of winning *Project Runway* was that it allowed me to continue to pursue my dreams by moving to New York, showing at Fashion Week regularly. I'm still able to wake up every day and make a living doing what I love so much—designing and creating clothes that women will love to wear. When I won, it also showed that you don't have to be a big diva or over-the-top "character" with an attitude to make it in fashion. I thought because I wasn't the loudest or craziest personality on my season I probably wouldn't win, but in the end it truly showed that talent, determination, and hard work do win out.

IRINA SHABAYEVA, SEASON 6 WINNER:

Irina was unavailable for comment at time of press; she has been busy since winning Season 6! In addition to showing at New York Fashion Week, she designed a collection for the Macy's INC line. Irina has designed for celebrities such as Lady Gaga, Selena Gomez, and Carrie Underwood, and has a line of bridal gowns.

SETH AARON HENDERSON, SEASON 7 WINNER:

Winning has been nothing short of amazing, and more then most could hope for, but I would have to say the most fantastic thing to date has been the moment Heidi said, "You just won *Project Runway*," and my two kids walked out. Aaron was thirteen at the time and Megann eleven. There was something about that moment that nothing else could compare. To see the look on their faces, that look you don't often see; that look that said, "My dad fucking rocks! Now what, bitch?!" Wow who could ask for more? I certainly could not. On that note, Thank you *Project Runway*, Lifetime, Weinstein, and Bunin/Murray. You are Fantabulous.

GRETCHEN JONES, SEASON 8 WINNER:

The best part about winning *Project Runway* was that it enabled me to take the necessary steps to reach my overall goals, both personally and professionally. Almost all of us designers come from very little, and fashion is a very expensive game to play. I felt that if I could get to the finale I would win and that would lead to my ultimate goal of being able to support my creative endeavors, which is what feeds my soul. Winning affirmed my belief that if you risk big, you can win big. Gambling is a part of life and if you embrace that you can make your dreams come true.

ANYA AYOUNG-CHEE, SEASON 9 WINNER:

There are so many competing answers to this question, but at the top of the list, from deep down in my heart, the best thing about winning *Project Runway* is knowing that I trusted myself and just went for it all! When I think back to the moment when I almost decided not to go onto the show I realize that my decision to take a big risk really changed my life—forever. In short, I loved every second of this experience and winning sealed my belief that my inner voice is always the wisest.

MONDO GUERRA, *PROJECT RUNWAY: ALL STARS* WINNER:

Winning *All Stars* has really helped to validate my work as a designer and has given me the confidence to earn my place in the fashion industry. I'm excited to work hard and produce pieces for people to wear. I feel like it's a gift to be able to offer my art—my designs—to all of the people who have supported me on this journey. I don't consider them "fans"—I view them as my friends instead.

WHAT HAS BEEN THE IMPACT OF *PROJECT RUNWAY?*

ZANNA ROBERTS RASSI:

I think it has brought fashion into the mainstream. Half of these kids would have never thought, "Oh, I could be a fashion designer!" Of course you can if you have the talent, the drive, the ambition, and you realize there are these amazing mentors around. It's catapulted fashion to the middle of America and it's made it accessible, achievable, and relatable. Fashion was quite a scary, almost sacred world that no one knew about and you kept the lid on it. You used to never learn about a designer's journey, or it was something that was passed down in the family and you became a designer; whereas now it can be very doable if you work hard to achieve the goal.

Project Runway is a real talent-based show. On the first episode I thought, this is real, there is not one minute of fixing, of lets go to the common room, whisper about this and speak to the producers to see whether something is a good decision. There's not one iota of that, and that to me was like, "Wow, that's why it's gone on for ten seasons, that's why it's such a strong show, and that's why people love it and they respect it—because it has integrity."

BARBARA SCHNEEWEISS:

I think that it's definitely engaged men in fashion more. It's easy for them to play along at home; to look at a series of dresses and then hear what Michael, Heidi, and Nina have to say. They like the competition aspect of it, too. One year I had someone tell me the *Runway* finale was airing up against the World Series, and they placed bets on both.

GEORGINA CHAPMAN:

In many ways the show has made fashion more accessible to a wide audience. People get a glimpse of all the hard work, inspiration, and dedication it takes to create a garment, and that really helps to show that fashion is an art form that should be appreciated.

DANIELA UNRUH:

I believe the impact of *Project Runway* is that a very "faraway, glamorous world" became "real." It showed the reality and drama of the fashion world. It got closer to everyone. Fashion became fun and people could realize their dreams!

SARA REA:

I think the show has been a huge part of pop culture and has brought the art of fashion design to the forefront of a lot of people's minds.

ELI HOLZMAN:

I think *Runway* has had an enormous impact in educating the average person about the fashion world. Designers known only to insiders have gained exposure to an audience of millions by appearing on the show. And we have all learned words like "ruching" and the proper pronunciation of "empire" waist dresses.

A few years after *Project Runway* premiered I called the dean at Parsons to ask whether the show was having a positive impact on them. I was shocked by her answer. She told me their enrollment had practically doubled, and that, industry-wide, design programs had seen a huge influx of new students. It was the first time I fully appreciated the power of television as a promotional medium. I was touched to realize that the little show I helped to create inspired young people to dream of a career they might not otherwise have known was a possibility for them. Maybe one of them will be a great designer someday. Undoubtedly, the industry has benefited from this influx of talent.

KALYN HEMPHILL:

Project Runway has made me appreciate each garment I wear and the hard work and creativity that it takes for designers to produce their pieces. Before *Project Runway*, I used to model and just take the clothes I was wearing for granted. Now I look at each piece of clothing as a work of art.

FERN MALLIS:

The show greatly impacted the enrollment in fashion schools. I know Parsons could barely handle the increase in applications. The show made everybody think if they could put two pieces of fabric together they could possibly become a designer. Ultimately, it is a great celebration of the fashion industry. The show made Michael Kors an incredible star designer. Same for Nina Garcia; now she writes books, makes all sorts of special appearances, and is a star editor.

HEIDI KLUM:

People definitely take more notice of the fashion industry now. I don't think before people thought about what it takes, how people constantly are thinking about new trends, and how you have to think about the new trend a year or a season in advance. People just see a skirt in the store and buy it. They don't know why the hem is like that or why it is knee length and not below the knee or higher, or why it's a certain color or a certain print. They see it and either they like it or they don't like it and that's it.

I think people love the magic of *Project Runway*. The designers have nothing to work with but what is in their heart and what is in their hands and they have to do it all by themselves. I think audiences love watching people

with talent and that's why shows like *Project Runway* have such longevity—because it's about the gift of talent that people can admire and appreciate.

MICHAEL KORS:

I think *Project Runway* has had an affect on the gay community—big time. Half of the people in my family were in the fashion business so there was never any kind of strange reaction to the idea that I wanted to sit in my room and sketch shoes when I was ten. Everyone thought that was totally great. In fact, most of the women in my family were excited they were going to get to have some new clothes and shoes in their lives. Still, knowing at an early age that you have different interests and starting to realize that you're gay, you do feel very isolated.

Growing up I was one of those kids who were glued to television. I could watch for hours on end. There were always these stereotype gay men on TV who never told you that they were gay. You watched Paul Lynde play Uncle Arthur in *Bewitched*, or Alan Sues going crazy on *Laugh-In*, and they were always kind of the clown; you never got to see successful, smart gay men. You got the humor, of course. Humor is great but you never heard anything about these men and their lives.

Look at the wide spectrum of gay people who are on *Project Runway*—different ages, different looks, and different points of view. It's not just funny Paul Lynde. Tim and I are very different from one another, the contestants are all very different. Mondo versus Santino versus Michael, the list goes on, and these are real people involved, not characters. The majority of the men on the show are gay, so I think it's revolutionary in that respect and it's revolutionary in lifting the veil. I think the light bulb goes off in their heads—even straight guys are like, "Wait a minute, I want to be a designer!" It's not just about being gay; it's about opening up the possibilities for young people.

We were launching a new fragrance a few years ago at the Herald Square Macy's. I was with Debra Messing. Debra and I were signing things together. Two teenage boys came up for signatures and both started crying. Debra and I thought, "Oh my God, what did we do?" And the two boys said, "The two of you changed our lives. Between *Will & Grace* and *Project Runway*, you made us feel like anything was possible and we weren't alone. We could see that there was a world for us." They were probably seventeen or eighteen, and they'd grown up watching both shows. I looked at Debra and said, "Oh my God, we've got such a responsibility." With television you are in people's homes and it's very personal. For kids who have had difficulties, whether with people at school or even within their own family, hopefully the show—without being preachy—says, "You can have a happy and productive life; you're not alone."

INDEX

#

7th on Sixth, 66
30 Vandam, 46
6126, 158

A

ABC, 55
Aberra, Amsale, 47, *47*
Abete, Elena, *139*
Academy Awards (Oscars), 53, 87, 191
Academy of Art University, 200
Accademia Italiana, 237
Access Hollywood, 47
Ackermann, Haider, 253
After the Runway, 186, 264, 270, 271
Agins, Teri, 99, *99*
Agstam, Karin, *247*
Aguilera, Christina, 150, *150*, 158, *158*, *162*, 170, 172
Akerman, Malin, 248, *248*
Alba, Jessica, 185, *185*
Alter, Amanda, *116*
Ambrosio, Alessandra, 72, *72*
amfAR, 235
America's Best Dance Crew, 55
American Express, 135
American Idol, 84
American Intercontinental University, The, 109, 236
Anderson, Clarissa, *94*, *97*
Anderson McDonald, Christina, *117*
Angjeli, Lorena, *175*, *180*, *182*, *183*, 193
Aparicio, Alyssa, *139*
Arace, Alex, *139*
Art Institute of Chicago, 36
Art Institute of Fort Lauderdale, The, 36
Art Institute of Portland, The, 174, 236, 265
Art Institute of Seattle, The, 130, 146
Ashcraft, Kasey, *3*, *180*, *183*
Askari, Shirin, 146, *146*, *148*, *149*, 152
Atlas, 32, 65, 198
Auld, Anthony Ryan, 107, 237, *237*, 238, *238*, *242*, 244, 252, *253*, 258, 262, 264, *270*, *287*, *289*
Ayoung-Chee, Anya, 18, 237, *237*, 238, *240*, 241, *241*, 243, *243*, 245, 246, *246*, *250*, *251*, 252-253, *252*, *253*, 255, 260, 261, 264, 270, *270*, 285, *285*, *287*, *289*
Azria, Max, 158, *158*

B

Badgley, Mark, 73, *73*
Badgley Mischka, 6
Balenciaga, 9, 276
Baltazar, Raymundo, 60, *60*, *61*, *62*, *74*, 85, 87, *288*
Banana Republic, 46, 65, 73, 77, 85
Barber, Tiki, 111, *111*, 118, *118*
Barboza, Josiane, *38*, *42*, *45*
Barneys, 126
Barrucci, Carla, *238*, *244*, *247*
Barungi, Camilla, *96*, *97*
Baum, Stephen "Suede," 130, *130*, *131*, 132, 136, *138*, *142*, *287*
Baumkirchner, Bradley, 88, *88*, *286*
Bebe, 280
Beckham, Victoria, 5, 16, 113, 119, *119*, 123, 126, 127, 129
Bell, Janine, *139*

Bell, Kristen, 213, *213*, 226
Bell, Sarah, *183*
Bendet, Stacey, 248, *248*
Bennett, Laura, 18, 24, 89, *89*, 92, *92*, 93, 96, 101, *104*, *105*, 106, 140, *140*, 191, 264, *286*
Berman, Paul, 46, *46*
Bernhard, Sandra, 140, *140*
Best, Robert, 88, *88*, *286*
Bewitched, 289
Beynon, Julia, *38*, 40, *44*, *45*, 50, *51*, 57-58
Beyonce, 87, 128, 129
Biassou, Katia, *94*, *97*
Bieber, Justin, 65
Bien Aime, Lindsay, *90*, *94*, *97*
Bill Blass, 77
Bilson, Rachel, 158, *158*
Bitten, 110
Black, Bryce, 236, *236*, *238*, *239*, *253*, *258*, 265, *287*, *289*
Black, Louise, 146, *146*, *148*, *162*, *173*
Blackburn, Chelsea, *238*, *244*, *247*
Blades, Lisa, *154*, *155*, *163*
Blair, Selma, 212, *212*
Blass, Bill, 12
Blige, Mary J., 52, 55
Bloomingdale's, 83
Blunt, Emily, 127
Bouwer, Marc, 158, *158*
Braiser, Melissa, *61*, *71*, *288*
Brandle, Emily, 130, *130*, *131*, *287*
Bravo, 6, 55, 63, 122, 148, 166
Braxton, Toni, 107
Breton, Malan, 88, *88*, *286*
British Airways, 87
Broadway Cares Equity Fights AIDS, 132
Brocks, Aviva, *117*
Broker, Alexis, *183*, *189*, *268*
Brooks College, 109
Brother International, 129
Brown, Heather, 61, 68, 69, 71, 75, *288*
Browne, Lauren, *114*, *117*
Browne, Thom, 253
Bryant, Joy, 55
Bryant Park, 33, 53, 54, 66, 107, 110, 170
Bryce, Keith, 130, *130*, *131*, 136, *287*
Bunim, Mary-Ellis, 166
Bunim/Murray, 6, 10, 26, 191, 271, 284
Burberry, 276
Burch, Tory, 184, *184*
Burkhardt, Brian, 272
Bye, Rich, 52-53, 58-59
Bynes, Amanda, 55
Byrne, Rose, 248, *248*

C

Cadenas, Mario, 36, *36*, *37*, *48*, *286*
California College of the Arts, 108
California State University, Long Beach, 108
California State University, Northridge, 60
Caliguri, Nora, 36, 36, 37, 38, 39, 48, 286
Calvin, Caroline, 119, *119*, *120*
Calvin Klein, 99
Calvin Klein Collection, 141, 184, 249
Calvin Klein Jeans, 58
Campbell's, 177
Carlota Alfaro College, 200

Carnegie Mellon University, 88
Carr, Peach, 200, *200*, *202*, *203*, 205, 229, 232-235, *232*, *235*, *289*
Cart, Sarae, *202*, *209*, 211
Casanova, Carlos, 200, *200*, *201*, *202*, 03, *203*, 205, 209, 229, 230-231, *230*, *231*, 234, *289*
Castiglioni, Consuelo, 227
Catholic University of America, The, 200
Cavalli, Roberto, 16, 119, *119*, 123, 253
Caven, Kaven Jo, 211
Ceccanti, Janeane Marie, 174, *174*
Celine, 195
Central Saint Martins College of Art and Design, 147, 237
CFDA, 13, 76
Cha, Jane, 6, *8*, *10*, 13, 15, 16, 17, 18, 19, 20, *20*, 21, 24, *24*, 26, *26*, *27*, 91, *104*, *143*, 148, *163*, 269, 270
Champion, Katie, *97*
Chanel, 128
Chapman, Georgina, 6, *58*, 141, *141*, 184, *184*, 212, *212*, 231, *267*, 274, 277, *277*, 278, *278*, 279, 287
Cheetah Girls, The, 55
Chihocky, Audrey, *38*, *42*, *45*
Chmura, Ben, 174, *174*, 235
Chorm, Eyen, 205, 209, 210, 211
Christensen, Joshua, 236, *236*, *238*, 240, *240*, *287*, *289*
Christiana, Kevin, 108, *108*, *109*, *286*
Chua, Celine, *153*, *155*
Chum, David, 236, *236*, *289*
Ciara, 128, 129
Clark, Tina Marie, *207*, *211*
Cleveland Institute of Art, The, 200
Coca-Cola, 107
Cohen, Andy, 107
Cohen, Matar, *149*, *152*, *155*, 156, *268*
Cohen, Sasha, 65, *65*, 67, 73, *73*, *75*
Cole, Kenneth, 248, *248*, 249, *249*, 272, *72*, 273
Coleman, Ra'mon Lawrence, 146, *146*, *148*, 152, 171
Coles, Joanna, 16, 176, 185, *185*, 86-188, *186*, *188*, 212, *212*, 233, 248, *248*, 271, 274, 276, *276*, 278, 279, 280-281, *280*
College of Charleston, 147
Collins, Christopher, 200, *200*, *201*, *202*, 04, *205*, *216*, 223, 224, 226, 229, *235*, *289*
Collins, Kenley, 131, *131*, 133, 134, *134*, 135, 136, *142*, *143*, *251*, 274, *274*, 276, 281, *287*
Columbia College Chicago, 108, 130
Columbia University, 89
Comme des Garcons, 277
Conner, Tara, 98, *98*
Cook, Rose, *3*, *209*, *211*, 226
Corbett, Sam, *238*
Corcoran School of Art, The, 60
Cosgrove, Miranda, 127
Costa, Francisco, 6, 16, 99, *99*, 141, *141*, 184, *184*, 249, *249*, 252, 253, 258
Costello, Michael, 191, 201, *201*, *202*, 03, 205, *205*, 206, *206*, 208, 209, *216*, *217*, 219, 221-224, *221*, 228, 260, 274, *274*, 277, *277*, *289*, *289*
Cox, Rafael, 236, *236*, 265, *287*, *289*
Crawford, Cindy, 159, *159*
Currie, Ewan, *238*
Cutforth, Dan 6

D

D'Aurizio, Nicholas, 200, *200*, *202*, 224
Da Conceicao, Serena 236, *236*, *289*
Dabo, Fatma, *155*, *268*
Danesewich, Brandise, *175*, *181*, *183*, *191*, *268*
Dao, Chloe, 18, 61, *61*, *62*, 64, *64*, *65*, 68, 70, *75*, 76-78, *76*, *78*, 81, 85, 86-87, 106, 282, *282*, *288*
DAO Chloe DAO, 78
Darton, Monique, *175*, *182*, *183*, 268
Daugherty, Alyssa, *61*, *71*, *288*
Davis, Dre, *202*, *211*
Davis, Megan, *183*
Dayrit, Lenka, *208*, *210*, *211*, 223
DeGeneres, Ellen, 113, 283
Deatherage, Gunnar, 236, *236*, *289*
Demarchelier, Patrick, 81
Demuelemeester, Ann, 277
Denardo, Erin, *38*, *45*, *48*
Diane von Furstenberg, 229
Diederich, Jennifer, 130, *130*, *131*, 145, *287*
Dion, Celine, 192
Disney, 55
Dolce & Gabbana, 16, 188, 203, 234
Dollhouse, 41, 54
Dominguez, Bonnie, 88, *88*, *286*
Donhoeffner, Alexandra, *97*
Douglas, Kyan, *102*
Dove, 78
Downing, Ken, *267*, 274
Draskovic, Bojana, *244*, *247*, 260
Dress for Success, 24
Drummond, Michael, 200, *200*, *201*, *202*, *203*, *204*, 205, *216*, 224, 228, 229, 231, 234, *289*
Duane Reade, 20
Dubuc, Nancy, 6, 229
Duran, Marla, 60, *60*, 61, *62*, 64, *288*
Dzienny, Cassie, 205, 208, 211

E

E!, 55, 87
Earthtec, 191
eBay, 46
Egan, Tara, *155*
Ehrig, Kirsten, 60, *60*, *61*, *62*, *74*, *288*
Elle, 13, 46, 52, 73, 81, 96, 106, 113, 127, 186
Emmy Awards, 19, 124, 216, 229
Eng, Diana, 60, *60*, *61*, *62*, 64, *64*, *65*, 76, *288*
Epperson, Rodney, 146, *146*, *148*, 149
ESOSA, 194
Estrada, Jesus, 174, *174*, *194*
Estrella, Stacey, 88, *88*, *286*
Evans, Ashley, *114*, *117*
Eve, 52, 55
Everine, Danielle, 236, *236*, *287*, *289*

F

Facebook, 187
Faris, Joe, 130, *130*, *131*, *134*, 137, 145, *287*
Fashion Careers College, 174
Fashion Inside/Out (Vosovic), 81
Fashion Institute of Design and Merchandising (FIDM), 60, 61, 84, 87, 130, 131, 146, 236
Fashion Institute of Technology (FIT), 14, 36, 61, 88, 108, 130, 146, 174, 200, 222, 237
Feld, Daniel, 130, *130*, *131*, *143*, *287*
Ferguson, Craig, 113
Ferretti, Alberta, 16, 119, *119*, 123
Field, Patricia, 16, 46, *46*

Fields, Amanda, *97*
Fierce Style: How to Be Your Most Fabulous Self (Siriano), 127
Filicia, Thom, *102*
Fish, Ari, 146, *146*
Fitzgerald, Vanessa, *152*, *155*
Florida State University, 131
Fluet, Shannon, *61*, 63, *71*, *75*, *288*
Ford, Tom, 191, 255
Foreign Affair, A, 135
Foxman, Ariel, 272, *272*, 273
Franco, Daniel, 36, *36*, *37*, 60, *60*, *61*, *62*, *64*, *64*, *67*, *286*, *288*
Frantsena, Polina, *139*
Frazier, Qristyl, 146, *146*, *148*
Full Picture, 6, 26

G

Gabbana, Stefano, 188
Gallo, Kenzie, *247*
Gap, 118
Garcia, Nina, 4, 5, 6, *8*, 10, 12, 13, *13*, *16*, *17*, 20, 22-23, *23*, 24, 26, *26*, *27*, *35*, *48*, *49*, 77, 80, 81, 83, 85, 101, *103*, *104*, *105*, 107, 112, *131*, 134, *143*, *150*, *158*, *159*, 160, 165, *165*, 167, 171, 179, 186, 187, 188, *188*, 191, 193, 205, 207, *207*, *212*, 14, *215*, *217*, 219, 223, 224, 234, 238, *238*, 240, 241, 242, *242*, 243, *248*, *250*, *251*, 253, 255, 257, 260, 261, 264, 281, 288
Gaultier, Jean Paul, 16
Gehlhausen, Gordana, 147, *147*, *148*, 149, *149*, 151, *151*, 153, 274, *274*, 88
GenArt, 17, 50, 174
Geoffrey Beene, 130
Georgia Southern University, 88
Gerdes, Katherine, 88, *88*, *286*
Gershwin's Porgy & Bess, The, 194
Gervais, Kelly, *183*
Giffin, Meghan, 241, 247, 262, 265
Gillaspie, Kayne, 88, *88*, 91, 94, *94*, *104*, 106, *286*
Gingerich, Alison, *183*, *189*, *199*, 268
Girls Just Want to Have Fun, 128
Givenchy, 128
Givhan, Robin, 102
Glassner, Zoe, 158, *58*, 221, 232
Glebova, Sveta, 3, 241, 246, 247, 252, 265, 285
Glee, 234
Goldson, Kimberly, 237, *237*, 242, 243, 244, *250*, 259-260, *259*, *260*, *270*, *87*, *289*
Gomez, Selena, 284
Gonzalo, Andrae, *20*, 60, *60*, *61*, *62*, 63, *63*, 64, *64*, 67, *67*, 69, *74*, *75*, 76, 77, 85, *288*
Goodwill, 226
Gottesman, Hannah, 238, *238*, *247*
Green, Olivier, 5, 161, 168, *168*, 237, *237*, 238, *238*, 240, *240*, 243, 244, 253, 258, *287*, *289*
Grier, Pam, 107
Griffin, Zulema, 60, *60*, *61*, *62*, 63, *63*, *64*, 65, *65*, 69, *75*, 86, *288*
Gristedes, 20, 38, 133
Gruber, Desiree 6, *8*, *10*, 11, 13, 14, 17, 18, 19, 20-21, 23, 25, 26, *26*, *27*, 29, *104*, *143*, *163*
Gucci, 77
Guerra, Mondo, 5, 18, *19*, 21, 24, 107, 191, 201, *201*, *202*, *203*, 205, *205*, 206, 207, 209, 210, *210*, *216*, 18-220, *218*, *219*, 223, 224, 229, 233, 234, 249, 252, 253, 264, 271, 274, *274*, 275, 277, *277*, 281, 285, *285*, 287, 289, *289*
Guess, 57, 58

Guggenheim Museum, 129
Guinness, Daphne, 256
Gullen, Ryan, *238*
Gunn, Tim, 5, 12, 13, 14-15, *14*, *15*, 17, *17*, 20, 25, *27*, *35*, 38, *40*, 41, 52, 3, 54, 62, 65, 66, 67, *67*, *74*, *75*, 6, 77, 85, *86*, 91, 92, 93, 101, *104*, *105*, 106, 107, 110, *110*, 111, 12, *120*, *121*, *131*, 132, *133*, 134, *34*, 135, *135*, 141, *141*, *142*, *143*, 49, 151, 160, *162*, *163*, 167, 168, 73, *178*, 186, *189*, 190, 191, 193, *98*, 202, *202*, *204*, 205, 206, *216*, 19, 221, 222, 223, 225, 227, 228, 230, 232, 238, *238*, 240, *240*, 241, 243, *250*, *251*, 252, 255, 256, 258, 259, 260, 264, *269*, 276, 278, 280, 281, *284*, *286*, 289

H

H&M, 26
Hairston, Javi, *97*
Hall, Mitchell, 146, *146*, *148*, *157*
"Halo," 128
Halston, 159
Halston, Roy, 12
Hanson, Leot, *238*, *246*
Haro, Melissa, 3, 38, 39, *39*, 42, 43, 44, 5, 48, 57, 58, 59
Harper, Althea, 147, *147*, *148*, 151, *151*, 152, 154, *162*, 169-171, *169*, *170*, *171*, *288*
Harper, Tanisha, *152*, *154*, *155*, 169, *268*
Harper's Bazaar, 129
Hartzog, Rachael, 61, 69, 71, 75, 288
Harvard Business School, 88
Haskins-Simms, Kristin, 200, *200*, 202, *202*, *203*
Hearst Entertainment & Syndication, 271
Heath, Toni, *97*
Heatherette, 119
Hedda Lettuce, 132, *132*
Helnwein, Kojii, *155*
Hemphill, Kalyn, 3, 153, 154, 155, 156-157, 156, 157, 268, *268*, *284*, 288
Henderson, Eden, 61, 65, 71, 75, 288
Henderson, Mary, *38*, *45*
Henderson, Seth Aaron, *19*, *165*, 175, *175*, *177*, 179, 181, 182, *189*, 190-191, *190*, *191*, 193, 252, 254, 263, 264, *284*, *284*
Hendricks, Christina, 127
Hermanovski, Mila, 175, *175*, 179, *179*, 180, 193, 195-196, *195*, *196*, *251*, 274, *274*
Hershey's, 21, 111, 129
Herzner, Uli, 89, *89*, 93, 94, 96, *96*, *104*, *105*, 264, 269, *269*, *286*
Higa, Ivy, 200, *200*, *201*, *202*, *203*, *204*, 205, *205*, 206, *206*, *216*, 222, 223, 224, 227-229, *227*, 231, *289*
Hightower, Kendall, *139*
Hilfiger, Tommy, 6, *58*, 159, *159*, *267*
Hill, Faith, 185, *185*
Hillman, David, 164-165, *164*, 271
Hilton, Nicky, 64, 72, *72*
Hoffman, Mara, 253
Holliday, Rebecca, 61, 68, 69, 70, 71, 75, 288
Holt, Shannone, *136*, *139*
Holzman, Eli, 6, *8*, 14-15, 20, 288
Hong, Victorya, 108, *108*, *109*, 114, 115, *115*, *120*, *286*
Honolulu Community College, 175, 201
Howell, James, 54
HP, 22, 205, 252
Hudson, Jennifer, 107
Hudson, Sarah, 46, *46*
Hutton, Lauren, 184, *184*

I

Ilzhoefer, Starr, 36, *36*, *37*, *286*

Iman, 73, *73*, 80, 81
IMG, 66, 100, 141
InStyle, 127, 273
Instituto De Allende, 88
Intel, 252
International Herald Tribune, The, 159
Ivy h., 229

J

Jackson, Janet, 77
Jacobs, Marc, 186-187, 223, 276
Jagger, Mick, 86
Jane, Eliza, 61, 71, 75, 288
Janx, Kara, 61, *61*, *62*, 64, *64*, 65, *65*, *75*, 77, 82-83, *82*, *83*, 85, 87, 274, *274*, 276, *276*, *288*
Jean Paul Gaultier, 58, 233
Jeanbart-Lorenzotti, Eva, 272, *272*
Jimenez, Elisa, 108, *108*, *109*, 110, *110*, *120*, 274, *274*, *286*
Jo-Ann, 225
John, Elton, 87
John, Kevin, 36, *36*, *37*, 39, *39*, 42, *286*
Johnson, Betsey, 6, 16, 47, *47*, 212, *212*, 231, 233
Johnson, Richard, 47, *47*
Johnston, April, 201, *201*, *202*, 205, 206, 209, *216*, 219, 222, 223, 225-226, 229, 233, 234, *235*, 274, *274*, 277, *289*
Jointer, Ebony, *155*, *268*
Jones, Erika Kimberly, *245*, *247*
Jones, Gretchen, 5, 18, 24, 165, *165*, 187, 188, 201, *201*, *202*, 203, 204, 205, *205*, 206, 207, 208, 210, *210*, *216*, 220, 223, 228, 231, 285, *285*, *289*
Jones, Ifeoma "Ify," *211*
Jones, January, 213, *213*
Jovovich, Milla, 158, *158*

K

Kahlo, Frida, 258
Kamali, Norma, 213, *213*
Kanellis, Maria, *3*, *116*
Kansas City Art Institute, 146
Kara Saun LLC, 55
Karan, Donna, 16, 52, 103, 118, *118*, 227
Kardashian, Khloe, 107
Kardashian, Kim, 248, *248*, *251*
Kashou, Rami, 78, 83, 101, 109, *109*, 113, *113*, 114, 115, *120*, 128, 191, 274, *274*, 277, 280, *286*
Kathleen, Laura, 237, *237*, 241, *241*, 244, 252, *253*, 261-262, *261*, *262*, *287*, *289*
Keeter, Bert, 101, 168, 237, *237*, 242, *242*, 244, 252, 255, 258, 261, *287*, *289*
Kelly, Alison, 88, *88*, 107, *286*
Kelsey, Grace, 61, 67, 68, 70, 71, 75, 77, 78, 288
Kennedy, Jacqueline, 205, *205*, 206, 228
Kenneth Pool, 140
Kent College of Art and Design, 36
Kerr, Miranda, 81
Keslar, Angela, 88, *88*, 92, 94, *104*, *105*, 106, *286*
Khan, Naeem, 213, *213*
King, Christiane, 174, *174*, *194*
KISS, 9
Klein, Calvin, 12, 52, 160, 227
Klum, Heidi, 4-5, *4*, 6, 7, *8*, 9-10, *9*, 10, 11, *11*, 13, 15, *15*, *16*, *17*, 19, *20*, 23, *23*, 24, *24*, 25, *26*, *27*, *33*, *35*, 38, *47*, 49, 52, 55, 58, 63, *75*, 80, 81, 87, *89*, 100-101, *103*, *104*, *105*, 110, *110*, 113, *121*, 123-124, *26*, 127, *131*, 134, *135*, *143*, *147*, *150*, 151, *158*, 161, *162*, *163*, 165, *165*, 167, 171, 172, 176, *176*, 179, *179*, *185*, 186, 188, *191*, 194, 195, 197, 206, *206*, 207,

207, 214, *215*, *216*, *217*, 218, 220, 222, 223, 224, *231*, 234, 238, *238*, 239, 240, *240*, 241, 243, *249*, *250*, *251*, 252, 253, 255, 256, 261, 268, *269*, *283*, *284*, *285*, *286*, 287, 288-289
Knight, Mychael, 88, *88*, 91, 93, 95, *95*, *104*, *105*, 106, *106-107*, 260, 269, *269*, *286*
Kononova, Olga, *38*, *42*, *45*
Kors, Joan, 92, 99, *99*
Kors, Michael, 4, 5, 6, *8*, 10, 11-12, *11*, *12*, 13, *13*, *16*, *17*, 18, 19, 20, 21-22, *22*, 23, *23*, 24, 26, *26*, *27*, *35*, 41, *41*, *48*, *49*, *74*, 77, 80, 83, 85, 90, 92, 99, 101, *103*, *104*, 123, *131*, 134, *143*, 148, *159*, 160, 161, *162*, *163*, *165*, 167, 171, 175, 177, 179, 188, 193, 204, *204*, 207, *207*, 214, 215, *215*, *216*, *217*, 220, 223-224, 231, 232, 238, *238*, 243, *250*, *251*, 253, 255, 257, 258, 263-264, *283*, 287, 288, 289
Kressley, Carson, *102*

L

L'Academies Des Couturiers Design Institute, 131
L'Oreal, 158, 252
La Miniatura Kids, 283
Lacamp, Ashley, *238*, *247*
Lachey, Nick, 55
Lady Gaga, 124, 127, 284
Lagerfeld, Karl, 128, 161, 191
LAIKA, 265
Lakshmi, Padma, 6
Lambert, Adam, 248, *248*, *250*, 258
Lang, Helmut, 195
Lanvin, 80
Laugh-In, 289
Lauren, Ralph, 128
LAX, 85, 87, 277
LeBlanc, Simone, 108, *108*, *286*
LeNoir, Jesse, 174, *174*, *189*, 193
Lechner, Kerstin, *244*, *245*, *247*
Lee, Marion, 108, *108*, *286*
Lee, Sophia, *183*, *189*
Lee, Spike, 194
Leiba, Freddie, 73, *73*
Leonova, Valeria, *181*, *183*, 190, 268
Lepore, Nanette, *280*
Levi Strauss & Company, 119
Lewis, Jillian, 109, *109*, 114, *120*, 128-129, *128*, 259, *286*
LG, 125, 127
Lhuillier, Monique, 118, *118*, 158, *158*
Libretti, Vincent, 78, 88, *88*, 90, 95, *286*
Lienhard-O'Malley, Michel Ann, *247*
Lifetime, 6, 26, 148, 161, 164, 165, 166, 191, 224, 229, 271, 278, 284
Lil' Kim, 55
Lim, Phillip, 195
Lincoln Center, 33, 203, 207
Lindenwood University, 200
Lindvall, Angela, *267*, 274, 278, *278*, 279
Lipsitz, Jane, 6
Lipstick Jungle, 132
Lisa Thon School of Design, 200
Liu, Lucy, 129
Liz Claiborne, Inc., 141
Lizalde, Ricky, 108, *108*, *109*, 111, *111*, 116, *286*
LL Cool J, 135, 141, *141*
Lloyd, Deborah, 46, *46*, 73, *73*
Lohan, Lindsay, 158, *158*
London College of Fashion, 36
Longoria, Eva, 159, *159*
Lopez, Jennifer, 135
Lopez, Mario, 55

Lopez, Sessilee, 125
Lorenzo De Medici Scuola De Arte, 88
Los Angeles Times, 149, 167
Los Angeles Trade Technical College, 89, 108
Lost in Translation, 133
Lot 8, 78
Louisiana State University, 237
Love Armoour, 262
Lucienne, Runa, *139*
Lucky, 129
Luna, Viktor, 237, *237*, 240, 243, 245, 246, *250*, 252, *253*, 257-258, *257*, *258*, 259, 260, 261, 263, *287*, *289*
Luz, Maya, 165, 174, *174*, 178
Lynde, Paul, 289
Lynett, Anna, 174, *174*
Lynn Sage Breast Cancer Foundation, 235

M

Macke, Erika, *155*
Mackenroth, Jack, 108, *108*, *109*, 111, *111*, 114, *120*, *286*
Mackie, Bob, 16, 150, *150*, 158, *158*, 172
Macy's, 98, 159, 191, 284, 289
Maddox, McKell, 200, *200*, 202, *202*, 203
Madonna, 280
Magalhaes, Thais, *246*, *247*
Magical Elves, 6, 17, 26, 53, 166
Maison Sapho School of Dressmaking and Design, 174
Majk, 107
Malandrino, Catherine, 6, 99, *99*
Mallis, Fern, 66, *66*, 99, *99*, 100-103, *100*, *102*, *103*, 141, *141*, 145, 288
Manzano, Leslie, *139*
Marc Jacobs, 87
March, Chris, 108, *108*, *109*, 110, 111, 112, *112*, 113, *113*, *115*, 116, *120*, 122-123, 269, *269*, *286*
Marchesa, 141, 212
Margiela, Martin, 195
Marie Claire, 127, 129, 158, 159, 160, 175, 185, 186, 187, 188, 191, 197, 203, 212, 238, 242, 248, 280, 281
Maritime Hotel, 39
Marni, 195
Maroo, 191
Marquee, 64
Marshall, Kristal, *112*
Marshall, Leanne, 78, 107, 131, 135, *135*, 137, 138, *142*, 191, 254, 283, *283*, *287*
Martin, Kelli, 130, *130*, *131*, 136, *287*
Martinez, Lily. 72, *72*
Massachusetts College of Art and Design, 88, 174
Mayen, Valerie, 200, *200*, *201*, *202*, *203*, 205, *216*, 227, 229
McAtee, Allison, 61, 71, 74, 75, 288
McCarroll, Jay, 36, *36*, *37*, 40, *40*, 44, *48*, 50-51, *50*, 54, 57, 58, 73, *73*, 78, 83, 171, 282, *282*, *286*
McCarthy, Emmett, 60, *60*, *61*, *62*, 64, 75, 76, 83, *288*
McCartney, Stella, 16, 227, 253
McKinley, Joshua, 79, 168, 237, *237*, *238*, 239, 241, *241*, 242, *242*, 243, 245, *245*, *250*, 252, 253, 254-256, *254*, *256*, 264, *270*, *287*, *289*
McQueen, Alexander, 191, 223, 253
McQuillan, Cerri, 177, *181*, *183*
Mellon, Tamara, 159, *159*
Melnitchenko, Elizaveta, *183*, 268
Mendel, Gilles, 118, *118*
Menkes, Suzy, 159, *159*
Merman, Varla Jean, *137*
Messing, Debra, 73, *73*, 289

Metropolitan Museum of Art, The, 59, 128
Miami Institute of Art and Design, 26
Miami University, 171
Michael, Keith, 88, *88*, 91, *91*, 94, *104*, *286*
Milde, Erica, *155*
Minaj, Nicki, 127
Minnelli, Liza, 249
Minnillo, Vanessa, 55
Miramax, 279
Miranne, Jacqueline, *114*, *117*
Mischka, James, 73, *73*
Mitchell. Marcia, *113*, *115*, *117*
Mitchell, Martinique, *38*, *45*
Miyake, Issey, 253
Mizrahi, Isaac, *267*, 274, 278, *278*, 279
Models of the Runway, 156, 268
Momolu, Korto, 21, 131, *131*, 136, 138, *142*, 144-145, 232, 269, *269*, *287*
Mood, 31, 81, 169, 173, 223, 231, 241, 243, 253
Motwani, Cecilia, 5, *236*, *236*, 240, 256, 265, *287*, *289*
Mouret, Roland, 185, *185*, 190
Mt. Hood Community College, 236
MTV, 55, 229
Munez, Katarina, *136*, *139*
Munn, Olivia, 229
Murphy, Eddie, 55
Murray, Jonathan, 6, *8*, 10, 11, *15*, 24, 166-168, *166*, 202, 206, 238, 241, 242, 277

N

Nargi, Lisa, 113, 115, 116, *117*
Nault, Wesley, 130, *130*, *131*, *287*
NBC, 55, 166
Negich, Becky, 47, *47*
Neiman Marcus, 78, 83, 127, 274, 280, 281
Neitzel, Logan, 146, *146*, *148*, *149*, 151, *151*, *163*, 170, *288*
Nelson, Katie, *117*
Net-A-Porter, 281
New Balance, 4, 5, 206, 223, 241, 255, 263, 264
New York Times, The, 53, 127, 206
Niekrasz, Sonia, 238, 239, 245, 247, 256
Nike, 107
NIKOLAI, 87
Nomi Network, 229
North Central College, 174
Nuo, 78

O

O'Dell, Nancy, 47, *47*
Ohno, Apolo, 133, *133*, 140, *140*, *142*
Oldehoff, Brittany, *175*, *181*, *183*
Oliver Twist (Dickens), 187
On the Road with Austin and Santino, 58-59, 275
Orange Coast College, 88
Orbit Gum, 87
Otis College of Art and Design, 36, 60, 88, 130

P

Palermo, Olivia, 249, *249*
Palmer, Alexandra, *202*, *208*, *211*
Paris Fashion Institute, 36
Parker, Sarah Jessica, 16, 66, 110, *110*, 118, *118*, *120*, 123, 125, 127, 128
Parsons The New School for Design, 11, 14, 15, 20, 29, 53, 60, 88, 101, 107, 108, 109, 130, 146, 147, 200, 204, 222, 237, 239, 278, 288
Pasek, Alyssa, *247*

Paul, David, 87
Payless, 19, 127
Peach Carr Designs, 233, 235
Pena, Topacio, *139*
Penn State University, 88
People, 127
"People," 67
Pepper, Wendy, 36, *36*, *37*, 39, 40, *40*, 41, 42, 44, 50, 51, 54, 76, *286*
Perez, Anna Lita, *117*
Perna, Amanda, 236, *236*, *289*
Perry, Katy, 87
Perry, Suwana, 221
Peters, Jonathan, 174, *174*, 177, 181, 234
Petland Discounts, 238
Pfeiffer, John, 81
Philadelphia College of Textiles and Science, 36
Phillips, Arianne, 159, *159*
Philo, Phoebe, 195
Piperlime.com, 249
Plotkin, Robert, 36, *36*, *37*, 40, *40*, 48, 49, 65, *286*
Polimoda Institute of Fashion Design and Marketing, 36, 108, 237
Portman, Natalie, 16, 140, *140*
Posen, Zac, 16, 99, *99*, 118, *118*, 226
Posey, Parker, 47, *47*
Poster, Meryl, 6, *8*, 10, *15*, *18*, 24, 279, *279*
Pratt Institute, 36, 88, 130, 174, 175
Pritchard, Candace, *97*
Project Accessory, 272, 273
Project Greenlight, 11, 25, 26, 53
Project Runway: All Star Challenge, 269
Project Runway: All Stars, 186, 187, 196, 198, 199, 219, 226, 274, 276, 277, 278, 279, 280, 281
projectrunway.com, 24
Ptak, Pamela, 174, *174*
Puma, 127
Pursell, Joy, *38*, *45*
Putvinski, Nicolas, 146, *146*, *148*, 150, 151, 153, *288*
Py, Ekaterina, *202*, *211*, 229

Q

Queen Latifah, 52, 55
Quinn, Morgan, *38*, 39, *39*, *45*, 49
QVC, 78, 279

R

Rade, Jennifer, *159*, 159
Rains, Traver, 119, *119*
Ralph Lauren, 129
Ralph's, 167
Rannells, Lea, *117*
Ratnavich, Vanessa, *202*, *211*
Rea, Sara, *8*, 15, 18, 22, 149, 239, 287
Real World, The, 166, 168
Reardon, Martine, 159, *159*
Red Hook Summer, 194
Red Lobster, 67
Red Rooster, 193
Rhode Island School of Design, 60, 88, 174, 175, 200
Ricci, Christina, 248, *248*, 258
Rice, Santino, 18, *20*, 58-59, 61, *61*, *62*, *64*, 67, *67*, 68, 69, *75*, 77, 82, 83, 85, 107, 191, 269, *269*, *288*, 289
Rich, Richie, 119, *119*
Richie, Nicole, 184, *184*
Ridings, Holly, *177*, *180*, *183*, 193, *268*
Rihanna, 124, 127

Riley, Vanessa, 36, *36*, *37*, 41, *41*, *48*, 51, *286*
Rinna, Lisa, 55
Rivera, Marilinda, *3*, *96*, *97*
Roberts, Cara, *61*, *71*, *75*, *288*
Roberts Rassi, Zanna, 159, *159*, 160-161, *160*, *162*, 186, 227, 232, 234-235, 248, *248*, 270, 271, *271*, 286-287
Robin Hood Foundation, 24
Robinson, Patrick, 118, *118*
Rocha, Coco, 187, 203, *203*
Rockstar, 191
Rodgers, Tarah, *61*, 63, *63*, 68, *71*, *75*, 85, 86, *86*, *288*
Rodriguez, Julia, *202*, *211*
Rolling Stone, 238
Romijn, Rebecca, 158, *158*
Rosengard, Steven, 108, *108*, *109*, *286*
Ross, Becky, 236, *236*, 241, *241*, 253, 255, 263-265, *263*, *264*, *287*, *289*
Rossum, Emmy, 127
Rowley, Cynthia, 6, 72, *72*, 141, *141*, 159, *159*, *165*, 185, *185*, 213, *213*
Roy, Rachel, 6, 213, *213*, 214-215, *214*, *215*, 248, *248*
Roy, Valerie, *155*
RuPaul, 140, *140*
Ruggiero, Samantha, *115*, *117*

S

Sajko, Kristina, *3*, 175, 180, 182, 183, 190, 268, 284
Sakalis, Johnny, 146, *146*, *148*, 151, *162*
Saks 5th Avenue, 78, 83, 127
Saldana, Zoe, 55, 249, *249*, 258
Salter, Marie, *117*
San Francisco State University, 200
Sander, Jil, 227, 277
Santiago, Maria Lucia, *61*, *71*, *288*
Santos, Jia, *97*
Sarabi, Amy, 174, *174*, 180, 189
Sario, Jay Nicolas, 175, *175*, *176*, 179, *179*, 180, 181
Sassa, Scott, 271
Saturn, 134
Saun, Kara, *20*, 36, *36*, *37*, 39, 40, *40*, 41, *41*, 42, 43, 44, 52-55, *52*, *55*, 78, *286*
Saunders, Clifford, 53
Savannah College of Art and Design, 60, 108, 146, 174, 201, 225, 236
Scarbo, Christina "Kit Pistol," 108, *108*, *109*, *111*, *115*, *286*
Scarlett, Austin, 4, 18, 25, 36, *36*, *37*, 38, 40, *40*, 42, 43, *48*, 51, 56-59, *56*, *57*, *58*, *59*, 78, 102, 133, *133*, 140, *140*, *142*, 188, 191, 218, *251*, 274, *274*, *275*, *275*, *286*
Schneeweiss, Barbara, 6, *8*, 10, 13, 14, 16, 17-18, *19*, 20, *20*, 24, *24*, 25-26, 29, 38, 269, 297
School of the Art Institute of Chicago, 146
Schriffen, Danielle, *97*
Scott, Jerell, 131, *131*, 132, *134*, 137, 138, *142*, 144-145, *144*, *145*, 274, *274*, 277, 281, *287*
Scott, L'Wren, 249, *249*
Sears, 87
Sebelia, Jeffrey, 19, 21, 89, *89*, 92, *92*, 93, *93*, 95, *95*, 96, *96*, *104*, *105*, 107, *121*, 269, *269*, 283, *283*, *286*
Segaro, Nazri, *94*, *95*, *96*, *97*
Sevigny, Chloe, 24
Sex and the City, 46, 110
Shabayeva, Irina, 147, *147*, *148*, *149*, 151, *151*, 153, 154, 156, *157*, 170, *171*, 172, *189*, 227, 284, *284*, *288*
Sharenow, Rob, 271
Sheepdogs, The, 238, *238*, 252, 253, 257
Shields, Brooke, 132, *132*, 140, *140*
Shipman, Tia, *136*, 138, *139*
Simons, Raf, 63

Simply Chloe Dao, 78
Simpson, Jessica, 24, 207, *207*, 213, *213*
Sims, Molly, 184, *184*, 272, *272*
Sing-Off, The, 55
Sinkevica, Tatjana, *238*, *247*
Siriano, Christian, 5, 18, 19, 21, 83, 101, 112, *112*, 113, *113*, 115, *115*, 116, *120*, *121*, 122-127, *122*, *123*, *126*, *127*, 128, 188, 191, 213, *213*, *217*, 258, 260, 262, 283, *283*, *286*
Slowey, Anne, 13, 46, *46*, 73, *73*
Smith, Cheron, *117*
Smithsonian Institute, 78, 195
Snow, Millana, 165, 202, 210, 211
Sosa, Emilio, 175, *175*, 177, 178, 179, 180, 181, 182, 192-194, *192*, *194*
South, Andy, 201, *201*, *202*, 205, *205*, 206, 207, 208, 210, *210*, *216*, *217*, 223, 224, 229, 231, 233, *289*
Spade, Kate, 98, *98*
Spiegel, 127
St. John Vianney High School, 112
Standard Hotel, 17
Standridge, Heidi, 60, *60*, 61, 62, *62*, 288
Stanford University, 88
Starbucks, 107, 127
Stephens College, 146
Steve & Barry's, 110
Stevens, Terri, 130, *130*, *131*, *287*
Sticksel, Katie, 152, 153, 155, 268
Stone, Lara, 226
Straub, Christopher, 146, *146*, *148*, *149*, *151*, 152, 171, *288*
Streisand, Barbra, 67
Strong, Collier, *163*
Strubegger, Iris, *116*, 125
Style Network, The, 55
Style Star, 87
Sues, Alan, 289
Sullivan, Wendi, *117*
Swift, Taylor, 127
Sylvester, Yosuzi, 155
Sylvia's, 193

T

Tam, Jerry, 130, *130*, *131*, *287*
Tam, Vivienne, 178, *178*, 185, *185*
Tangoren, Mehmet, 98, *98*
Target Corp., 236
Taylor, Elizabeth, 57
Theory, 229
Thouvenot, A.J., 200, *200*, *202*, 205, 206, 223, 224, 229, 234, *289*
Tierney, Julie, 236, *236*, 240, *287*, *289*
Tisci, Riccardo, 128
Tk, Amare, *211*
Today Show, The, 111, 118
Toledo, Isabel, 185, *185*, 192, 195
Tom Ford, 77
Tony Awards, 194
Top Chef, 6
Topstick, 206
Toth, Jenny, 38, 43, 44, 45, 54, 55
Toys "R" Us, 64
Treacy, Philip, 5, 21, 204, 212, *212*, 223, 224, 227-228, 233
TRESemmé, 113
Troisi, Jason, 200, *200*, *202*
Trost, Sarah, 200, *200*, *202*, *203*
True Beauty, 55
Trump, Ivanka, 98, *98*

Trump Organization, 98
TV Guide Network, 87
Twitter, 187
Two Part Affair, A, 129
Tyler, Richard, 99, *99*
Tytler, Xaviera, *139*

U

Underwood, Carrie, 284
University of Alabama, The, 174, 236
University of Arizona, The, 108
University of California at Berkeley, 108
University of Cape Town, South Africa, 61
University of Chicago, 108
University of Cincinnati, 147
University of Houston, 89
University of North Texas, 146
University of Rhode Island, The, 174
University of Southern California, 60
University of Texas at Austin, The, 108
Unruh, Daniela, 6, 287
Unzipped, 278

V

Valentino, 125
Van Noten, Dries, 16
Varvatos, John, 159, *159*
Vaughn, Kathleen, "Sweet P," 108, *108*, *109*, 110, *115*, *120*, 269, *269*, 274, *274*, *276*, *286*
Ved, Zhanna, 210, 211
Verreos, Nick, 18, 60, *60*, *62*, 64, *64*, 65, *65*, 68, 70, 75, 77, 83, 84-87, *84*, *86*, 158, *158*, 171, 191, 221, 270, *288*
Versace, Donatella, 16
Victoria's Secret, 9, 72, 81, 127
Vidal, Alexandra, 36, *36*, *37*, 48, *49*
Vidal, Guadalupe, 60, *60*, 61, 62, 64, *288*
Vien, Malvin, 146, *146*, 171
Viktor & Rolf, 191
Vilmenay, Danyelle, 61, 63, *63*, 71, 75, 288
Vitamin Water, 191
Vogue, 127, 129
Vogue Italia, 127
Volorioz, Germaine, *136*, *139*
von Furstenberg, Diane, 6, 16, 72, *72*, 76, 83, 98, *98*, 135, *135*, 141, *141*, 145
Vosovic, Daniel, 18, 61, *61*, *62*, *64*, 68, 69, 70, *74*, *75*, 77, 79-81, *79*, 83, 85, 86, 254, 269, *269*, *288*

W

W, 129
Wade, John, 60, *60*, 61, 62, *62*, 85, 87, *288*
Wakeema, Hollis, *283*
Wall Street Journal, The, 99, 127
Walmart, 221
Walsh, Blayne, 130, *130*, *131*, 145, *287*
Wang, Alexander, 227
Wang, Vera, 16, 98, *98*, 279
Washington, Kerry, 158, *158*, 248, *248*
Washington Post, The, 102
Wasson, Erin, 248, *248*
Watanabe, Junya, 227
Waterman, Anne, 11
WB, 55
Webb, Chris, 134, *134*, *142*
Webber, Carmen, 108, *108*, *109*, *286*
Webster, Stephen, 184, *184*, 195
Wei, Shen, 59

Weinstein, Harvey, 6, *6*, *24*, *49*, 166, 279
Weinstein Company, The, 6, 191, 278, 279, 284
Wells, Fallene, 236, *236*, *238*, 265, *287*, *289*
West, Karalyn, *3*, *137*, *139*
Western Kentucky University, 237
Westwood, Vivienne, 16, 227
What I Like About You, 55
Whitaker, Keisha, 55
White, Constance, 46, *46*
Whitfield, Carol Hannah, 147, *147*, *151*, 154, *163*, 171, 172-173, *172*, *173*, *288*
"Who Will Buy?," 187
Wicked Quick, 265
Will & Grace, 73, 289
Williams, Anthony, 174, *174*, *175*, 176, 177, 178, *178*, 180, 182, 188, 193, 197-199, *197*, *198*, 225, 274, *274*, 276, *276*
Williams, Lesley Ann, 61, 71, *75*, 288
Williams, Vanessa, 55
Williamson, Matthew, 185, *185*
Wiltz, Emarie, *151*, *155*, 268
Windsor, 87
Winfrey, Oprah, 283
Women's Wear Daily, 127, 129
Woodbury University, 174
Works and Process, 129
Wu, Ping, 174, *174*, *189*
WWE, 4, 112, 129

Y

Yamamoto, Yohji, 253
YouTube, 231
Yung, Moon, *97*

Z

Zaager, Nicole, *137*, *138*, *139*
Zac Posen, 229
Zajarias, Samantha, *211*
Zara, 26
Zebelian, Allison, *38*, *45*
Zoe, Rachel, 99, *99*, 107, 141, *141*
Zotis, Stella, 130, *130*, *131*, *287*

CREDITS

This book was a co-production between The Weinstein Company, Weinstein Books, and Running Press Book Publishers. Special thanks go to writer Eila Mell for all her work and tireless spirit. All involved in the book's production give special thanks as well to all interview subjects featured throughout these pages, who so generously shared their time, insights, and memories.

Publishing Director, Weinstein Books: Georgina Levitt
Editorial Director, Weinstein Books: Amanda Murray
TWC Consultants: Barbara Schneeweiss and Meryl Poster

Writing and Interviews: Eila Mell
Editor and Project Manager: Cindy De La Hoz
Interior Design: Melissa Gerger
Cover Design: Frank Sipala and Frances SooPingChow

THANKS

Teresa Bonaddio, Ken Byers, Jack Cesarano, Mike Cesarano, Jane Cha, Bradley Cherna, Joanna Coles, Claire Congleton, Aaron Day, Celeste Fine, Nina Garcia, David Gewirtz, Desiree Gruber, Eli Holzman, Jennifer Hozer, David Hutkin, Bill Jones, Michael Kors, Heidi Klum, Jennifer Leczkowski, Shari Levine, Jennifer Love, Mark A. Lyons, Chris Navratil, Barbara Nitke, Sue Oyama, Clare Peeters, Kate Prescott, John Radziewicz, Stacy Shuck, Shea Sinclair, Sydney Snyder, Iris Soricelli, David Steinberger, Will Swann, Monica Torero, Daniela Unruh, Harvey Weinstein, Kannie Yu LaPack

PHOTOGRAPHY CREDITS

Page 4: Heidi Klum by Robert Erdman
Page 6: Harvey Weinstein: AP Photo/John Carucci
Page 22: Casting photos by Marvin Orellana
Page 88: Nick Verreos by Johnny Nicoloro
Page 50: Patricia Field, AP Photo/Jennifer Graylock
Page 51: Amsale Aberra: Jason Kempin/Getty Images
Page 51: Nancy O'Dell: Mathew Imaging/WireImage/Getty Images
Page 104: Fern Mallis by David S. Rubin
Page 122: Monique Lhuillier: AP Photo/Dan Steinberg
Page 122: Patrick Robinson: AP Photo/Jennifer Graylock
Page 122: Gilles Mendel: Dimitrios Kambouris/WireImage/Getty Images
Page 122: Donna Karan: Robin Marchant/Getty Images
Page 123: Alberta Ferretti: AP Photo/Dan Steinberg
Page 123: Roberto Cavalli: Denise Truscello/WireImage/Getty Images
Page 159: Suzy Menkes: Katy Winn/Getty Images
Page 173: Althea Harper by Andrew Werner
Page 194: Seth Aaron Henderson by Timothy J. Parks
Page 277: Ariel Foxman by John Shearer
Back jacket flap: Eila Mell by Felicia Lebow
All photographs from *Project Runway* Seasons 1–5 courtesy NBC/Universal.
All photographs from *Project Runway* Seasons 6–9 and series spin-offs courtesy The Weinstein Company.